The
Search
for Lost
Habitats

The Search for Lost Habitats

30 Years of Exploring for Rare and Endangered Plants—Book I

Perry K. Peskin

ORANGE FRAZER *PRESS*
Wilmington, Ohio

The Three-Hour Press Company

ISBN: 1-933197-16-1

Additional copies of
The Search for Lost Habitats, 30 Years of Exploring for Rare and Endangered Plants—Book 1
may be ordered directly from:

Customer Service Department
Orange Frazer Press   or   The Three-Hour Press Company
P.O. Box 214   3559 Strathavon Road
Wilmington, OH 45177   Shaker Heights, OH 44122

Telephone: 1.800.852.9332 for price and shipping information.
Website: *www.orangefrazer.com*

Book and jacket design: Lynn Margalit, Margalit Studio

Peskin, Perry K.
    The search for lost habitats: 30 years of exploring for rare and endangered plants.
    Book 1 / Perry K. Peskin.
        p. cm.
    Includes bibliographical references (p.).
    ISBN 1-933197-16-1
        1. Rare plants--Ohio. 2. Endangered plants--Ohio. 3. Rare plants--Lake States.
        4. Endangered plants--Lake States. I. Title.

QK86.U6P47 2006
333.95'32--dc22

                                                                        2006046420

Printed in China

To my wife **Carolyn**, who is briefly mentioned in only five out of seventeen chapters (and not always by name), this book is humbly dedicated. When she acquired her personal computer in 1997, she rewrote several of my longer articles in computer format for the first time, helping my editors considerably. Ever since then, although I still labor away on an antique Smith-Corona, correcting all my many typos with dry-line, it's a great relief to send out her perfect copies to magazine editors and know that they are so readable.

Our post-retirement fields differ greatly (Hers is composing and arranging music.), but she still takes time out of her busy schedule to read over parts of my manuscript for clarity and style, whenever I ask her.

From Alaska to Newfoundland, from Britain to the Galapagos, and all points in between, we have trudged along together on so many eco-tours that we've lost count. At home or away, while I am glued to the typewriter or behind the camera, her patience, good humor, and common sense make searching for endangered species (and actually finding many of them!) truly one of the pleasures of life.

Author's Note: Except for the editors, who are listed under their publications, all the people who helped me are arranged alphabetically by last name under their respective specialty (field botanists, etc.). Donors of photos are credited in the captions.

In a book such as this, which took over 25 years to evolve, I hope that I can be forgiven for not remembering every person who helped me in the course of writing the various chapters. Until ten years ago, I had no intention of collecting the individual chapters into a book; they were written as separate essays destined to become magazine articles. In some cases I gave credit to individuals within or at the end of each article, but usually I acknowledged only the printed sources of my information. In the past few weeks I have been hurriedly writing down all the names that I can still remember—a difficult task at any age, let alone for a senior citizen—and I trust that anyone whom I have neglected will understand.

First, the **editors**. Starting with the *Explorer* magazine of the Cleveland Museum of Natural History, I salute **Aaron Leash** and **Megan Harding**, former editors in the '80s and '90s, and their staff photographers, **Bruce Frumker**, **Dan Flocke**, and **Greg Petuskey**. **Dr. Barbara Andreas**, Professor of Botany at Kent State University, accepted my article on sedges (Chapter 14) when she was editor of the Ohio Nature Conservancy's *Newsletter* in the 1980's. In the spring of 2003, she also lent me a copy of the invaluable reference for correct scientific and common names of Ohio plants *The Seventh Catalog of the Vascular Plants of Ohio, 2001*. The editors of *On the Fringe*, the newsletter of the Northeast Ohio Chapter of the Native Plant Society—**Laurel Giblock**, **Tom Sampliner**, and **Ann Malmquist**—accepted many articles of mine for publication. The first article I ever wrote for publication was accepted by the editor of the *Sunday Plain Dealer Magazine*, **Richard Bilotti,** for its July 30, 1978, issue, and entitled "White City … What a Dump!" I remember Mr. Bilotti asking me, "Why does a guy from Shaker Heights have any interest in a lakeside dump in Cleveland?" Chapter 9 may supply an answer. Ever since I joined the Association of American Field Botanists (AAFBees, for short), many articles of mine were accepted by this mostly Southern group, centered in Chattanooga, Tennessee, for their *AAFBee Newsletter*. **Chuck Wilson** was the last editor of this fine newsletter before the group disbanded, to my great regret. My editor at *Wildflower* magazine, a Toronto, Ontario, quarterly devoted to the native flora of all North America, has been **Jim Hodgins** for the past 15 years or more. The art editor is Jim's wife, **Zile Zichmanis**, who has offered many of her own slides to supplement mine, as well as excellent line drawings. My most recent associate in the publishing field is my co-publisher **Marcy Hawley** of the Orange Frazer Press of Willmington, Ohio. I wish her the best of luck in our joint venture.

Field botanists: These are the people who have led guided tours through nature preserves, given lectures, and written and edited books and newsletters on rare habitats and the endangered plants encountered in them. They are the experts associated with two fine organizations—the Ohio Department of Natural Resources, Division of Natural Areas and Preserves (simply referred to as ODNR in this book) and The Nature Conservancy, Ohio Chapter (referred to as TNC) For 20 years before their recent retirement, **Allison Cusick** and **Guy Denny** have held top positions in ODNR, led many field trips that I've attended, given lectures on Ohio plants, and written articles in the ODNR *Newsletter* on rare Ohio plant species as well as co-authored several standard Ohio botanical references. (See Bibliography.) Cusick has also written several scientific-journal articles that I've found very useful. In fall 2003 Cleveland Metroparks naturalist **Dave Dvorak** showed me many plants in Kentucky that are rarities in Ohio. The Heritage List, a database of rare Ohio plants and animals, has been operated by ODNR specialists, such as **Victoria Hugo**, for over 25 years. I'm grateful for the maps of plant locations she has sent me, as well as historical material on plant distribution in the past. **Marilyn Ortt** of Marietta has been active in both ODNR and TNC and has given me important information on southeastern Ohio locations of rare plants as well as taken me on field trips in the area. Other ODNR personnel who aided me include **Jim McCormac**, who led walks through Scioto State Forest, as described in Chapter 15 and kindly offered to double-check the text and captions for errors; **Dan Rice**, a zoologist, who was in charge of the Heritage List in 1978, when it was first being compiled, and contacted me to send in my sightings of rare plants by using this list; and **Jennifer Windus**, who led a trip through the Lake Kathryn Preserve in 1995.

State park and nature preserve managers: Some of the excellent field botanists who have guided me around ODNR and TNC properties include **Bill Hudson**, in northeastern Ohio; **Mary Huffman** in the Toledo area; **Terry Jaworski** at Cedar Swamp in west-central Ohio, a preserve owned by the Ohio Historical Society; **Dave Minney** in extreme southern Ohio; **Peter Whan,** manager of TNC's Edge of Appalachia Preserves; and **Phil Zito** of the Lake Kathryn Preserve.

Professors of botany in Ohio: Professor of botany (now retired) at Kent State University, **Dr. Tom Cooperrider** gave me a list of important references on parasitic plants for Chapter 8. Retired professor of botany at Kent State University, **Dr. Clinton Hobbs** has encouraged my writing of articles on endangered Ohio plants and has introduced me to a group of wildflower enthusiasts in Stark County— the Botanizers. I don't know how I could have written Chapter I without the help of **Dr. Ronald L. Stuckey**, retired professor of botany at Ohio State University, who compiled a complete bibliography of Lucy Braun's scientific papers, wrote a valuable biography of Braun, and is now engaged in reprinting all of her scientific-journal articles with his own press. Meeting professor of botany **George Wilder** of Cleveland State University, now teaching at a Florida university, was a valuable introduction to the urban flora of the Cleveland region, which he specialized in, resulting in his discovery of many rare species. Whenever I accompanied him and his classes through the inner city and suburbs of Cleveland, he always sighted unsuspected rarities on these informal field trips.

Professors of botany outside Ohio: Dr. Gwynn Ramsey, professor (retired) of botany at Lynchburg College, Lynchburg, Virginia, introduced me to the Kankakee mallow at a site on the James River in Virginia, which he had discovered some years before. (See Chapter 6.) **Dr. A. A. Reznicek**, Director of the Herbarium of the University of Michigan, identified plant specimens accurately for Chapters 7 and 8.

Staff of the Cleveland Museum of Natural History: Bob Bartolotta of the Education department showed me Ninety-Acre Prairie in Erie County and, in the summer of 2003 and 2004, many rarities along the Lake Erie shoreline. **Jim Bissell**, curator of botany and director of the herbarium, has helped the museum acquire many nature preserves, mostly in the form of donations from land-owners, through his Natural Areas Division. Jim also organized the Northeast Ohio Naturalists (NEON). Its object was to find plants designated as rare by the state of Ohio on the Heritage List. I participated in many field trips over the years with this group. Jim was also the first to introduce me to the literature on halophytes (Chapter 5). **Dr. Shya Chitaley**, curator of paleobotany, where I have volunteered for over 20 years, supplied most of the illustrations for Chapter 11. **Joe Hannibal**, curator of invertebrate paleontology, gave me some valuable references on the animal life of the Paleozoic Period.

Friends and acquaintances: so many botanically knowledgeable people, including many personal friends have helped me out that I can only briefly mention their names and accomplishments. **Dan Boone** of southwestern Ohio, a lineal descendant of the famous trailblazer and a trailblazer in his own right. **John Barbour** of Akron guided me in 1979 to Willow Bog (See Chapter 2.) to show me a stand of arethusa orchids. Jim and **Sandy Davidson** of Columbus guided me around Rhododendron Cove. **William Eillis** (now deceased) and his wife **Jane Anne** guided me around Conkle's Hollow and their own property, Crane Hollow, which they donated to ODNR. **Cal Frye** of Kent, formerly of the Education Dept. of the Cleveland Museum of Natural History, helped me find the bunchflower. **Jim Heflich** of South Euclid accompanied me in finding Brown's Lake Bog the hard way—wading through the lake instead of using the boardwalk. **Dr. Arthur Herrick** (ret.) of Kent State University showed me a big-leaved magnolia in flower, so that I could photograph it. **Chuck Hammer** of southeast Ohio, who gave me directions for finding a rare species of lily. All the Minnesota people mentioned in Chapter 7 deserve recognition: **Nancy Sather**, **Julie Muehlberg**, **Jay Hutchinson**, **Alden "Mack" McCutcheon**, and **Orwin Rustad**. **Kenny Pheasant** of Traverse City, Michigan, gave me background on the Odawa people of Manitoulin Island, Ontario, where he was born. **Brian Parsons** of Holden Arboretum, Lake County has given me much information on the growing conditions for certain federally endangered species. **John Pogacnik**, naturalist for Lake County, Metroparks, relocated a lost plant—the bearberry—on the shores of Lake Erie. **Trella Hemmersley Romine** of Caledonia, Ohio, helped with data on Lucy Braun (Chapter 1) and railroad prairies in central Ohio, such as Claridon Prairie, which she helped save (Chapter 3). She is still going strong in the conservation field in her mid-90's. **Fritz and Alice Schmitthenner** of Wooster helped me find the site of the prairie fringed orchid. **Jack** and **Florence Selby** took me on many field trips where we found rare orchids. Also, Jack's collection of plant photos supplemented mine in many chapters. **Bob Shaper**, former president of the Kirtland Bird Club of Cleveland, was the first person to show me a real fen in Ohio—Herrick Fen of Portage County. **Bert Szabo**, retired park naturalist of Summit County Metroparks, gave ODNR my name in 1978 as a possible contributor of rare plant sightings. He also helped me find the northern monkshood in Cruickshank Glen (Chapter 2). **Chuck Thomas** of Lakewood helped me find the rare stout goldenrod in one of the Cleveland metropolitan parks. **Gordon Vujevic** of Youngstown guided me to a wetland near a railroad track, where I saw my first quillwort (*Isoetes*). (See Chapter 11.) **Dr. Joel Wachtel** of Columbus guided me around Rhododendron Cove. **Tom Yates** of the Holden Arboretum showed me the inconspicuous downy rattlesnake-plantain, a woodland orchid.

Sadly, in a long-term project such as this, some of the people who helped me the most have passed away before the project was completed. **Bill Baughman** was the editor of the *Explorer* who accepted the three articles that later became Chapters 1,

2, and 3 of this book. On the advice of ODNR, he suggested that I disguise the names of fragile habitats with pseudonyms. In a class by himself, **Benjamin "Pat" Bole**, associate professor of botany at Case Western Reserve University in Cleveland, presented to his students a type of botany with a "human face." His course Classification and Evolution of the Flowering Plants, which I took one summer, had as its "lab" the flower garden and woodland around his home. I have never taken a botany course before or since that presented so enjoyably the many details about the 100 main plant families of North America and the world. **Dave Corbin**, former president of the Kirtland Bird Club, showed me rare orchids in Ohio and Pennsylvania, especially the showy lady's-slipper. **Mary Ann Fox** of West Bay, Ontario, on Manitoulin Island, gave me a great deal of information on the Odawa people for Chapter 4. **James Irwin "Bus" Jones** of Chattanooga, Tennessee, as first editor of the AAFBee *Newsletter*, accepted many of my articles that were too long for the *Explorer's* format and serialized them. **Lindley Vickers**, a park naturalist, who was the first professional botanist to take the time to show an amateur like myself the fragile habitat known in Chapter 2 as Moorhead Forest. **Dr. James H. Zimmerman** of the University of Wisconsin corresponded with me on the northern monkshood.

Last but not least, I wish to thank my designer, **Lynn Margalit** of Margalit Studio, Peninsula, Ohio, for turning this book into a work of art.

Introduction: The Three-Hour Walk   page 2

Chapter 1: A Walk Through Lucy Braun's Prairie   page 16

Chapter 2: Four Species in Search of a Habitat   page 26

Chapter 3: Ohio's Invisible Prairies   page 40

Chapter 4: Fire and Ice in the Lair of the Manitou   page 54

Chapter 5: The Halophytes Are Coming? The Halophytes Are Here!   page 70

Chapter 6: Mallows   page 78

Chapter 7: Faribault Diary   page 94

Chapter 8: The Knotted Dodder and Other Curiosities   page 114

Chapter 9: White City ... What a Dump!   page 130

Chapter 10: Orchidophilia   page 144

Chapter 11: Pennsylvanian Nature Trail   page 158

Chapter 12: The Elusive Gentians   page 170

Chapter 13: Let's Look at the Grasses   page 178

Chapter 14: Why I Won't Write about the Sedges   page 186

Chapter 15: Ohio's Rarest and Fairest Plants...and How to Find Them page 194

Epilogue: Putting Back the Pieces   page 214

Appendix A:
Illustrations with Captions, of Plants Not Mentioned in the Text

    1. Northern Ohio (NO)   page 232
    2. Southern Ohio (SO)   page 240
    3. Upper Great Lakes (GL)   page 246

Appendix B:
Federally Listed Plant Species of Ohio and the Upper Great Lakes States   page 252

Selected Bibliography   page 254

Index   page 261

The
Search
for Lost
Habitats

In-1 **A Gallery of Northern Ohio Habitats. Dunes: The lighthouse at Mentor Headlands** on Lake Erie, 30 miles east of Cleveland, marks the site of a state bathing beach and nature preserve. Dominated by **cottonwoods, sandbar willows** (*Salix interior,* sometimes called *exigua*) and **American beach grass** *(Ammophila breviligulata–T),* the dunes are the site of many rare strand plants, mostly of Atlantic Coast origin.

In-2 **The Girdham Road dunes at Oak Openings Park,** west of Toledo, is one of many dune, prairie, and marsh areas in northwest Ohio left over when prehistoric Lake Warren shrank in size to become Lake Erie. These **interior sand dunes** support a remarkable flora, not seen in the rest of the state in such concentration. (See Chapter 15.)

introduction

The Three-Hour Walk

How I got myself involved in searching for rare and endangered plants, photographing them, and writing articles about them, I'll never know exactly, but I think it happened gradually in the '60s and '70s.

I remember that in the '60s, every year around October, I would assign my senior English classes at Maple Heights High School, located in a suburb of Cleveland, Ohio, a three-hour walk that each student should take, unaccompanied, on foot. The students could choose their own time and itinerary; record their thoughts, feelings, and observations in a small notebook; and write them up as a unified essay of at least 300 words, using as many details and sense impressions as they wished. Although a few of them turned in strongly worded essays that were unified only in one aspect—that they thought the project was a total waste of time, the majority was more tolerant, using the assignment as a chance to get away from school problems, pressures from home, and unwanted interactions with friends. Many of them chose streets in their home neighborhoods, but others preferred the natural world of the nearby local and metropolitan parks, where they could be alone with their thoughts. One girl even chose a cemetery!

I'm not sure what prompted this assignment. I was always a rather introspective person myself, having gone through a Thoreauvian period in high school when at first I wanted to become a park naturalist and then later a farmer. In college I was introduced to three-hour field trips when I took courses in botany, fresh-water biology, and ecology, all leading to a minor in biology on my teaching certificate. However, the schools where I taught never asked me to teach biology, since English, my major field, was always a required course and needed the most teachers. Perhaps this type of assignment involving the outdoors reflected my own needs as a frustrated biology teacher.

In-3 **Disturbed Areas:** The Conrail freight train going by **Claridon Prairie near Marion, Ohio**, illustrates the largest habitat for plants in Ohio: the **disturbed area**. See Chapter 3 for more details on **railroad prairies**, sheltering many plant species displaced by agriculture.

On weekends I would sometimes accompany friends on three-hour hikes along the forest trails of the Cleveland Metropolitan Park System. I marveled at the foresight the directors of this wonderful system had used in purchasing forest land in the early 1900s, because now all the major parks were surrounded by suburban housing, on streets with typical names like Metropark Drive and Parkview Road, and there was little open space left for expansion.

Although I enjoyed roaming through the beech-maple forests of the metropolitan parks, in the '60s I became interested in exploring more unfamiliar habitats: the dunes of Lake Erie, abandoned farm fields, disturbed areas along railroad tracks, and city dumps. I was amazed at the great diversity of plants and animals in these places and equipped myself with a reflex camera to take color slides of unknown plants that could be identified later.

One important turning point occurred in the '70s, when a group of amateur naturalists in Erie, Pennsylvania, invited a friend of mine and myself to join them at Titus Bog. Never having explored any wetland before, let alone a bog, I bought a pair of canvas shoes for walking in deep water, took along a notebook, but for safety's sake left the camera at home.

A peculiar wetland containing the very rare and beautiful red-purple **orchid** called the **dragon-mouth**, or **arethusa**, Titus Bog was located on a hilltop, instead of in a bottomland, amid rolling farm country south of Erie. To reach it, twenty bog-fanatics and I had to slog along in a "moat" of cold, knee-deep water the color of tea, looking like fugitives escaping through the sewers of Paris, until we reached an incline. Here we pulled ourselves up to a sort of plateau, where a wholly new natural world greeted us.

In-4 An ore boat, passing a gravel yard on the **Cuyahoga River near downtown Cleveland**, in an industrial area locally known as the Flats, also illustrates the **disturbed-area habitat**. Once notorious for containing such a great volume of polluting hydrocarbons that it caught fire, the Cuyahoga River has been cleaned up to such an extent that fish swim in from Lake Erie. Foreign and native plants, including some that are endangered, grow along its banks.

At first sight, the bog resembled an extensive short-grass meadow, surrounded by a ring of tall conifers—**American larches**, or **tamaracks** (*Larix laricina*). However, close up, the "grass" turned out to be quaking mounds of sphagnum moss, a plant which I had never seen before, which alternated with bare spots of wet gravel and small pools containing white water-lilies in full bloom. It took me some time to realize that there was no soil in this habitat. Our leader explained that the bog started as a **kettle hole**, meaning a lake created by melted ice from the glacier 12,000 years ago, that was slowly filled in by plant life growing atop layer upon layer of dead sphagnum moss. We were advised to walk on the wet gravel because the sphagnum mounds were treacherous, sometimes covering knee-deep holes.

The plant life was as peculiar as the habitat. Feeling as if I had been suddenly whisked 1,000 miles north to Arctic Canada, I noted down the names carefully as our leaders identified strange plants that I never expected to see within 90 miles of Cleveland. Most were growing right out of the sphagnum mounds. Here was **small cranberry** (*Vaccinium oxycoccus*) in leaf. Over there was a strange white puffball of a seedhead, much silkier than that of a dandelion, which the experts were calling **green cotton-grass** (*Eriophorum viridicarinatum*), really a sedge. An unfamiliar plant resembling a tiny stem with a cone on top was **bog clubmoss** (*Lycopodiella inundata*). A group of botanizers were crowding around a clump of tiny, ground-hugging leaves shaped like ping-pong paddles and covered with tiny drops of sticky red glue. This proved to be the famous **round-leaved sundew** (*Drosera rotundifolia*), the first carnivorous plant I had seen in its natural habitat.

But interest in all other plants gave way to silence when the first **arethusas** (*A. bulbosa*) were spotted, growing singly on sphagnum mounds. An unreal, red-purple glow seemed to stream out of the sphagnum as if the flowers were incandescent. This was the first large-flowered, really colorful orchid I had ever seen close up, and as all the camera buffs closed in with their single-lens reflexes and tripods and flash attachments, going slightly crazy over these floral gems, including several albino specimens with pure white flowers, I promised myself two things: that I would never again go plant hunting without a camera, and that I would continue to look for new habitats, since rare habitats yielded rare plants.

It was also in the '70s that I started to use as a reference one of Lucy Braun's major works, *The Vascular Flora of Ohio, Volume I: Cat-tails to Orchids*, the first volume in a projected series by this eminent Ohio botanist that would illustrate and describe every flowering plant in Ohio. Because its illustrations and distribution maps were so clear, I started referring to it whenever I saw sedges, grasses, and obscure aquatic plants, and

In-5 Colonies of **black-crowned night herons** (*Nycticorax nycticorax*–T), a fish-eating species, are a familiar sight near the mouth of the Cuyahoga. (Photo from Yucatan.)

In-6 **Wetlands. Bogs and Fens:** These are among Ohio's most endangered habitats. Shown here is the boardwalk area of **Herrick Fen in Portage County**. Tall trees in the background are **American larch**, or **tamarack** (*Larix laricina*–P), a northern tree found sparingly in Ohio. Neither bogs nor fens have conventional soil. **Bog plants** grow on a peaty base composed of layers of pressed sphagnum mats, which are acidic. **Fen plants** grow over an alkaline gravel, covered by layers of compressed sedges.

in time I taught myself how to use the identification keys. Later on, I found out that many of these unglamorous plants were useful as **index species** in identifying habitats, especially the many rare wetland habitats that were being drained and bulldozed out of existence at this time for agriculture, industry, highways, suburban housing, and shopping malls.

Countering this destructive trend in American life was a new environmental movement, which also took shape in the '60s, and '70s and was embodied in the revolutionary Endangered Species Act of 1973, the first legislation designed to protect the habitat of rare plants and animals.

Shortly afterwards, I wrote to the US Department of the Interior, asking how a private citizen like myself could help promote the goals of the 1973 Act, and I was told that each of the 50 states was required to set up an agency that would catalogue the plant and animal rarities within its borders, publish its findings, and endeavor to protect these species. In Ohio this agency was the Division of Natural Areas and Preserves of the Ohio Department of Natural Resources (ODNR).

Although ODNR already had a staff of professional biologists, I found out that they welcomed amateurs who could locate endangered plants and report their scientific name, location, and habitat annually to Columbus. In the case of really obscure species (sedges and grasses again), a voucher, meaning a plant specimen, should be collected (with an ODNR permit, of course) and deposited in any one of the many **herbaria** (collections of pressed plants) in the state. I chose the **herbarium** of the Cleveland Museum of Natural History because I had already gone on many of the field trips offered by the Department of Botany, under the curatorship of Jim Bissell, who, as I later found out, is regarded as one of the finest field botanists in Ohio. In 1977 and every year since, I have turned in a report to ODNR on my findings.

Once in the field, I learned how to collect specimens in a plastic bag and label them by location and date. When I returned home, I would record the date, place, and habitat of the specimens in my record book and put them in a plant press. Later I would unload the plant press at the museum herbarium, try to identify the species, and place all important information on a **herbarium slip** (where and when found, by whom, with what other plants, in what habitat), without which no collected specimen has any scientific value. For recording data on all the plants I observed, I used old-fashioned, cloth-bound record books of the type that was once popular for single-entry bookkeeping, and so far I have

In-7 **Titus Bog, near Erie, Pennsylvania**, photographed in 1984 on my second visit, this time with the Northeast Ohio Native Plant Society. Notice how this bog resembles a short-grass prairie from a distance, but the "grass" is a mat of **sphagnum moss** (*Sphagnum sp.*). Tamaracks form the background.

In-8 **A white water-lily** *(Nymphaea odorata)* of the kind found in Titus Bog. Normally found in **ponds** and **shallow lakes**, where its large roots are anchored in a mud bottom, this is the first and only water-lily species I've seen in a bog habitat. Recent fossil discoveries reveal the oldest flowering plant was a member of this family. (Photo taken at North Chagrin Reservation, east of Cleveland.)

accumulated three of them and am halfway through the fourth. After a while I began to depend on these notebooks for supplying many of the details in my articles.

The Endangered Species Act requires that rare plants be classified by a special system. **Plants labeled E, for endangered (close to extinction)**, have very low populations in the country as a whole, and are confined to very few areas and to one type of habitat. **Plants labeled T, for threatened (not quite so close to extinction)**, have relatively larger populations although still few in number, and live in a greater number of areas and often in more than one type of habitat.

Ohio and the Upper Great Lakes region have very few *federally* endangered or threatened species, but they do have many rare plants, marked E or T, called "Heritage plants" in Ohio, that are *locally* endangered or threatened. As expected, these are plants dwelling in rare habitats, such as bogs, or else common plants in other parts of the country that reach Ohio at the very edge of their range. Certain northern forest plants common in Canada are found only in extreme northeast or northwest Ohio (Ashtabula or Lucas Counties, typically), while certain plants from the Deep South or the Appalachians are found only in the extreme southern counties along the Ohio River (Adams and Scioto Counties, typically). In addition, ODNR has also instituted two other categories: **X, for extirpated**—not documented for **20 years or more**—and **P, for potentially threatened**—losing population and habitat though still abundant.

In the rest of the book, I will follow every scientific name of a plant with the initial of its appropriate category of rareness (E,T,X, or P). If no initial is used, the reader must assume the plant is common or not native to Ohio.

In the twenty-two years since I began sending annual reports to ODNR, I have noticed how the ratings continually change. More often than not, E becomes T, then P, and sometimes just disappears off the list. Perhaps more intensive plant-searching is involved, or more areas with rare habitats are acquired. Conversely, new native species never reported before for Ohio suddenly appear, or species marked X return from the dead. Both types will then be rated E.

During the '70s, I started exploring distant parts of Ohio, especially the Lucy Braun country of Adams County, and the prairies and sand barrens of Oak Openings Metropolitan Park outside of Toledo. Later I went farther afield and visited other parts of the Great Lakes region: Michigan's Upper Peninsula and Ontario's Bruce Peninsula, both famous for orchids; Wisconsin's Door Peninsula and its wildflower hot spot called the Ridges Sanctuary; the Indiana Dunes National Lakeshore; Michigan's Isle Royale National Park in Lake Superior; and Ontario's Manitoulin Island in Lake Huron. My record books were getting fatter with all the new data.

In preparing for these trips, I had originally supposed that there were plenty of guide books on the market that pinpointed and described choice botanical locations in the same manner that the Pettingill series and others had accomplished for bird-watchers, but no luck; if I was curious about good areas for rare plants, I either had to hear about them through word of mouth, or else write to agencies in other states equivalent to ODNR in Ohio. Or else, I could start the ball rolling by writing articles on my own for would-be plant hunters, incorporating all the best three-hour walks I've taken in unusual habitats; providing observations, thoughts, and feelings on the rare plants I encountered; and mentioning the environmental pressures on these species and their chances for survival.

While I was wondering what style to use and what format the articles might be modeled after, the staff of the *New Yorker* magazine answered my questions. By an odd coincidence, the January 12, 1976, issue came out with an article on the search for one rare tree—the **round-leaved birch** (*Betula uber*), which was found in southwest Virginia and nowhere else, and had been lost for about 60 years since its original discovery in 1914. "The Search for *Betula uber*," by New Yorker staff writer Eugene Kinkead, had all the elements of a good personal essay (Kinkead was one of the search party.) plus the suspense of a mystery story. In style, it was strictly journalistic, with quotations from local farmers as well as from the botanical experts who had invited Kinkead along. Lastly, it was scientifically accurate but lacked the stuffiness of much botanical writing, and it even had touches of humor here and there.

In-9 **Sphagnum Plants: Wild Calla** (*Calla palustris*-T) of the **jack-in-the-pulpit family**, or **aroids**, near a lake in Portage County.

So now I had all the elements for writing my own articles. I had found my subject: endangered species (mostly of plants, but including any unusual animals present) and their habitats, which I had personally observed, often after some difficulty; my purpose: conservation of rare species within their habitats; my medium: the three-hour walk type of personal essay; my style: journalistic, although scientifically accurate (but not stuffy or loaded with technical jargon and unexplained scientific terms); and my readers: average people who liked plants but were not very familiar with them. All I had to do now was consult my record books, full of raw data, and put together essays that people would want to read. Oh, yes, I would also have to find a publisher.

In this I have been lucky. Since the late '70s, I have written about thirty articles on rare species and their habitats—amounting to one or two a year, not exactly a frantic pace—but I have always had a publisher. My first articles of a medium length and a more serious nature, including the first three in this book, appeared in the *Explorer*, the magazine of the Cleveland Museum of Natural History. Later on, I sent my longer essays to the *Newsletter* of the American Association of Field Botanists, headquartered in Chattanooga, Tennessee. The AAFBees, of which I'm proud to be a member, are a very informal type of group and originally concentrated on the flora of the Southern Appalachians, the most diverse and perhaps the oldest in North America, but lately have extended the range of their field trips to the rest of the continent and even into Europe. The editors of the *Newsletter* have also been very accommodating to long articles submitted to them: they simply serialize them.

In the late '80s, I was invited by the editors of *Wildflower* magazine, published in Toronto, Ontario, to submit essays to them, because they liked the way my articles in the *AAFBee Newsletter*, with which they had an exchange agreement, stressed conservation. Although Jim Hodgins, the editor-in-chief, has named me on the masthead as "contributing editor of Great Lakes, South," I turn in essays on all parts of the continent.

As for my shorter, less researched articles, they have appeared in the newsletters of two conservation organizations I belong to: the Native Plant Society of Northeastern Ohio and the Ohio Chapter of the Nature Conservancy. Lastly, one article—on a dump on the east side of Cleveland on the Lake Erie shore—appeared in *Sunday* magazine of Cleveland's newspaper *The Plain Dealer*. This is reprinted here as Chapter 9.

And now a few words about the chapters. Each essay selected for this book was written independently of the others and was meant to stand on its own without additional explanation. To this end I try to keep scientific terminology to a minimum and explain all technical words. The longer, more serious, and more detailed articles usually involve one specific habitat type, like a prairie, or a specific location, like Manitoulin Island

In-10 **Large cranberry** (*Vaccinium macrocarpon* of the **heath family**) in Willow Bog in Portage County. Very typical of northern bog plants, it was first gathered for its fruit by Native American tribes.

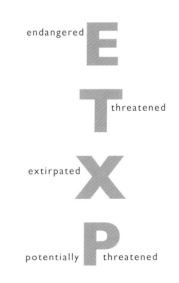

endangered **E**

T threatened

extirpated **X**

potentially **P** threatened

or the Driftless Area. The shorter, less serious, and less researched articles are usually on a single family of plants, such as orchids, and the conservation message is played down.

I chose Chapter 1, "A Walk through Lucy Braun's Prairie," to set the tone for the whole book. The article, in picture-frame style, starts and ends with Lynx Prairie, but the middle part focuses on the life of a remarkable woman, E. Lucy Braun, a special person and an influential scholar and writer, who epitomizes the environmental movement in Ohio. Not only in my travels through Adams County, where Lucy Braun did much of her important field work, but in my attempts to popularize her environmental message, I have followed in her footsteps.

"Four Species in Search of a Habitat" (Chapter 2) shows the influence of the Endangered Species Act of 1973 on my writing as I investigate the habitats of four very rare and unusual plants of Ohio. The section on the arethusa orchid represents the happy ending of a quest begun several years before when I first saw this colorful species in Titus Bog in Pennsylvania and always hoped to find it in Ohio. In gathering material for this article, I realized more than ever before the importance of knowledgeable guides. I could never have found these four species and their locations without them.

"Ohio's Invisible Prairies" (Chapter 3) focuses on just one habitat mentioned in the previous article, the **prairie**, but includes numerous field trips I have taken throughout Ohio to see all the various kinds of prairies in the state. I also introduce the concept of biodiversity, the great array of both plant and animal species that can coexist in one habitat if it isn't altered by man.

My only article on a region of Ontario, Canada—Manitoulin Island in Lake Huron—is included here as Chapter 4, based on a weekend visit I made with the Canadian Native Plant Society. This was an opportunity to write about the *alvar* habitat, natural limestone pavements more common to the Great Lakes region, including Ohio, than elsewhere. Writing the article also gave me an opportunity to tie together elements of field biology, geology, ecology, ethnology, travel, history, and conservation. I feel that while this mixture may increase the length of an article, it also increases its readability.

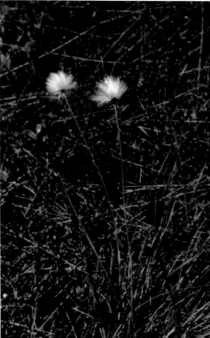

In-11 **Bog cotton**, now called **green cotton-grass** (*Eriophorum viridicarinatum*–P), is neither cotton nor a grass, but a sedge, one of the few in this large family whose tiny fruit is carried aloft by silky hairs. Very common genus in Arctic regions.

Both "The Halophytes are Coming?..." (Chapter 5) and "White City...What a Dump!" (Chapter 9) deal with what is now the commonest habitat of the Great Lakes region—the disturbed area, now populated by introduced species of plants and animals, including **halophytes**, or salt-tolerant species. In Chapter 5, I point out the effect of habitat change by salt pollution in the soil and water of an area and the economic damage to its human residents.

"White City..." was actually the first article I ever wrote on rare plants, and its journalistic style reflects the fact that it was submitted to a daily newspaper for publication. My observations of a former Lake Erie bathing beach turned into a dump are equally divided between rare migrating birds and unusual plants, including some species, oddly enough, that I would never see anywhere else. In content it is mostly straight description, with no attempt to comb the scientific literature to explain the facts. If I were to rewrite this article, I would certainly contact the many fine Ohio ecologists who have been investigating the changes affecting the Lake Erie shoreline in the past quarter-century.

"Mallows" (Chapter 6) describes the mallow family in general but zeroes in on the four rarest mallows of the eastern U.S., three of which are found in Ohio and the Upper Great Lakes states. I could have omitted the fourth, the Peters Mountain mallow of Virginia, but its successful comeback from near-extinction, due to the implementation of a **recovery plan** (as mandated by the Endangered Species Act), was too important to neglect. It's always satisfying to report a success story.

"Faribault Diary" (Chapter 7) follows a trip I took to Minnesota in 1995 to see the Driftless Area and the federally endangered dwarf trout lily. Since this journey to a typical small town brought back memories of my own small-town upbringing, in the pre-television days, I chose details that would convey the parallel between the rarity of the lily and the decline of Main Street and its values, as urbanization spreads over the countryside.

The tongue-in-cheek tone of Chapter 8, "The Knotted Dodder ...," matches a similar attitude in Chapter 9, "Orchidophilia." Both articles were prompted by reading about the amazing lifestyles of orchids and non-green, leafless plants, such as dodders, which make both groups almost human, or at least animal-like. With the non-green plants I concentrate on their complex life histories, while with orchids, I describe their effects on the behavior of certain amateur botanists, whose main object, like that of certain birders, is to increase their life list. Although the orchidophobe described at the end of the article is, of course, fictitious, many readers will no doubt subscribe to his philosophy of "the wholeness of life," which is basically what **ecology** is all about.

About Chapter 11, "Pennsylvanian Nature Trail," I won't say anything except that the first word of the title has a double meaning to students of geology.

In-12 **Northern bog club-moss** (*Lycopodiella inundata*) is a spore-bearing plant, whose ancestry goes back to the Devonian Period of 400 million years ago. (See Chapter 11) Not a moss, it is more closely related to ferns. The expanded part of the stem at top, commonly called the "club," is actually the spore-producing tissue.

The next three chapters (12 through 14) are a light-hearted overview of three plant families in Ohio: gentians, grasses, and sedges. The discussion of the latter two families is designed especially to help readers who like plants to know more about some of the commonest but least spectacular species in Ohio. Chapter 14 on sedges takes the form of a letter to an editor and mirrors some of my own experiences as a volunteer for 10 years in the herbarum of the Cleveland Museum of Natural History.

Chapter 15, "Ohio's Fairest and Rarest Plants...and How to Find Them," written in 2003, summarizes the main theme of the book: that searching out rare habitats will always result in finding endangered species in need of protection. Although I emphasize Appalachian-type habitats in the Lucy Braun country of southern Ohio, which ties in well with Chapter I, I also mention wetlands found in other parts of Ohio. These are the northern habitats that are familiar to plant-hunters all over the Upper Great Lakes region.

In the Epilogue I go back to the book's beginning and try to show how successful Ohio's Natural Heritage Program has been in promoting conservation and exploration for rare species and their habitats. I also recount adventures in other states, in which I first encountered some of the plants Lucy Braun originally discovered.

The appendix is a list of the 1999 *federally* endangered and threatened plants found in Ohio and the five Upper Great Lakes States. Of the eighteen separate species named, I've covered, or at least mentioned, eight in various chapters. I've also discussed species that were on the federal list in previous years but have been removed, due to discoveries of additional populations.

All the illustrations were originally meant to be placed in a second appendix, but I thought it would be easier for the reader to refer to them if they were placed throughout the book. The numerals of the illustrations refer to the chapter where they first appear. "In-" refers to this introduction, and "Ep-" refers to the Epilogue.

Since I possess so many slides of plants not discussed in the text of the book, I have included some of the best at the end in a separate photo appendix. "NO" refers to plants in northern Ohio not mentioned before. "SO" refers to southern Ohio plants, and "GL" refers to plants seen around the Upper Great Lakes that barely reach Ohio, or did so in the past.

I have been retired now for twenty-three years, over half of the time that I spent behind the teacher's desk, but through writing these articles and fourteen others (covering habitats in other regions of North America), I feel that I'm still teaching, but

"We wanted

In-13 **The round-leaved sundew** (*Drosera rotundifolia*), surrounded by strands of dried-up (brown) and living (green) **sphagnum moss**, is a **carnivorous plant**. (See Chapter 8.) It has been found in so many sphagnum wetlands that it has been taken off the **Heritage List**, Ohio's roster of rare plants.

to see

In-14 **The dragon's-mouth**, or **arethusa**, orchid (*Arethusa bulbosa-E*), seen from the side, is generally considered the rarest of the three pink bog orchids. The others are the **rose pogonia** (*Pogonia ophioglossoides—T*) and the **grass-pink** (*Calopogon tuberosus—T*). The only place I've found all three is Willow Bog, but not in bloom at the same time. (See Chapter 10.) This view of the dragon's-mouth shows the **tongue** (actually the lowest petal, usually called the **lip**), which is multicolored to attract pollinators.

through a different medium. Also, I'm still learning, not only about rare and endangered plants and their habitats, but also about the importance of the natural world in our lives.

Whenever the Endangered Species Act comes up for renewal, many scientific writers justify its continuance on the basis of the beauty and genetic uniqueness of the species that are being protected from extinction; on their scientific and educational value, which are just becoming known; and on their present and potential economic importance in medicine, agriculture, and industry. All these are extremely important, but one doesn't have to be an expert to add another reason to the list: that the natural world, even our own back yard, sets a standard for reality.

The Greeks understood this—one character in mythology lost all his strength if he couldn't feel the earth under his feet, and Thoreau called contact with nature a high point on our mental "Realometer," a kind of gauge for judging human activities and attitudes. He took the name from Nilometers in Egypt that measured the daily depth of that country's only river and its source of life. One wonders how he would react if he were to observe how much of our life nowadays is spent watching the flickering lights and shadows on our personal computer and TV screens and digesting the relentless messages from the media, bombarding us with symbols, clichés, slogans, stereotypes, and illusions. He would probably recommend a personal Realometer to free our minds.

He would also relish the following story: in 1985, when my wife Carol and I had just returned from a weeklong Nature Conservancy convention in Orlando, Florida, we were telling some friends about many of the wonderful natural areas that this fine organization is saving, and which we had spent much time exploring on foot—tropical forests of cabbage palmettos and slash pines; magnolias and live oaks, with butterfly orchids and resurrection ferns growing on their branches; cacti and strange-looking cycads clustered on the ground. One of our friends asked,

"How could you visit Orlando and not see Disneyworld?"

Our reply was without apologies: "We wanted to see the real world."

Shaker Heights, Ohio
February 2006

the real world."

In-15 The **leather-leaf** flower close up. Note the tall drooping cluster of white, semi-closed flowers, very characteristic of the heath family. Heaths, club-mosses, sedges, sundews, and orchids are all typical of northern wetlands, such as **kettle-hole bogs**. (See next photo.)

In-16 Another type of bog, such as pictured here at **Triangle Lake**, in Portage County, is the **kettle-hole lake**, which fills up with rain water and is replenished from underground springs. Note the zonation: **tamaracks** to the rear, and a shrubby heath called **leather-leaf** (*Chamaedaphne calyculata*–P) in front.

In-17 **Rocky Slopes** in northern Ohio. The most common building blocks that form slopes and ledges are sandstone, limestone (especially as one goes further west), and hard clay. Shale, a sedimentary rock, is fairly uncommon. Here is a shale slope overlooking the Chagrin River in Gates Mills, Ohio, 20 miles east of Cleveland, with oaks changing to autumn colors. The slope supports, among other plants, a stand of the **small fringed gentian** (*Gentianopsis procera*–P). (See Chapter 12.)

A Walk Through Lucy Braun's Prairie

Slowly, as if someone were idly running his finger along a pocket comb, the ascending chromatic scale of a bird's song came from the top of a tall red cedar. The prairie warbler, certainly, but where was he hiding? As we stood in the grassy clearing surrounded by shrubs and tall trees, we could not help feeling the appropriateness of the occasion: here was Lynx Prairie with its resident bird.

1-1 **Lynx Prairie, a Series of Forest Openings: North Prairie** is the first of ten prairie openings the visitor comes upon. The grasses and broad-leaf plants are typical prairie species. The surrounding forest is dominated by **eastern red-cedar** (*Juniperus virginiana*), a tree typical of limestone soils.

1-2 **Eastern red-cedars** close up. Note the unbranched, columnar shape of the younger trees.

It had not been easy finding the prairie. Lying not far from the Ohio River on a slope in Ohio's Adams County, it consisted of ten grassy patches of several acres apiece separated by thick woods. Oddly enough, the only entrance path led from a country cemetery, near the village of Lynx. No directional arrows had been posted; no signs at all except the dedicatory plaque were visible, and even that was half concealed by vegetation. A conspiracy of silence seemed to block easy entrance to this nature preserve, as if screening out all but the most dedicated hikers.

And then it began to rain. Fighting the urge to give up this exploration and return to something more civilized—say, a guided tour through nearby Serpent Mound—we began stumbling our way through the jungle of wet shrubs, trying to hold on to botany books, camera, map, and the guide pamphlet issued by Ohio Nature Conservancy, which owned the area.

"Not much of a prairie," observed the youngest of our party, as we emerged into a vest-pocket opening in the midst of scrub pines, oaks, and cedars. But it was a prairie, nevertheless, an isolated grassland in the hills of southern Ohio, explored and studied over the years by the indefatigable Lucy Braun, ultimately preserved by her efforts, and

1-3 A typical plant of Ohio prairies, the **prairie-dock** (*Silphium terebinthinaceum*) has flowers resembling those of the **common sunflower** (*Helianthus*) in the same family. The specific, or second, name refers to the resin in the stem. Note the large basal leaves.

1-4 Close-up of the flowers of **prairie-dock**.

dedicated to her memory. Here she identified and catalogued the strange assortment of Southern, Appalachian, and Western plants, found nowhere else in such a congenial association. Here she pondered over the environmental factors—temperature, soil, rainfall, and others—that made such an association possible. From here she branched out to other parts of the Ohio Valley to unravel its geological history and to conclude that the last two **glaciers** played as important a part in the distribution of plants as the present environment. Thus she accounted for the region's peculiar **relict plants**— formerly widespread but now surviving in a relatively few nooks and crannies where pre-glacial conditions prevail, and its odd **disjuncts**—plants separated by great distances from their main centers of abundance.

Fortunately the rain had stopped, and I took out the camera, ready to record any of the strange inhabitants of Lynx Prairie. It was late June, not the prime viewing time of August, but even now patches of huge leaves were elbowing their way into the open. From visits to other Ohio prairies, I recognized them as forerunners of prairie-dock (*Silphium terebinthinaceum*), an aggressive sunflower-like **composite**, which would soon compete with the prairie grasses and lift up yellow flowers, nodding on five-foot stems. Typical of prairies, I thought, and rather expected.

More of the prairie flora began to appear out of the grass. Here bloomed **whorled milkweed** (*Asclepias verticillata*), a common roadside plant in northern Illinois, but not in Ohio. With small, grayish-white flowers, it was a shorter, slimmer version of the common milkweed familiar to northern Ohioans. Scarlet **Indian paintbrush** (*Castilleja coccinea*) provided spots of hot color among the browns and greens. **Lance-leaved loosestrife** (*Lysimachia lanceolata*) reminded us of the other loosestrifes of northern Ohio except for the narrow leaves. Familiar types of plants, all, but where were the relicts and disjuncts?

I knew that we would not find in Lynx Prairie the most famous relict of southern Ohio—**mountain lover** or **cliff-green** (*Paxistima canbyi–E*) of the **bittersweet family**. This is a tiny, ground-hugging shrub found locally atop cliffs in only six states: Ohio, West Virginia, Virginia, Kentucky, Tennessee, and Pennsylvania. Its closest relative lives in the Rocky Mountains of Montana. This strange distribution seemed to be telling Lucy Braun a familiar story: a plant with no apparent special adaptations to a changing environment such as in post-glacial eastern North America, would ultimately find itself restricted to a few scattered areas of the continent and perhaps become extinct if its habitat were not preserved.

Disjuncts were a different matter. In Lynx Prairie we kept running across a "foreigner," so to speak. We examined the tall spike of flowers, the strap-shaped succulent basal leaves. A yucca? We were almost right. Thanks to Lucy Braun's pamphlet in our hand, we could identify this as **false aloe** (*Agave virginica–T*). Here was actually one of the century plants that had made its way east and north from its desert home in the America Southwest

1-5 **False aloe** (*Agave virginica–T*) is the only century-plant in northeastern US. One of the smallest members of its genus, this specimen displays the typical tube-like petals exceeded by the long stamens.

1-6 Basal leaves of the **false aloe** have hardly any teeth, compared to the wicked spines of the Southwestern species of *Agave*.

1-7 Looking down at **Indian paintbrush** (*Castilleja coccinea*). One of the few Eastern species of a huge genus that dominates prairies out West, it has colorful scarlet bracts that attract insects to the inconspicuous flowers.

1-8 **Leather-flower** (*Clematis viorna*) is a vine with nodding, wine-colored sepals. Petals are lacking. It climbs over shrubs, tall grasses in open woodlands mainly in southeastern US.

and Mexico during a dry, interglacial period and now stood incongruously in a well-watered grassland. Yet for it and other Far Western plants, Lynx Prairie was home.

An unusual vine, **leather-flower** (*Clematis viorna*), lacking petals, but with thick, half-opened, wine-colored sepals, was clambering over the shrubs and tall grasses. We had never before seen this denizen of the South and Midwest with its nodding, bell-shaped flowers. Keeping it company were two other unfamiliar vines native to the Deep South: **anglepod** (*Matelea obliqua–T*) of the milkweeds and yellow **passion-flower** (*Passiflora lutea*). The unexpected was becoming the usual thing.

Even the trees and ferns were different. Like the flowering dogwood in the North, redbud (*Cercis canadensis*) was the dominant understory shrub here, reminding us of its great abundance in the Pennsylvania Appalachians. But that other tree with the white blossoms was unfamiliar and had to be keyed out as **Carolina buckthorn** (*Rhamnus caroliniana*), found south of the Ohio River, except for stations in Adams and Scioto Counties. The ferns draped over the large dolomite boulders scattered in the woods looked promising, and they were. Both were widespread in eastern North America but confined to limestone and similar rocks. One was the **bulblet fern** (*Cystopteris bulbifera*), familiar to northern Ohioans as an inhabitant of cool gorges, a companion to hemlock and Canada yew. However, the other one, almost blue in color with lower leaflets divided twice, was **smooth cliff-brake** (*Pellaea glabella*), never seen in northeast Ohio.

From prairie patch to forest to rocky ledge to swamp, all within the confines of a small area, we were following the footsteps of Dr. E. (for Emma) Lucy Braun, who, decades before, had first laid out these trails and named each prairie after its typical occupant (Dock Prairie, Liatris Prairie). One prairie is named after her sister Annette. This is appropriate when one realizes the two sisters lived together in the same Cincinnati house, worked together in the natural sciences—Lucy as professor of botany at the university, Annette as free-lance researcher in entomology—and traveled together over the country in pursuit of their respective specialties.

Early in childhood the Braun sisters had acquired a love of nature from their schoolteacher parents, and this never left them. With a rare singlemindedness they determined their area of specialization (Annette in tiny moths, or microlepidoptera, and Lucy in plant distribution), and both obtained their doctor's degrees at the University of Cincinnati, which, in a sense, became their lifetime home.

Together as students they roamed the Cincinnati region, Annette collecting minute moths and their larvae, Lucy measuring, analyzing, and photographing plant habitats for her doctor's thesis, "Physiographic Ecology of the Cincinnati Region." It was during this time that she became interested in the relict and disjunct flora of Adams County. When she began teaching at the university before World War I, she would take her classes to Lynx and other prairie locations. Perhaps the last of Ohio's horse-and-buggy naturalists, Lucy would make countless trips to Adams County by train. After being let off at a railroad crossing, she would be met by a horse-drawn wagon to take her the rest of the way. Often she would have correspondents at strategic locations let her know when a certain rare plant was in bloom so that she could schedule a visit to study and photograph it.

Field trips could become adventurous. In Kentucky, moonshiners occasionally blocked choice botanical valleys with their stills. "You can go up this hollow, but not that hollow," they would tell her.

As a teacher and friend, she was patient, very exacting, but never pompous. Reserved and soft-spoken in the classroom, she was more informal in the field. In all her publications the one picture of herself she permitted to appear, next to a giant arbor vitae, shows her dressed in slacks, boots, and open-necked shirt. (Characteristically the caption refers to the tree and neglects to identify the author.) Often she would be accompanied on field trips by her mother, then in her 80s, who would amaze Lucy's students with her vigor and wide knowledge. Admired and respected by her students, Lucy was open and companionable to friends who shared her interests. They called her Braunie.

During the 1920s she developed a style of living that combined a Spartan personal life and a public life totally dedicated to botany. Articles for magazines and scholarly journals appeared in revolving-door succession from her pen. She was the founder, editor, and chief writer of a magazine called *Wildflower*, which at first was mainly descriptive but soon took on a crusading tone as she deplored the many man-made pressures threatening to obliterate the plant habitats she had painstakingly catalogued. Before the name became popular, Lucy Braun had become an environmentalist.

In private she lived an almost ascetic life. One friend noted that although a big double bed occupied her bedroom, she preferred sleeping on a small cot at its foot. She preserved a somewhat puritanical attitude, especially when she took her college students out on long weekend field trips. Once at Mineral Springs, in Adams County, a former student recalls, a dance was in progress at a hotel where she and her pupils were staying overnight. Dr. Braun permitted the young people to join in the festivities but after a while had second thoughts and took them away. She was heard saying to one young woman, "How can you let strange men put their arms around you?"

1-9 At the northern end of its range, Ohio's yellow **passion-flower** (*Passiflora lutea*) represents an exotic tropical family of vines, well known as ornamentals. (Photo taken on Lookout Mountain, in eastern Tennessee.)

1-10 The glamorous purple **passion-flower**, or **maypop** (*P. incarnata-T*) reaches southern Ohio in only 6 counties, including Adams. Since it favors open woodlands, it might be found in Lynx Prairie, but I've never seen it in bloom in Ohio or anywhere in the US. (Photo taken in Costa Rica.)

21

1-11 The **redbud** (*Cercis canadensis*), a tree of the legume family with beautiful pink flowers, seems to take the place of the **flowering dogwood** as an understory tree in much of the southern Ohio and the Appalachians.

To her, the pleasures of the mind took precedence. At home on Mt. Washington in Cincinnati, her greatest joys were to cultivate in her garden many of the rarities that she had picked up in her travels. Travel throughout the Ohio Valley and later the whole country became her passion, as she searched out unusual habitats and probed the geological history of each region, from which all the facts were to be organized into her greatest work, *The Deciduous Forests of Eastern North America*.

In the course of many trips throughout Kentucky, she had the pleasure that fewer and fewer botanists of the twentieth century have shared—finding, describing, and naming new plant species. As an Ohioan, she was probably a little disappointed that she had found no species new to science in her own state although she discovered some remarkable disjuncts. A good example was the startling appearance of *Erythronium rostratum*, a bright yellow fawn-lily never before found north of Tennessee. Lucy was the first to find it in southern Ohio in 1963. However, Kentucky proved a more fertile ground for new species of plants. It became the type locality for four new species and four new subspecies, duly reported by Lucy in the journal *Rhodora*. She found and named *Rhododendron cumberlandense*, a spectacular scarlet azalea from the Cumberland Plateau of Kentucky and West Virginia. It resembled the familiar flame azalea but bloomed later and had smaller, more brilliantly colored flowers with no color variations. Lucy theorized that it had crossed with the flame azalea to produce as hybrid offspring the enormously varied azaleas of the Blue Ridge further south. Another new Kentucky plant was a peculiar goldenrod, *Solidago albopilosa*, found in two counties and confined to so-called **rockhouses**, overhangs resembling the mouths of caves and commonly occurring in sandstone cliffs above rivers. With a sandy floor and a rock roof cutting off light and rain from overhead, a rockhouse provided a demanding environment for plants. Another rockhouse plant she discovered was a boneset, *Eupatorium deltoides*, which Merritt L. Fernald renamed, for his 1950 edition of *Gray's Manual of Botany*, *Eupatorium luciae-brauniae* in her honor.

After thirty-four years on the faculty, Lucy retired from the University of Cincinnati in 1948 at the age of fifty-nine. From exhaustion? Hardly. Early retirement was her opportunity to put into final form *The Deciduous Forests*, a reference on forest ecology that has never been surpassed in wealth of descriptive detail. With her solid grounding in geology and genetics, Lucy advanced the theory that all the forest types of the East evolved from the cove forest of the southern Appalachians after the last Ice Age. The difference in forest makeup (**oak-hickory**, **beech-maple**, and others) was due mainly to geological and environmental factors which favored certain species of trees over others in each region of the country. Her theory was disputed but never successfully challenged, at least during her lifetime. (The few times the usually reserved Lucy Braun was ever observed in a heated argument was with scholars who questioned her conclusions.) As a grand synthesis, it provides a reason for the distribution of not only all the important forest trees but also many of the plants associated with them.

With her life's work behind her, Lucy Braun now turned to a huge project never tackled before: a comprehensive **flora** of every vascular plant found in Ohio, with illustrations, keys to identify species and subspecies, and distribution maps to include each county. This colossal undertaking, made with collaborators, illustrators, and special contributors, required a thorough check of every major herbarium in the country as well as much supplementary exploration in the field. The results were *The Woody Plants of Ohio* (1961) and *The Vascular Plants of Ohio: Cat-tails to Orchids* (1967), regional flora acclaimed as models of their type. As necessary references, they are to be found on the shelves of every plant scientist who works in Ohio and yet can be understood by any amateur botanist who wants the name of a strange tree or grass.

Who knows how many plant hunters, coming across **bottle-brush grass** or **plantain-leaved sedge** for the first time, as I did, have been encouraged by the well-drawn illustrations in Lucy's book to go out and investigate on their own the grasses and sedges ignored by the standard plant guides? The book is so useful that one wonders how Lucy herself got along without it! Thus it was that in her retirement years, she became a teacher to the world. But, as one associate remarked, "Lucy never really retired."

Time was taking its toll. Her last published work, in 1969, was a journal article, "*An Ecological Survey of the Vegetation of Fort Hill State Memorial, Highland County, Ohio.*" The reader gets the picture of a doughty lady in her late '70s, climbing the steep hills of her beloved southwest Ohio with her assistant, directing transect lines, staking off quadrats, photographing habitats, supervising the diagrams, graphs, profiles, and maps, and comparing all the information obtained with the store of data stretching back to her first visit in 1923. Her conclusion? Much research still has to be done to explain this ecosystem and its peculiarities of plant distribution. To Lucy Braun, long past retirement age, the mysteries of plant communities were still as intriguing as they were to the teenage girl entering the university sixty years before.

In 1971 she died at the age of 82, having received a multitude of honors and awards for her scientific work and yet aware of its incompleteness. *The Vascular Plants of Ohio* was yet to be finished, although a number of scholars were working on it. (It still hasn't been completed at this writing—in 2006!) Her concern over preservation of habitats, starting with the articles in *Wildflower*, has led to many concrete results. Lucy's favorite prairie locations in Adams County, beginning with Lynx Prairie and continuing with Buzzardroost

1-12 **Smooth cliff-brake** (*Pellaea glabella*), one of the many ferns that favor the pitted limestone-like rock known as **dolomite**, very prominent in Adams County. The bluish color of its tiny fronds makes it distinctive.

1-13 **A Rare Southern-Ohio Lily**: To Lucy Braun goes the credit for discovering the **golden-star** (*Erythronium rostratum—E*), a type of **fawn-lily**, in a single river valley in one county in Ohio. As of this writing (2003), this distribution pattern still holds true. (See Chapter 15.)

1-14 **Biographical Photos, Courtesy of OSU Prof. (Ret.) Dr. Ronald Stuckey:** At the age of 61, **Lucy Braun** had been retired for two years from the University of Cincinnati to work on *The Deciduous Forests of Eastern North America*.

Rock, Red Rock, The Wilderness, and others, have all been preserved by an organization she encouraged and advised, the Ohio Chapter of The Nature Conservancy. A future project combining all these holdings into one large nature preserve, to be called **Edge of Appalachia**, was begun around this time. The one small voice that spoke up within an obscure magazine in the 1920s has been joined by hundreds of thousands, eighty years later, concerned lest our own quality of life approach the relict and disjunct stage if our environment is not improved.

1-15 In an Adams County prairie, **Lucy Braun** smiles as she demonstrates the extraordinary height of **big bluestem** (*Andropogon gerardii*).

1-17 **Lucy and Annette Braun,** in hiking clothes, relax in an Adams County forest.

1-16 In a family photograph taken in front of the Braun's Cincinnati home, probably in the World War I era, **Lucy**, on the right, and her sister **Annette**, on the left, stand beside their **mother**. Annette, a lifelong lepidopterist, died in November 1978.

1-18 Standing next to a large oak tree in Pennsylvania, **Lucy Braun** in 1944 had begun traveling throughout Eastern North America to do research for her book on forest ecology.

As we searched for a sight of the prairie warbler in the treetops, the bird flew off. Thanks to a modest, dedicated woman, there will be a prairie for it to return to next year, a place where the Carolina buckthorn and the yellow passion-flower will grow next to the false aloe and the other curious plants of an association spanning untold centuries. Botanists and plant geographers will be able to return to Lynx Prairie to ferret out its mysteries. Ordinary people listening for the unchanging heartbeat of our beautiful land may find it here.

Four Species in Search of a Habitat

2-1 **The Swamp Forest: Spreading globeflower**
(*Trollius laxus—E*) is shown at the height of bloom
in Moorhead Forest. It is reputed to be highly toxic.

2-2 A single **globeflower** close up. What appears to be a row of **petals** are really
sepals; the real petals circle the central core of stamens and pistils and function as
nectaries to attract insects.

"Rare...extremely local...nearly extinct..." For years readers of natural-history guides and wildlife manuals have resigned themselves to these dreary labels, usually applied to the larger, more attractive plants and animals of any group, whether fresh-water fish, birds, butterflies, or trees. **Ecology,** like economics, had become the gloomy science.

However, since the passage of the Endangered Species Act of 1973, we hear a new message of hope: with government protection rare species can be saved. The Postal Service has issued stamps picturing rare species; the Smithsonian Institution has drawn up large lists of endangered species for the whole country; individual states have set up special offices to identify species warranting protection; and the wheels of government have slowly turned in recognition of this neglected branch of the environment. In Ohio, for instance, over 700 species of plants have been labeled as extinct, endangered, threatened, or potentially threatened. Under the state's Natural Heritage Program the computerized inventorying of the endangered species is rapidly progressing, to be eventually followed by their protection. The goals of generations of naturalists and environmentalists seem now within reach—except for the nagging question: "How do we protect a species if we have no knowledge of its habitat requirements?" As one authority puts it, "The threatened and endangered species are one of the poorest-known assemblages of plants in the United States."

2-3 One of the rarest native plantains in the US, the **heart-leaf plantain** (*Plantago cordata*–T) lives only in shallow streams of swamp forests, a highly specialized and endangered habitat.

To answer this problem, it has been generally conceded that since rare plants cannot be saved by transplanting them to greenhouses, botanical gardens, or other artificial environments, the best approach is to acquire a whole plant and animal community and maintain it in its original condition. The search for rare plants has thus evolved into a search for rare habitats.

Unlike beauty, rarity is not only in the eyes of the beholder. It can be measured by the decline of known localities for each rare plant. To illustrate the scope of the problem, let us follow the fortunes of four Ohio plants whose numbers have declined in the past fifty years. Each is considered endangered in that only one or two locations are now known for it, and each requires a different habitat. The **globeflower**, the **small white lady's-slipper**, the **arethusa orchid**, and the **northern monkshood** are the kind of plants often vividly described and illustrated in field manuals but seldom encountered in the wild. All four are glamorous with large, colorful, and uniquely shaped flowers. All have an ancient lineage with relatives in Europe, Asia, and Western North America. All but the arethusa are rare in all parts of their range and are thus on the national endangered list compiled by the Smithsonian Institution.

To find the "last known address" of these rarities, one need not go far from the teeming cities and sprawling suburbs of industrialized northern Ohio. By some fluke of geography and local history, locales that I will call Moorhead Forest, Mill Prairie, Willow Bog, and Cruickshank Glen are not so much removed from modern Ohio by distance as by time. Time has stood still in these localities, allowing their plants and animals to enjoy the original conditions for growth and survival.

2-4 Providing a golden display of flowers every spring in wetlands throughout northern Eurasia and North America, the **marsh-marigold** (*Caltha palustris*) enjoys a success completely opposite to that of the globeflower, yet both are in the **buttercup** or **crowfoot** family.

To discover these original conditions at first hand, I visited each locality during the blooming season of its most celebrated inhabitant. In late April I journeyed to Moorhead Forest to find the **spreading globeflower** (*Trollius laxus*–E) in its last stand in Ohio. After meeting my guide, a soft-spoken retired park naturalist, I entered the wet woods, cut by many streams and pools. We stood under tall trees, whose leaves were just expanding, and marveled at the long vistas of **Virginia bluebells** (*Mertensia virginica*) carpeting the forest. Many of the trees were **American elms**, either dead or suffering Dutch elm disease. Their trunks littered the ground. By a strange twist of fate, my guide explained, the elms' misfortune had helped the globeflowers by giving them more light and space to grow in. Not many years before, the only other Ohio colony, growing in a nearby park, had been extirpated when park managers, not realizing the rarity of *Trollius*, decided to plant tulip trees in the midst of a thriving patch. It was soon shaded out.

As we threaded our way down wet banks and over fallen logs, I could not help feeling that this swamp forest had changed little since the earliest days of settlement. **Marsh marigolds** (*Caltha palustris*) were in their glory, their golden clumps dotting the pools and streamsides. On higher ground the strange-looking **toadshade** (*Trillium sessile*) with dark maroon flowers tightly closed, stood close to **swamp saxifrage** (*Saxifraga pensylvanica*) with its large, white-hairy leaves and unfurling blossom stalk.

2-5 Close-up of a colony of **blue-eyed Mary** (*Collinsia verna*), a bicolored member of the snapdragon family fond of lush forests.

Proceeding through this rich understory, I felt lucky to have an experienced guide. Otherwise, I would have never noticed the blue and white flowers of **blue-eyed Mary** (*Collinsia verna*), a member of the snapdragon family that grows on wet ground, sometimes in large colonies. Also, in the same brushy corner of the swamp forest was a large plantain in flower with a typical spike of dried brownish flowers without petals, similar to, but twice as tall as, that of the **common plantain** (*Plantago major*), the notorious lawn weed, originally from Europe. My guide called it "water-plantain," and we moved on.

(Later, after my slides came back from the developer's, I remembered that **southern water-plantain** is the common name of an aquatic plant in the arrowhead family, *Alisma subcordatum*, which has open panicles of white-petaled flowers but no relationship to the true plantains, although the leaves are shaped the same. But what was this plant, which was obviously in the same family as that of the true plantains, but much taller?

Finally I was told by an expert, whose name I can't remember, that this was indeed a true plantain and, what's more, the rarest one in Ohio at that time—**heart-leaved plantain** (*P. cordata*–T). Found in only ten counties in Ohio, it is becoming rare throughout its range in the Southeastern and Midwestern states because it is adapted exclusively to well-shaded swamp forests, such as Moorhead, and its seedlings usually take root in rocky stream bottoms that are alkaline or neutral.)

Suddenly I realized we stood in the midst of large, two-foot-high clumps of globeflower. Despite their finely dissected leaves and pale yellow blossoms they could have easily been dismissed as faded marsh marigolds. The flowers were of the same size and shape. The American species is unlike the typical globeflowers of Europe and Asia, often seen in the garden catalogues, with their golden or orange color and tight globular shape. In our species the globe shape, in which the tips of all the **sepals** touch, is preserved only in the green, immature stage. When fully developed, the flowers spread their sepals (The real petals are reduced to tiny **nectaries**.) and somewhat resemble their cousins in the **crowfoot family**, the marsh marigolds.

Whatever the reason, the globeflower as a species is not doing well. The Smithsonian Institution lists it as endangered throughout its range: Maine, New Hampshire, Connecticut, New York, New Jersey, Pennsylvania, Delaware, and Ohio. **Endangered**, in the language of the 1973 law, means in immediate danger of extinction unless protected. Endangered species have a small range and a restricted habitat within that range. On the other hand, species labeled as **threatened** are in danger only in part of their range. Usually they exist in larger numbers and in more varied habitats.

As I glanced around at the thriving clumps of globeflowers, it was hard to realize that these fifty or so plants within an acre of woodland were the last remnants of the species west of the Appalachians. Why did it thrive only here? Similar wet woods could be found in many other parts of the state. Why did its relatives seem to do well in Europe and the Rockies? Suddenly Moorhead Forest assumed a fragile, impermanent cast, its very lushness denying its own mortality. Within its protected boundaries, could such a small plant population withstand predators, disease, adverse weather, or the insidious genetic conditions that produce defective mutations or sterility through inbreeding?

*　　　*　　　*　　　*　　　*　　　*　　　*

It was a far cry from the cool, well-watered forests of Moorhead to the dry, sunny stretches of Mill Prairie. Even in May the temperature soared above 80, with high humidity and no breeze. The tall grasses and composites which distinguish the prairie in late summer had hardly put in an appearance. The ground seemed baked, and although the shade under the trees and bushes along the edge of the prairie looked inviting, the air there was as parched as elsewhere. Yet the native prairie plants were thriving. Two kinds of violets covered the baked clay. **Starry Solomon's plume** (*Smilacina stellata*) lifted sprays of white flowers, of a larger size than those of the commoner woodland species,

2-6 My mentor, the late **Lindley Vickers**, was the first expert in rare wetland plants to guide me around their habitats. He is shown here looking at a colony of the sedge known as **green cotton-grass** (*Eriophorum viridicarinatum*–P).

false Solomon's seal (*S. racemosa*). The **yellow star-grass** (*Hypoxis hirsuta*) seemed to be hiding among the other plants. By contrast, the real attraction of Mill Prairie, the **white lady's slipper** (*Cypripedium candidum–E*) was out by the hundreds of clumps (Someone estimated 5,000 blossoms.) along the dirt road, tucked away in the grass, or in the hot shade of bushes, each with a few stalks of white-pouched flowers, one or two on a stalk, in such abundance as if to suggest all the other Ohio prairies must be now bursting with these white orchids.

Such is not the case. Although the plant was once reported from nine counties, Mill Prairie is the only prairie in the state that has a population of the lady's slipper and only one of four sites in Ohio where one can find it at all. (One other is Willow Bog.) Why a species is so abundant in certain sites and completely absent in others with apparently similar conditions is one of the agonizing problems of plant distribution, a mystery made more disheartening as the plant's present range continues to shrink throughout the country. The Smithsonian lists it as threatened in thirteen states from New York to North Dakota south to Nebraska and Kentucky.

As an orchid, the white lady's-slipper has evolved one of the most ingenious methods of pollination of any family of plants. The attractive pouch is simply a petal turned into an insect trap. In finding its way out of the pouch, the insect inadvertently pollinates the flower. Plant systematists believe it to be a close relative of the **yellow lady's-slipper** (*C. parviflorum var. pubescens*), which became isolated as a species between advances of the glacier. In early spring the flowers unfold before the leaves develop, which is an arctic-alpine trait. Adapted more to grasslands than any of the other lady's-slippers, it has always been local, even in the prairie regions of Michigan, Wisconsin, and Illinois, where it used to be found in its greatest abundance. As with most of the prairie flora in Ohio, its former habitats have been drained and converted to fields of corn and soybeans. ("Succotash!" one environmentalist has scornfully called them.) Fortunately, since Mill Prairie is protected, its character will not change through human encroachment, but it must be "managed" to prevent trees and shrubs from taking over. For this reason, the ancient Indian method of **fire** has been revived. Every two or three years Mill Prairie is judiciously burned.

2-7 **The Tall-Grass Prairie: Mill Prairie** in August. Here can be seen **big bluestem** (*Andropogon gerardii*) or **turkey-foot grass**; **prairie-dock** (*Silphium terebinthinaceum*); and other native plants. It has a thriving population of the **small white lady's-slipper** (*Cypripedium candidum–E*).

2-8 Close-up of the small white **lady's-slipper**.

2-9 **The Bog or Fen**: Willow Bog is named for the **hoary willow** (*Salix candida*-T), a northern type of small tree with frosty-white undersides to the leaves. Northern Ohio is at the extreme southern edge of its mostly Canadian range.

*   *   *   *   *   *   *

For a long time it has been known that white lady's-slippers will sometimes live in bogs if conditions are alkaline enough. Willow Bog is one example. Technically an **alkaline bog** or **fen**, it consists of a **sedge meadow** growing over a well-drained substrate, probably gravel. As the sedges turn into peat, mats and mounds of **sphagnum moss** grow over the peat to nourish acid-loving plants, such as the arethusa orchid (*Arethusa bulbosa*–E). Here, in the only location in Ohio now inhabited by the arethusa, it coexists peacefully with alkaline-tolerant plants, which are growing in a different **soil horizon**, a neutral dry peat or a mineral soil on the alkaline side.

Approaching the bog in mid-June, we passed through a thick, second-growth forest containing a few clumps of **early azalea**, also called **northern rose azalea** (*Rhododendron nudiflorum var. roseum*–P) a potentially endangered species in Ohio. A few pink flowers were still blooming, giving off a glorious fragrance. The seldom-seen **weak aster** (*Aster infirmus*) would bloom in this same woodland later in the summer. Willow Bog itself was a hard-to-find opening surrounded by cat-tail marshes, sedge meadows, and red-maple swamps. Not the ugly pit of quicksand of the popular imagination, guarded by poisonous snakes and insects, this fen was a fairly dry sphagnum mat covered by a fascinating plant community. Nearly every plant we encountered here was a Canadian species, and many were on the endangered list, because only a small number of Ohio fens have escaped commercial exploitation, through agriculture or **peat mining**. We threaded our way through mounds of the dominant woody plant, **shrubby cinquefoil** (*Potentilla fruticosa*), some of its yellow flowers already appearing in the midst of blue-green foliage. Everywhere the distinctive compound leaves of **Canada burnet** (*Sanguisorba canadensis*), also of the rose family, indicated where stalks of fuzzy white flowers would be in bloom the following month.

At our feet, the spongy, light-green sphagnum moss provided the basis for this strange, soilless habitat. Ecologists see bogs and fens as **succession stages** between aquatic habitats and swamp forests. In this sense, all the typical bog plants, including the arethusa orchid, are living on borrowed time.

The term quaking bog was brought home to us vividly every time we took a step, when all the nearby hummocks would shake in unison. The absence of frogs and nesting birds made the bog strangely quiet. The only reptile we saw was a garter snake lying under a cinquefoil bush, digesting a heavy meal, apparently some sort of rodent, judging from its bulging belly. Mosquitoes and black flies were absent, we gratefully noted, and our butterfly expert was waxing ecstatic over such northern rarities as **Harris' checkerspot** (*Melitaea harrisii ssp. liggettii*) and the **eyed brown** (*Lethe eurydice ssp. eurydice*).

We began to concentrate on the more conspicuous plants. Shiny **alder-leaved buckthorn** (*Rhamnus alnifolia*) crowded through rare sedges and grasses. Along with **poison sumac** (*Toxicodendron vernix*) and the European **highbush cranberry** (*Viburnum opulus var. opulus*) unfamiliar stunted willows dotted the bog, adding a touch of the Arctic. Here was **autumn willow** (*Salix serissima–P*) and **hoary willow** (*Salix candida–T*). With its inrolled leaves, white-hairy on the underside, and sunken veins, all adaptations for retaining water, the latter provided a perfect example of an arctic plant designed to withstand the cold, desiccating winds of the tundra.

Peeking above the sphagnum, the pink, swept-back petals of the **large cranberry** (*Vaccinium macrocarpon*) hinted at an abundant harvest in the fall. On the same sphagnum mat, tiny leaves dotted with red, sticky hairs gave evidence that at least one carnivorous plant, the **round-leaved sundew** (*Drosera rotundifolia*), was at work capturing small insects.

As we rounded one hammock, a magenta-pink glow on a six-inch stalk proved that the arethusa orchid (*Arethusa bulbosa–E*) still survived in Ohio. The fanciful imagination of early botanists had seen in the petals of this bizarre-shaped species the horns, face, and gaping mouth of a dragon, thus the common name of dragon's-mouth. The lower lip with its red and yellow crests did suggest the outstretched tongue of a beast but actually served the more prosaic function of attracting pollinators such as bumblebees.

The bees had done their work well at Willow Bog. There were at least fifty of the dragon's-mouths scowling at us from scattered points among the sphagnum hummocks. The abundance of this strange but beautiful plant may be misleading. In Michigan, where it is far more abundant, a low bumblebee population sometimes determines a poor crop of orchids in certain years. We felt uneasy that through some accidents, Willow Bog, privately owned and unprotected, had become the only sanctuary for the orchid in Ohio. In its silent fight for survival, an uneasy truce had prevailed for the moment.

*   *   *   *   *   *   *

Searching for another plant survivor, in August, with a group of hardy plant-hunters, I gingerly reached for footholds and handholds as we clambered down the slippery sides of Cruickshank Glen. Our destination was a ledge in the sandstone cliffs. Where soil had

2-10 A much more common bog plant, **shrubby cinquefoil** (*Potentilla fruticosa*) of the rose family is native to both North America and Eurasia. Commonly seen as a garden plant.

2-11 Closeup of the flower of **shrubby cinquefoil.**

2-12 A less welcome inhabitant of bogs and fens, **poison sumac** (*Toxicodendron vernix*) bears large inflorescences of greenish flowers that soon turn into whitish berries similar to those of its notorious cousin, poison ivy (*Toxicodendron radicans*). Bog explorers should be warned that all parts of this species are poisonous, even the roots, which pollute the water of ponds surrounding bogs. From personal experience, I've learned to wear boots when wading through wetlands where this species is found.

accumulated, natural springs had kept it moistened to an almost mud-like consistency. Edging our way down, we reached the narrow rocky outcrop to find **Canada yew** (*Taxus canadensis*) and **mountain maple** (*Acer spicatum*). As in Willow Bog here was another pocket of northern plants. Among the plant associates in this specialized habitat was a tall, slender grass which later proved to be an endangered species, the **northern wood reed** (*Cinna latifolia*–E), not seen in Ohio for forty years and formerly listed as extirpated. Where the ledge widened was the plant we had journeyed to find, the **northern monkshood** (*Aconitum novaboracense*–E), growing in a large stand as densely as if planted.

The three-parted seedpod resembled closely that of the larkspurs, close relatives, and the leaves looked like those of *Trollius*, also of the crowfoot family. However, the blue flower was unique. One **sepal** had grown over the other four to imitate a helmet or bonnet, thus the common name. The petals, as in *Trollius*, had been reduced to tiny **nectaries**. The slender, weedy-looking plants looked as if a moderate wind would topple them all, yet for untold years they had been thriving under this particular sandstone cliff (and one other in a nearby county) and nowhere else in Ohio. Indeed, they rank among the most strangely distributed plants of North America: a few counties in the Catskills in New York, three localities in Ohio, and several counties in Iowa, and Wisconsin, where the two states come together in the so-called **driftless area**, believed to be the only part of the northern Midwest that the last glacier did not cover. (See also Chapter 7 on the driftless area.)

Northern monkshood is rare, but it is also of clear potential worth to mankind. Notorious for their deadly action on the nervous system, the monkshoods have been known as swift poisons since the Greeks. ". . . It doth work as strong as **aconitum**," is a line from Shakespeare. No group of plants besides the poppies have been studied so intensively for their medicinal value. Like all its close relatives in the crowfoot family, monkshood contains deadly alkaloids, in this case, aconitine, which perhaps evolved to make it unpalatable to mammal and insect herbivores. This toxicity seems to be strongest in Eurasian species, of which there are many, mostly in mountainous and Arctic habitats.

"There must be hundreds of similar places like this in northern Ohio," one member of our party speculated, as we talked about the strange success of the plant at Cruickshank Glen and its complete absence elsewhere. By an odd coincidence the second location of northern monkshood in Ohio—one that had been forgotten for over a generation—was rediscovered the same year by a young graduate student at Kent State University, Barbara Andreas. Using astute detective work, she found the herbarium

2-13 Willow Bog is one of the few dependable sites where the **dragon-mouth or arethusa orchid** (*Arethusa bulbosa*–E) can be found in Ohio. The photo shows three sepals, resembling horns to early botanical explorers, and a **lower petal**, or **lip**, extending like a tongue of a fire-breathing dragon.

2-14 Flowers of the **northern rose azalea**, also called the **roseshell azalea** (*Rhododendron nudiflorum var. roseum*–P). This showy, fragrant flowering shrub is not strictly a bog plant but is found frequently in woods and stream banks at the edge of bogs.

2-15 **Wet Sandstone Ledges**: at Cruickshank Glen, where I took this photo of sandstone ledges, I found a variety of plants.

slips with the name of the original collector. Although he himself was long deceased, his relatives pointed out the general area where he had done most of his field work. Then followed a long series of treks to all the sandstone cliffs that seemed likely sites of the monkshood until Barbara found one small ledge containing the long-lost plants.

Finding rare plants is but the first step in understanding their special requirements. Out of the four Ohio rarities described so far, only the monkshood has been researched in a thorough way to offer some conclusions. A Wisconsin botanist, the late Dr. James H. Zimmerman, called it a hybrid derived from arctic, Rocky Mountain, and Appalachian species which were brought together by glacial upheavals. Their offspring were then isolated after the glacier receded. One of these populations, which we now call the northern monkshood, survives only in places that resemble the habitat its arctic ancestors preferred; porous sandstone or damp gravelly slopes that give off constant moisture into the air; cliffs and ledges that block off the drainage of cold air during the day and cause cool nighttime temperatures; unusual soil high in lime and low in phosphorus; and steep terrain that discourages grazing by herbivorous animals, for "despite its reputed toxic alkaloids," Zimmerman states, "the monkshood is freely browsed by deer and cattle."

Its arctic character may have made it intolerant of fluctuations in climate such as the hot, dry spell called the Xerothermic Period of around 5,000 to 3,000 years ago, when many western prairie plants invaded northern Ohio. Thus, ancient climatic changes may account for the elimination of northern monkshood from many cliffside sites that seem suitable now.

Aconitum is a slow grower. It may take from five to fifteen years to grow from seedling to flowering size. Such a life cycle prevents the plant from competing with fast-growing plants on more favorable sites. Therefore, the plant has developed a large taproot to store up carbohydrates and scarce minerals, which would give it an advantage in a mineral-poor location. This perhaps explains why it exists in such pure stands unthreatened by any other plants in its particular habitat.

The study of the northern monkshood—its chemical makeup, physiology, anatomy, and reproductive cycle—may shed light on the other three rare plants. The globeflower, in the same family as the monkshood, apparently shares similar alkaloids and arctic-alpine plant behavior. Its swamp-forest habitat may also have been a victim of the Xerothermic Period, a warm, dry spell, which gave the advantage to Southern and Western species. Its reproductive cycle is not known, but it too may be slow to flower. The fact that it increased when the elms in Moorhead Forest died shows that as a species it has a great deal of vitality left, given the right conditions of sunlight.

Competition with woody plants is perhaps the source of the problems of the two rare orchids. Not only do trees and shrubs take away light but they also remove water through transpiration. Prairies and bogs, in Ohio at least, need a high water table to maintain their characteristic plants. In prairies ditching and draining will lower the water table as will, paradoxically, the lack of fire. According to one theory, fire is the most important factor in maintaining all the tall-grass prairies east of the Mississippi. As the early successional stages of prairies and bogs merge into the shrub and tree stage, more water will be removed by the roots of woody plants. The plant succession has become "too successful," according to Zimmerman. By contrast, fire, by killing off the woody plants, may actually benefit other plants, like the white lady's-slipper, in the long run.

The science of ecology teaches us to ask better questions—not "Why is this plant rare?" but "What are its limiting factors?" Temperature seems to limit northern monkshood; temperature and light in the case of the globeflower; and ground water for the two orchids. We can see that human intervention will not help in the first two cases. Their rarity was decided by warming trends thousands of years ago. However, the ground-water supply of the two orchids can be maintained if ditching, draining, damming, or large construction projects are prevented from taking place. In unprotected Willow Bog, once threatened by power line construction, the two orchids are thus living on the edge of survival.

As we learn more about endangered species, let us hope that their habitats continue to provide the necessary stability to maintain the complex plant and animal communities living upon them. In the struggle to survive, granting these four species a reprieve in the form of a few acres of bog, prairie, cliffside, and forest seems a simple enough task. For these rare plants are survivors—veterans of past glacial upheavals, climatic changes, and other ecological crises, as well as present-day use and abuse of the land. Like stone tablets left behind by ancient civilizations, the black dots on a distribution map for each species tell the story of environmental change if we can only read it. Once we learn how certain species survived under past conditions, we will have a better understanding of the chances for all species—including our own—in the future.

2-16 One of these was a rare grass, which I later keyed out as the **northern wood-reed** (*Cinna latifolia*–E), formerly known from only one Ohio county, again proving that rare habitats yield rare species.

2-18 Side view of the **northern monkshood flower**. The arrangement of the petals is supposed to be attractive to bees.

2-17 The flowers of **northern monkshood** (*Aconitum novaboracense—E*) resemble faces looking out from under a bonnet.

Author's Postscript (2006): In the last decade ownership of Willow Bog has been transferred to ODNR, and its name has been officially changed. It is to be hoped that its new protective status will improve the chances for survival of the arethusa orchid, the small white lady's-slipper, and the many other rare plants documented there. Also, this acquisition may set a precedent to protect the other three habitat areas in northern Ohio mentioned in this chapter.

2-19 **Rock-harlequin** (*Corydalis sempervirens*–P) of the **fumitory family**, at one time placed with the poppies, grows in rocky places across northern North America and into the Appalachians. I took this photo in the Nolichucky River Valley of Tennessee, not realizing it was a rarity in Ohio. (At that time it was called **pale corydalis**.) Since then, it has been discovered on sandstone ledges of Cuyahoga Valley National Park, not far from my home.

To make a prairie it takes a clover and one bee—
One clover and a bee,
And reverie.
The reverie alone will do
If bees are few.

—Emily Dickinson

chapter 3

Ohio's
Invisible Prairies

3-1 **Northern Ohio Prairies:** One of the finest remaining wet prairies in Ohio is located at **Irwin Prairie Preserve**, outside of Toledo. It is dominated by **twig rush** (*Cladium mariscoides*), a sedge.

Emily Dickinson might have been writing about the state of present-day prairies in Ohio when she penned this observation. Lately it takes not only reverie in visualizing the huge tracts of prairie now turned into farmland; it also takes a great deal of imagination in recognizing a prairie remnant even when standing within it.

In the nineteenth century the prairie plants of Ohio, as well as other Midwestern states, retreated to unlikely-looking refuges, where they still survive as holdover species from the past and as colonizer species for a dubious future. In effect, like tough guerilla fighters hiding out from an oppressive government, they have chosen an "invisible" type of habitat—unwanted or unusable parcels of land, abandoned fields, clay banks, railroad rights of way, old cemeteries, and even islands of rocky soil on the tops of cliffs.

When the Ohio Biological Survey took a census of prairies in 1978, it found 155 areas that qualified, in fifty of the eighty-eight counties. Most of the locations were in the western third of the state but with some outposts almost as far east as the Pennsylvania line.

To determine if a site was prairie, the compilers of the survey would examine an area to see if it had at least four out of eight typical prairie species as indicators: three grasses—**little bluestem** (*Schizachyrium scoparium*), **big bluestem** or **turkeyfoot** (*Andropogon gerardii*), and **Indian grass**, (*Sorghastrum nutans*)—and five composites— prairie dock (*Silphium terebinthinaceum*), **gray-headed coneflower** (*Ratibida pinnata*), saw-**toothed sunflower** (*Helianthus grosseserratus*), **purple coneflower** (*Echinacea purpurea*), and **blazing star** (*Liatris sp.*). If the area qualified, a plant census was made Ultimately 265 plants were found to be associated with the prairie habitat in some degree.

Exactly what sort of habitat is congenial to these plants? In Ohio it must be a grassland where trees and shrubs can not gain a foothold and become dominant, shading out the herbaceous plants or using up precious ground water. Thousands of years after the retreat of the last glacier, during the dry, warm climatic era called the Xerothermic Period (from about 6,000 to 2,000 B.C.), conditions favored the expansion of prairie habitat at the expense of forests. Many of Ohio's prairie plants may have entered then from centers of distribution in the Midwest.

As the climate became wetter and colder, up to the present day, the forests started to regain their lost territory except in a few places where shallow, soggy, rocky, or sandy soil limited the growth of trees. The slow swing back to forest habitat was complicated by fires, either set by lightning or by Ohio's Indians, seeking to maintain prairies as hunting areas. In fact, many authorities in plant ecology maintain that all the tall-grass prairies east of the Mississippi survived mainly through fire. In the nineteenth century the see-saw struggle between the two habitats ended when the settlers removed both prairie and forest for farmland. Until that time about 300 prairies took up 1,000 square miles of territory, or two and a half percent of Ohio's land area.

3-2 A characteristic wet-prairie plant, **Michigan lily** (*Lilium michiganense*) is the northwestern-Ohio analogue of the **Turk's-cap** lily (*L. superbum*–P), found mainly in wet habitats of northeastern Ohio.

So much for reverie. To preserve what is left, only about 1,000 acres, such organizations as Ohio's Department of Natural Resources and the Ohio chapter of The Nature Conservancy have quietly moved in. Since the late 1970s, the Ohio Natural Heritage Program has been busy inventorying rare and endangered species of plants and animals, along with their communities, and assigning top priorities to fragile ecosystems in danger of being lost to plow or bulldozer. Many of these communities, such as shorelines, bogs, rocky gorges, climax forests, and especially prairies, have been acquired for preservation, to join other ecosystems earlier obtained for state and local parks. Thus, in one way or another, many grasslands have been preserved.

Visits to Ohio prairies reveal the impressive variety this habitat may assume, given the differences in groundwater, soil, elevation, and human disturbance. What at first glance looks like a vacant lot or a weedy wasteland often turns out to be a prairie community of great complexity, with plants and animals markedly different from those of the usual disturbed areas. Take Irwin Prairie in north-western Ohio, for example. One of the wettest of Ohio prairies, its high water table supports not only the usual prairie species but also a remarkable meadow community dominated by **twig-rush** (*Cladium mariscoides*), a close relative of the **saw-grass** of the South (*C. jamaicense*). These plants are neither rushes nor grasses, but sedges. When the wind ripples across the acres of twig-rush at Irwin Prairie, the scene looks vaguely familiar. Then it hits the viewer: this is a northern version of the Florida Everglades, with twig rush replacing saw-grass, and groves of oaks replacing hummocks of palmettos.

Among the twig-rushes grow many rare, showy plants, such as **Riddell's goldenrod** (*Solidago riddellii*), named for its discoverer, Ohio botanist John L. Riddell. Along the edges of Irwin Prairie one may also find the stately **Michigan lily** (*Lilium michiganense*), the prairie analogue of the **turk's-cap lily** of northeast Ohio (*L. superbum–P*).

Late summer and fall are the best times to view prairie plants. "The later, the taller" might be a rule of thumb in prairie ecology because the flowering plants have to keep their heads up above the maturing prairie grasses; otherwise, they may be skipped by the insects, their chief pollinators. Mill Prairie in north-central Ohio is one of the best places to observe the changes throughout the seasons. One of the more "visible" prairies, it consists of wet tracts of grassland with scattered groves of trees near drainage ditches, dug years ago in a futile attempt to turn the area into farmland. "Unused land" is the visitor's first impression, reflecting our national obsession with economic values. It is true that Mill Prairie is a rather unpromising, weedy-looking tract, but a close look produces some surprises.

3-3 The most common *Liatris* of northern-Ohio prairies, **dense blazing star** (*L. spicata*) is familiar to gardeners as a cultivated plant that livens up the mid-summer doldrums.

3-4 **Prairie coneflower** (*Ratibida pinnata*) is often found growing in huge colonies, as shown here in Mill Prairie.

The giant composite, prairie dock, for instance, takes over in midsummer. It is a good example of a **forb** (non-grassy, non-woody plant) that has evolved to compete with the tallest prairie grasses, even big bluestem, on their own terms. Not only does it lift its large, yellow, sunflower-like blossoms up to ten feet off the ground, but it breaks the rule about prairie plants having narrow, compound, or finely dissected leaves. Rivaling those of skunk cabbage in size and shape, the leaves of prairie dock establish a beachhead early in summer while its grass rivals are relatively small and weak. This strategy, like that of dandelions taking hold in a lawn, gives it an advantage in obtaining living space, which it never loses. In a prairie, as in every natural community, the beauty of form and color masks the fierce struggle for existence.

At the other end of the size scale, the **small white lady's-slipper** (*Cypripedium candidum–E*) also makes Mill Prairie its home. Since it blooms early, it follows the rule of matching height to season by growing only six to twelve inches high. With its green, corkscrew-like side petals and large lower petal shaped like a pouch, this small orchid is unique among prairie plants. Once locally abundant in fifteen states from New York to North Dakota south to Nebraska and Kentucky, this plant is better adapted to grasslands than any others of its genus. However, it is declining in numbers throughout its range even in Illinois and Wisconsin, where it once grew most abundantly, and has been put on the national endangered-species list by the Smithsonian Institution. Apparently the wet prairie habitat where it feels most at home has become too desirable for farmland in recent years and is being cleared and drained. Formerly found in nine Ohio counties, the orchid is now confined to two.

3-5 With its grayish leaves, **ashy sunflower** (*Helianthus mollis-T*) is well named. Preferring the dry prairies of Illinois, Indiana, and the South, this species occurs in only seven widely scattered Ohio counties. Photo taken in Erie County. (left image)

3-6 A true prairie anomaly, the **Virginia meadow-beauty** (*Rhexia virginica-P*) is the only Ohio representative of a huge tropical family, the melastomes, occurring throughout the southern Hemisphere. (center image)

3-7 Not rare, but certainly one of the showiest of its genus, **Liatris scariosa**, or **large blazing-star**, was photographed at Mill Prairie. (right image)

One reason that trees and shrubs offer little competition to the prairie plants of Mill Prairie is that the state of Ohio, the present owner, deliberately burns over the area every two or three years. Young woody plants perish, but the specialized grassland flora, which has evolved to cope with fire, survives. The **crown**, or growing point, of these plants is at or below the surface of the soil. Even after a destructive fire, the grasses and *forbs* will flourish during the next growing season.

Throughout northwest Ohio, scattered sand dunes and barrens, such as at Oak Openings Park, attract prairie plants that favor a dry habitat. Lying on a former lake bed, large stretches of the Oak Openings originally consisted of oak forests interspersed with a great variety of prairie plants. **Switch grass** (*Panicum virgatum*) and **sand dropseed** (*Sporobolus cryptandrus*), which are also found on the Lake Erie dunes, grow beside typical dry-soil plants such as **scaly blazing star** (*Liatris squarrosa–P*) and **butterfly-weed**

(*Asclepias tuberosa*). Seeing a grassy stretch mixed with the tall spires of **yucca** (*Yucca filamentosa*) and **prickly-pear** (*Opuntia humifusa–P*) makes one wonder whether he is still in Ohio or somehow transported to Arizona. The yucca is an Atlantic coastal species which has escaped into Ohio from cultivation, but the cactus is a native Ohioan, probably an immigrant during the Xerothermic Period.

One of the most unlikely-looking prairies is a **clay slump**, such as the one overlooking the Cuyahoga River in Summit County south of Cleveland. As pieces of the clay bank slowly erode or slide down toward the river, barren patches of soil are colonized by a host of prairie species. Among the Indian grass grow the brilliant orange **Indian paintbrush** (*Castilleja coccinea*), three kinds of blue gentians, as well as the pink **downy phlox** (*Phlox pilosa*). Woody plants of the beech-maple climax forest can not grow on such inhospitable soil, but two unusual shrubs from the far North are found here: **Canada buffalo-berry** (*Shepherdia canadensis–P*) and **common juniper** (*Juniperus communis var. depressa–E*). In fact, the disjunctive feature of their distribution in northern Ohio can be explained by their preference for clay slumps wherever these occur.

* * * * * * *

The scarcity of prairie sites in the central part of Ohio is probably due to the high value of agricultural land. In the rich Darby Plains west of Columbus, for example, the prairies have undergone transformations into cemeteries and railroad rights of way. Bigelow Cemetery is a case in point. Used by farm families of British stock and Episcopal persuasion, the cemetery fell into disuse when the old families died off or moved away. After German Lutherans moved into the township and chose another site for their burial ground, Bigelow Cemetery became overgrown with weeds for lack of proper maintenance. However, the weeds were almost all native prairie plants seeking living space. Now, with state protection, Bigelow Cemetery is being maintained as a historical site without harming the native flora. Walking through the cemetery gate in mid-August, the visitor is greeted by a large stand of the rare **royal catchfly** (*Silene regia–P*), fire-engine red in color. This tall relative of the carnation is a Southern species that prefers prairies and dry woods. Bigelow Cemetery is apparently the northernmost point of its range. Here it stands cheek to jowl with **purple cone-flower** (*Echinacea purpurea*) and rare prairie grasses and legumes. The survival of this colorful prairie proves that the cause of ecological diversity and local history can both be served by an imaginative state administration.

3-8 A scene from Arizona? No, but the short-grass prairie on the **inland sand dunes of Oak Openings Park** near Toledo looks very much like the Sonoran Desert, with its yuccas and cacti. The **yucca** species shown here (*Y. filamentosa*) is actually an East Coast plant inhabiting the sand dunes of New Jersey south to Georgia. One of its common names is **Adam's needle**. Considered a garden escape in Ohio.

3-9 A **yucca flower** close up. Once considered lilies, yuccas are now placed in the agave family.

3-10 An actual native cactus of eastern US and extreme southern Ontario (Point Pelee), the **common prickly-pear** (*Opuntia humifusa*–P), shown here at Oak Openings Park, is the eastern relative of dozens of prickly-pears in the West.

3-11 Close-up of the flower of the **common prickly-pear** with its many **stamens,** pollen producing organs.

A few miles away in the next county, utility corporations have proven that they too can be enlightened custodians of prairie plants. Here in a long narrow strip between cornfields, prairie species have taken refuge in the only land available to them—a railroad right of way. Here is another location of royal catchfly as well as the single Ohio station of **wild pea** (*Lathyrus venosus–E*), a purple-flowered sweet-pea that prefers a dry habitat. After the railroad abandoned the right of way, a utility company took title and strung power lines, with an understanding with the state that no disturbance, such as mowing or spraying with herbicides, would be permitted. Through such enlightened land management, thirty-nine prairie species are being protected, including six endangered in Ohio.

❋   ❋   ❋   ❋   ❋   ❋   ❋

No description of Ohio prairies would be complete without mentioning the hillside or **hanging prairies** of Adams County. This rural county on the Ohio River east of Cincinnati is a sort of physiographical crossroads where portions of the Appalachian Plateau, the blue-grass region, and the central plains meet. Long studied by the Ohio botanist Dr. E. Lucy Braun, Adams County has proven to be a natural botanical garden, where, in the hilliest terrain of the state, different forest and prairie habitats have attracted a varied assortment of plants from the Deep South, the Appalachians, the Midwest, and the arid Southwest, all mingling with a native Ohio River Basin group.

Among the areas Dr. Braun studied were Lynx Prairie with its ten pocket-sized prairie patches alternating with forest; the Wilderness Preserve, a complex of limestone hills and hollows with a few prairie patches near the summit; and Buzzardroost Rock, which has a dry cliff-top prairie in the process of splitting away from the mountain—literally a hanging prairie. In the course of time the Ohio Nature Conservancy has

3-12 **Butterfly-weed** (*Asclepias tuberosa*), characteristic of prairies and grasslands throughout Ohio, has attractive globes of orange flowers. Juice within stem is watery, not milky, as in other members of the milkweed family.

3-13 **Clay Banks:** Often seen above rivers and creeks, clay banks (also called **slumps** and **slippage slopes**) are unstable habitats, in which the clay, after heavy rains, moves downslope and creates open ground, to be quickly filled in by highly specialized, prairie-loving plants. Shown here is a slump habitat above the Chagrin River in northeast Ohio.

3-15 **Ground juniper** (*Juniperus communis–E*), a rare Northern evergreen, usually seen growing as a mat or low bush, ranges from Canada to just south of the Great Lakes and into the Appalachians, and favors a variety of treeless habitats, including slumps. Ohio specimens are assigned to variety *depressa*.

3-14 **Downy phlox** (*P. pilosa*), shown here above a slump in Summit County, south of Cleveland in the Cuyahoga Valley National Park, is one of the most attractive species of the clay-bank community.

acquired these and some of the sixteen other prairies in Adams County, assuring these properties protection against development or encroachment.

In visiting the Adams County prairies, the average Northern Ohioan may be surprised by the Southern nature of the plant life, as indicated by the tobacco farms lining the main highways. The prairies themselves are so small and inconspicuous, usually hidden by dense forest of second-growth **scrub pine** (*Pinus virginiana*) and **Eastern red-cedar** (*Juniperus virginiana*) that one wonders why they are not swallowed up entirely by forest. The most obvious answer is that the thinness of the soil above the limestone bedrock discourages trees from taking root.

One of Adams County's most inaccessible prairies, Buzzardroost Rock sits on a steep cliffside overlooking a wide valley in a setting reminiscent of the Skyline Drive of Virginia. Beginning incongruously in a farmyard, the path climbs steeply and enters a thick woodland. At the summit, where the trees thin out to reveal a panorama of farmland and low hills, stands Buzzardroost Rock, a treeless cliff separated by a four-foot crevice from the rest of the hilltop. True to its name, the rock attracts, as its only wildlife, ominous, low-flying turkey vultures. Huge piles of limestone at the bottom of the Rock attest that nearby cliffs have split off and fallen into the valley and that the crevice here will also eventually widen.

Nonetheless, a fairly safe "jumping-off place" can be found. Once over, the visitor will discover that the Rock is a typical prairie of medium to short grasses, with a few woody plants, mainly red-cedar and **redbud** (*Cercis canadensis*, of the legumes), anchoring their

3-16 A clump on a slump. **Yellow vetchling** (*Lathyrus ochroleucus–T*), related to garden sweet peas, is shown here on a clay slump above the Grand River in Ashtabula County, where I saw it in 1981.

3-17 Multiple flower stalks of **Cooper's milk vetch** (*Astragalus neglectus–E*). This wild legume is found only in one site in Ohio, where I saw it in 1982—on a clay slump above the Grand River in Lake County. For more on Grand River rarities, see supplemental illustrations under Northern Ohio (with NO- numbers).

roots in the thin alkaline soil. The Rock has been documented ever since 1835 as a prairie. Despite the loss of some plant species, perhaps due to trampling, one can still find the rare prairie grass, known as **side-oats grama** (*Bouteloua curtipendula*), and a colorful composite, the **slender blazing-star** (*Liatris cylindracea–T*). The blazing-stars are a North American group that are especially adapted to prairies, dunes, and other dry habitats, and each Ohio prairie seems to have its typical species.

*   *   *   *   *   *   *

From Irwin Prairie in the north to Buzzardroost Rock in the south, Ohio is preserving its prairie remnants. Like a natural greenhouse, they may serve to restock depleted grasslands in other parts of the Midwest. Currently there has been much discussion about using prairie grasses and forbs to tie down the soil in and around superhighways. Adaptable to dry soil, these plants will not brown out in the summer and will provide an eye-pleasing spectacle in the fall. Unless we want a one-crop flora, such as the imported crown-vetch, lining our median strips and road shoulders, mile after monotonous mile, use of the state's native prairie plants makes a great deal of sense.

Although it may be presumptuous to think of our invisible prairies as harboring plants of great potential in medicine, industry, or agriculture, the possibility is not to be ignored.

3-18 **Central Ohio Prairies**: One of Ohio's staunchest defenders of railroad prairies, **Trella Romine** of Caledonia, near Marion, helped save the nearby Claridon Railroad Prairie from destruction. She and her friends from the community persuaded Conrail to stop spraying herbicide along the tracks and thus preserve a thriving natural community.

3-19 **One of the signs** prohibiting the spraying of herbicides by personnel of the Conrail system.

3-20 At the **Claridon Railroad Prairie**, the white spikes of the **prairie false indigo** (*Baptisia alba var. macrophylla–P*), a large flowered member of the **legume**, or bean family, are testimony that preservation is possible, even in a highly industrialized environment.

3-21 Named after the discoverer of the species, William Starling Sullivant, a prominent Ohio botanist, **Sullivant's milkweed** (*Asclepias sullivantii*) occupies prairie sites in a large, north-south band of counties in central Ohio. At the extreme eastern edge of its range in the Midwest.

3-22 Fire-engine red, the flowers of **royal catchfly** (*Silene regia*-P) of the pink family, attract notice in the three central-Ohio prairie habitats shown here: **railroad tracks**, **power-line corridors**, and **cemeteries.**

To cite recent examples, certain tropical plants from Madagascar have been found useful in fighting cancer. A wild perennial maize plant, found in three small locations in Mexico, may revolutionize the growing of corn and help increase the world's food supply.

In addition, many endangered mammals, birds, reptiles, and insects are to be found only in a prairie habitat. Although the prairie chicken has become extinct in Ohio, the badger still survives in the Oak Openings and may be increasing. It is known to prey on destructive rodents. When the prairies are studied more intensively, they may be found to harbor many other natural enemies of agricultural pests.

Finally the psychological effects of prairies cannot be ignored. By saving what is left of Ohio's prairie flora, perhaps our most handsome and eye-catching wild plants, Ohio's protective agencies are contributing to the variety and the spirit-lifting qualities of the environment.

3-23 View of **Bigelow Cemetery**, near Columbus, with prairie plants forming a colorful backdrop to the tombstones in front.

3-24 **Composites** are members of the daisy family. Shown here is a close-up of **purple coneflower** (*Echinacea purpurea*), a composite of a dark pink hue rather than purple, now very popular in gardens. The scene is Bigelow Cemetery.

3-25 **Milford Center Prairie** in west-central Ohio is an abandoned railroad right of way, now a power-line corridor, which shelters many prairie species. The power company does not mow or spray.

3-26 An ODNR Prairie Open House in 1980 introduced me to the power-line corridor at Milford Center Prairie, but all I saw of the rarest inhabitant—**wild pea** (*Lathyrus venosus*-E)— were the compound leaves. Shown here are the handsome purple flowers that I finally saw in West Virginia in 1988.

3-27 Southern Ohio Prairies: **Buzzardroost Rock** in Adams County from the side, showing the steep cliffs. A few red-cedars are the only woody plants. The prairie on top of the Rock has been documented since the nineteenth century.

3-28 The *Liatris* species that usually frequents **hanging prairies**, such as the top of Buzzardroost Rock, is **slender blazing-star** (*L.cylindracea*–T), known for its sparse petals and long, cylindrical flower base.

Today, with only 1,000 acres of our prairie heritage remaining, Ohio's Department of Natural Resources and other protective agencies are showing how it is possible to accommodate to the natural environment and by astute management save an important habitat from needless destruction. Ohio's invisible prairies are adding a new twist to Emily Dickenson's observations:

To make a prairie it takes space
That corn and soybeans must not replace.
Reverence for nature's plan will do
If spaces are few.

3-29 **Rattlesnake-master** (*Erygium yuccifolium*–T) of the parsley family can usually be found in Lynx Prairie. Its globular flower clusters differ radically from the **umbels**, or flat-topped clusters, of the better-known members of the parsley family, such as Queen Anne's lace.

4-1 **Manitoulin Island Shoreline Species: The Great Lakes sand cherry** (*Prunus pumila var. p–X*): a close-up of the white flowers and slender leaves, wider toward the tip.

Fire and Ice in the Lair

chapter 4

To explore Manitoulin Island successfully for plants, one needs an elementary knowledge of Great Lakes geology, helpful guides to lead one to the rare species, and —how can I put this?—a healthy respect for the Manitou.

Looking back on early June of 1990, when I came to Manitoulin for a plant-hunting weekend conducted by the Canadian Wildflower Society, I now realize how ignorant I was about the place. All I really knew was that it was the largest freshwater island in the world (about 100 miles by 40) and nearly divided Lake Huron in half; that it contained a large Ojibwa population, who call themselves Odawa (related to the name Ottawa); and that somehow the island's name was connected to the Manitou, or Great Spirit of Nature.

It wasn't until much later, long after I returned home to Ohio, that I found out that Manitoulin literally means in Odawa "the lair of the Manitou." Like many islands, mountain peaks, and caves around the world, Manitoulin is considered holy.

"But why was this one island out of many hundreds in the Great Lakes singled out and designated as holy?" I asked my two Odawa informants: Kenny Pheasant, a Michigan accountant who was born and raised on Manitoulin; and Mary Lou Fox, a lifetime resident of the island and familiar with its legends.

4-3 **Heart-leaved willow** (*Salix cordata*) is a low shrub with very woolly white fruits.

of the Manitou

They told me that in one legend the Manitou carved a great chunk of ice into the form of an island and hurled it into Lake Huron. Another legend describes a great fire that burned down much of the forest cover of the island and proved that such power could have been exercised only by the Manitou itself.

Kenny went on to explain that after the fire "cleansed" the island, the Manitou allowed all the plants and animals to return. The Manitou favors harmony between man and nature, and not vengeance. Except when the balance of nature is disturbed, the Manitou remains serene and looks benignly on anyone living on his home grounds who respects the environment.

However, all this discussion lay in the future when I disembarked from the *Chi-Cheemaun* (Odawa for "great canoe"), the huge car ferry that plies Lake Huron between Tobermory, Ontario, on the Bruce Peninsula, and South Baymouth, on Maniotulin. As I drove slowly down the two-lane asphalt road on my way to Hideaway Lodge on the shores of West Bay, I was surprised how ordinary the scenery appeared at first glance. Instead of the heavily forested wilderness of my imagination, dotted with fishing camps and Odawa settlements, Manitoulin was mostly rolling, hay-and-dairying country, such

4-2 Blossoms of the **Great Lakes sand cherry** against a blue-gray mat of lichens.

4-4 The **yellow color phase** (*forma lutescens*) of the parasitic **scarlet Indian paintbrush** (*Castilleja coccinea*) is more common on Manitoulin Island than the reddish-orange phase. Plant perhaps parasitizes sand cherry and heart-leaved willow.

4-5 At West Bay a wreath of **Canada anemone** (*A. canadensis*) encircles a smooth granite boulder, probably a **glacial erratic**.

4-6 Close-up of the flower of the **Canada anemone**, showing the masses of golden **anthers** in the center.

as one might see in northern New England and New York State. Nothing seemed out of the ordinary in the numerous black-and-white Holsteins nor in the typical Ontario towns like Mindemoya, a little four-corners place where I stopped to buy some Canadian dollars at the local bank.

Actually the most mysterious thing about Manitoulin was how unspoiled the scenery appeared despite the island's popularity as a summer vacation spot, and how few billboards cluttered up the landscape. In the distance at nearly every turn of the road, I could see a low ridge, mostly tree covered, that I later learned was the Niagara Escarpment, the backbone of Manitoulin Island.

On the road, I thought over all the possibilities the weekend may hold: rare orchids, especially the **calypso**; Great Lakes endemics, such as **Pitcher's thistle**; and above all, the **alvars** (natural limestone pavements, covered with thin soil), with their specialized flora. Here was to be found one of the rarest plants of eastern North America: a daisy-like composite with large yellow flowers, known here as **Manitoulin gold** and in the prosaic world of botany as *Hymenoxys herbacea*–E.

Originally found only in four sites, *H. herbacea* goes under several aliases. On the Marblehead Peninsula, on Ohio's Lake Erie shore, where it occupies a former prairie turned into a limestone quarry, it is called the **Lakeside daisy**, after the nearby village of Lakeside. On the Bruce Peninsula of Ontario, on alvars near the main highway, it is called the **rubberweed**, because of its flexible leaves. In Tazewell and Will Counties, south of Chicago, Illinois, in a now heavily strip-mined area, it became extinct before anyone could give it a common name; and on the south shore of Manitoulin Island near an inlet called Misery Bay, where it flourishes so prodigiously that its flowers give the alvars a golden cast, it became known as Manitoulin gold.

What sort of plant is *H. herbacea* that it occurs only in four scattered locations in the Great Lakes area and nowhere else in the world? Superficially its flowers resemble those of the cultivated **golden coreopsis** (*Coreopsis tinctoria*) although it's from a different tribe of the composite family. These showy blossoms, almost two inches wide, bloom at the end of long stalks above a rosette of inconspicuous narrow leaves, and the whole plant looks so neat and well shaped that the first impression of a colony is that some philanthropic horticulturist decided to turn the alvars into a giant rock garden.

Looks are deceiving, however. *H. herbacea,* because of its demanding habitat preferences, does not take to ordinary cultivation easily. Most of the colonies I had seen sit on hot, glaring-white limestone rocks with no soil or water evident. In the still-active limestone quarry at Marblehead, Ohio, where thousands of Lakeside daisies bloom at once toward the end of May, I had found piles of discarded limestone slabs covered with blooming plants. How do they survive? Apparently all they need is a few cracks in the rock into which water from winter snows and spring rains has seeped down and has carried enough nutrients to support a seedling.

Brain Parsons of the Holden Arboretum, thirty miles east of Cleveland, Ohio, raises Lakeside daisies under a federally-supported program that aims to learn more about endangered species. He reports that he has no problems growing the plants in any rock-garden type of soil—acid or alkaline; sandy, rocky, or gravelly—as long as the plants have good drainage. Their **crowns**, where the stems and roots meet, will tolerate any kind of soil except organic, which retains water.

Because this extremely dry type of soil is now rare in eastern North America, the unusual distribution pattern of *H. herbacea* has resulted. Where did it come from, though, and what are its ancestors? Plant geographers believe it originated in the high prairies of the western Great Plains and on the slopes of the Rockies, both areas with very low rainfall. Even today the **stemless goldflower** (*H. acaulis*) of the Rockies looks almost identical to *H. herbacea* and probably served as its ancestor.

Apparently the stemless goldflower migrated eastward when North America underwent a drastic change of climate in the years 6,000 to 2,000 B.C., known as the Xerothermic Period. As the name indicates, the weather became hot and dry; many forested areas in the East gave way to tall-grass prairies; and many prairie plants invaded areas around the Great Lakes. In its new environment, the Great Lakes population of *H. acaulis* acquired so many new characteristics that a former geographical variety evolved into a new species.

Many other western plants followed the "fire trail." Ancestors of the newly-evolved eastern **prickly-pear cactus** (*Opuntia humifusa–P*) found their way to nearly every state in the US east of the Mississippi. In Ohio it grows near the western end of Lake Erie, and in southern Ontario at Point Pelee. There are hundreds of other examples, and I would be seeing many of them on Manitoulin.

Ecologists have discovered that dry-weather prairie-type plants will survive under wet conditions as long as the soil is suitable, and trees and shrubs do not take over and turn the prairie habitat into a forest once again. Fires can delay this process, called **succession**, by killing the young shoots of woody plants but sparing the deep roots of grasses and other prairie plants. The great fire on Manitoulin of the Odawa legends may be a tribal memory of huge, lightning-induced forest fires during the Xerothermic Period that swept away the coniferous and hardwood trees and brought in grasslands and the deer that fed on them. On these animals the Odawa prospered, as if from a gift of the Manitou. And when natural fires failed to occur, the Odawa themselves, as well as many other tribes, set fires to the forests and brushlands to make way for the grasses the following year.

The first prairie plant that I observed after I arrived at our hotel was an armful of pure white flowers that Ann and Trudy, my fellow northern Ohioans and the only other Americans on the trip, brought in. None of the Canadians at the hotel were familiar with the species. After I puzzled over the irregularly-toothed leaves, I consulted *Gray's Manual* and discovered that this new plant was *Leucophysalis grandiflora*, or **large white-flowered ground-cherry**, of the potato family, closely akin to Chinese, western North American, and Andean South American plants. Preferring sunny, open, or disturbed land, such as the roadside where Ann and Trudy found it, it seemed more like an introduced weed than a native. I neglected to take a picture of it, thinking we would frequently see it growing abundantly beside the roads, but I never observed it again. This seemed strange at the time.

Our lodge turned out to be ideal for the weekend: the rooms were comfortable; the food, all on the American plan (meaning breakfasts and suppers included in the bill), was delicious; and the natural setting of West Bay, framed in evergreens and with unexpected plants and animals to be seen along the trails, was a delightful introduction to this northern island. Even before supper was ready (and the dining room staff in an American-plan hotel takes a dim view of latecomers), I had found on a tall evergreen an osprey nest with the two parent birds in attendance, and down by a muddy part of the shore a bulky turtle with yellow speckles on a dark-gray shell and a bright yellow patch under the chin. This was Blanding's turtle (*Emydoidea blandingi*), common only around the Great Lakes, but very scarce in Ohio because of the overdeveloped Lake Erie shorelline.

The plants around West Bay, though mostly typical of the northern forests, also held a few surprises. I was immediately drawn to the abundant **Canada anemones** (*Anemone canadensis*), twining themselves like a Japanese flower arrangement around the boulders on the muddy shore. In Ohio these white-petaled plants inhabit overgrown wetlands, such as riverbanks, and never seem to look as big and conspicuous as those at West Bay.

Nearby, on a muddy stretch, was growing an unfamiliar buttercup, **creeping spearwort** (*Ranunculus reptans*), a tiny amphibious plant, at home in running water or on mud flats when the source of water dries up. At intervals, its threadlike stem, creeping along the mud, sends down roots and puts out a tuft of narrow leaves and a flower stalk with usually a single, small, yellow-petaled flower.

4-7 **Creeping spearwort** (*Ranunculus reptans*) appears as such an inconspicuous plant that it is hard to believe that it is a missing link between the two great divisions of flowering plants—the **monocots** and **dicots**; but note the grass-like leaf, typical of monocots.

4-8 Close-up of **Blanding's turtle** (*Emydoidea blandingii*): with its heavy shell and yellow patch under the chin, it is rare everywhere except in undisturbed habitats on or near the Great Lakes, as in Canalway Metropolitan Park, about three miles south of Lake Erie in a suburb of Cleveland. (Photo taken at West Bay.)

4-9 The **dunes of Carter Bay** are among the highest on the Great Lakes.

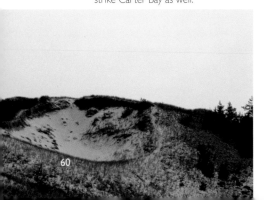

4-10 A hollowed-out area, called a **blowout**, at **Grand Sable Dunes**, in the Upper Peninsula of Michigan. If ground cover, such as **American beach grass**, fails to hold the sand particles, then such a disaster could strike Carter Bay as well.

This admittedly unexciting plant represents two concepts of great significance. First, it belongs to a group of buttercups that some plant evolutionists believe to be close to the "missing link" between the **dicots** and the **monocots**, the two great divisions of flowering plants. Its flowers with no fixed number of stamens and pistils closely resemble those of *Sagittaria*, the **arrowhead**, a primitive monocot, while its long narrow leaves approach in form and venation those of grasses, sedges, and rushes, other typical monocots, some of which have adapted to a semi-aquatic way of life.

Secondly, to Great Lakes ecologists, the spearworts are very typical in their geographical range: mainly Arctic (Greenland to Alaska) and as far south as Newfoundland, the Maritimes, New England, the states of the Upper Great Lakes, and mountainous areas of the West. All these areas were covered by the last great glacier, the **Wisconsinan,** up to 12,000 years ago; subsequently, the spearworts, along with hundreds of other Arctic species, have reclaimed their territory when the glacier receded.

Archeological excavations indicate that human settlements have existed on Manitoulin for many thousands of years. Do tribal memories of the glacier account for the other Odawa myth about Manitoulin's creation, that it was carved out of ice by the Manitou and thrown into Lake Huron? Perhaps; or was it due to a lingering covering of snow and ice on the Niagara Escarpment, long after other parts of the Great Lakes area became ice-free?

On the shore of West Bay I found my only parasitic plant— the yellow- flowered variety of the **scarlet Indian paintbrush** (*Castilleja coccinea forma lutescens*). It was probably feeding on the roots of the two common trees on the shore: **heart-leaf willow** (*Salix cordata*) and the tiny **sand cherry** (*Prunus pumila var. pumila–X*), both just coming into bloom at this late date with conspicuous white catkins and flowers.

Next morning when Jim Hodgins announced that we would visit the sand dunes at Carter bay and the wet evergreen forests behind them, he also, to my surprise, informed me that I had been "elected" as one of the guides, since I had visited various islands and peninsulas on the Great Lakes several times in the past. In case anyone had questions about plants with little green or brown flowers, I was supposed to be "the answer man."

I took the job with misgivings, knowing that all the islands and peninsulas of the Great Lakes that I had visited differ greatly in the type and number of species in their individual floras. No two areas are the same. I recalled **devil's club** (*Oplopanax horridus*), an extremely thorny bush related to the ginsengs and native to the Pacific coastal rain forests. Two thousand miles east, one finds devil's club on Ile Royale in Lake Superior and on the nearby Keweenaw Peninsula of Upper Michigan—and nowhere else. What about lake iris (*Iris lacustris*), a dwarf species typical of Lower Michigan shorelines bordering the Straits of Mackinac? Where was it on Manitoulin? In one location far to the east, as I found out later. What about **Huron tansy** (*Tanacetum bipinnatum ssp. huronense*), a strong-smelling composite with fernlike leaves and flowerheads shaped like yellow buttons? It was all over Tobermory harbor when I left yesterday on the *Chi-Cheemaun*, but nowhere to be seen on Manitoulin. With these crazy distribution patterns, I didn't expect that previous experience would count for much.

However, I was relieved when we arrived at Carter Bay, with one of the highest and most extensive sand dunes on the Lakes, that most of its plants looked rather familiar. The rare endemic, **Pitcher's thistle** (*Cirsium pitcheri*), which I had first seen several years before on the Lake Michigan dunes of northern Indiana, was conspicuous with its silvery rosette of highly dissected leaves and spiny flower buds in the center. Unfortunately the large, cream-colored flowers, differing from the reddish-purple of most species in this large genus, hadn't yet opened.

4-11 A federally endangered species, **Pitcher's thistle** (*Cirsium pitcheri*) is an endemic of the Upper Great Lakes. It has white flowers and silvery green, highly dissected basal leaves. Named for Dr. Zina Pitcher, who was serving in the US Army when he discovered the plant on the shores of Lake Superior. Photo taken at Indiana Dunes National Lakeshore, near Michigan City.

4-12 **Swamp Forest Behind the Dunes at Carter Bay**: Bearing the largest flowers in its genus, **striped coral-root** (*Corallorhiza striata*), a **saprophytic orchid** lacking leaves and green stems, prefers wet, boggy habitats like roadside ditches and swamp forests. (See Chapter 8.)

However, when people started to question me about the dune grasses, I realized that the taller of the two major species, a very graceful and leafy plant, was an "unknown." It seemed to be stabilizing the dunes, whereas the other grass, **American beach grass** or **Marram grass** (*Ammophilia breviligulata—T*), a shorter, no-nonsense type, grew in dense colonies like a field of wheat, and was stabilizing the shoreline.

Also, like ripened grain, it had a short, thick panicle of yellow spikelets. It is a **halophyte**, or salt-tolerant species, originally native to coastal sands from Labrador to North Carolina, and probably moved into the Great Lakes region from the Atlantic coast at the end of the glacial period, defying the west-to-east trend of so many other plants. Ecologists acclaim beach grass as a sturdy "pioneer species" that seeds into beaches swept clean of vegetation by heavy windstorms or hurricanes and quickly establishes a colony whose roots anchor down the sand and prevent further erosion by the waves. The dunes at Carter Bay are, in effect, created by beach grass and prevent the waters of Lake Huron, after an occasionally violent storm, from encroaching on or flooding out the swamp forests which spring up behind dunes, and which we were to visit next.

4-13 **Limestone Cliff Species:** The white limestone cliffs of the **Niagara Escarpment**, seen from the Cup-and-Saucer Trail. The escarpment, also a landmark of the Bruce Peninsula and other parts of Southern Ontario, shelters many rare ferns.

4-14 A limestone-loving fern, the **slender cliff-brake** (*Cryptogramma stelleri*) bears two kinds of fronds: wider leaflets (above) indicate the **sterile fronds**, while narrow leaflets (below) are **fertile**, i.e., bearing spores.

In the dense shade of **northern white-cedars** (*Thuja occidentalis*—P), we stumbled into a wet, muddy paradise abounding in snipe and spring wildflowers, and strangely free of the mosquitoes and black flies I had come to expect in Michigan or on the Bruce Peninsula. I could actually take a picture of the **striped coralroot** (*Corallorhiza striata*), the most photogenic of this leafless, **saprophytic** group of orchids, without retreating before the onslaught of hostile insects. There was no problem, either, with the great beds of golden-flowered **marsh marigolds** (*Caltha palustris*); the n**aked miterworts** (*Mitella nuda*), with tiny flowers shaped like snowflakes; and the shrubby **Kalm's St. John's-wort** (*Hypericum kalmianum*—P), virtually a Great Lakes endemic. The **western anemone** (*Anemone multifida forma sanguinea*), with its blood-red flowers and yellow centers, was the first member of this genus that I had ever seen whose flowers were not white or greenish.

In the afternoon we had some free time to act like conventional tourists and visit the old settlement of Gore Bay; Bridal Veil Falls at Kagawong; and the small Odawa crafts store in the village of West Bay. For a souvenir of the island, I chose a small, hand-sized model of a Canada goose, uniquely constructed from flexible reddish-brown twigs of the Northern white-cedar. These were cleverly bent and tied into shape by almost invisible threads. I had never before seen such a piece of sculpture.

Even now, many years later, I look at the little model and wonder how the Odawa artists created it. Did they hold the twigs together with one hand and tie them with needle and thread with the other, or did they have to have help? What if the threads wore out or were broken—how many would have to break before the shape collapsed and all the tiny pieces scattered?

In a sense, all the habitats of Manitoulin Island, such as the Carter Bay dunes, are constructed of individual plants and animals tied together to the soil and the climate

4-15 A small, elegant fern, the **maidenhair spleenwort** (*Asplenium trichomanes*) grows out of cracks in limestone rocks.

and the limestone bedrock and to each other, as if by invisible threads. Would the tall, unknown grass hold the dunes down if the beachgrass washed away or was broken up by a marina? Would the white-cedar forest survive if the waters of Lake Huron broke through the gap and flooded out all the plants? Without forest cover, would the snipe be able to nest in the open without fear of raccoons? Would the Manitou be able to restore everything as before, as after the great fire?

I think that nowadays, in the face of beach development, housing projects, and timber and pulpwood operations, even the Great Spirit of Nature would need some help.

On the last day of our trip, the schedule called for a visit first to the Cup-and-Saucer Trail, then to Foxey Prairie, and lastly to the much-anticipated alvars of Misery Bay. The Cup-and-Saucer Trail climbed a well-known landmark on the island: part of the Niagara Escarpment that looked in profile like a teacup turned upside-down on its saucer. On the "saucer" path within a heavily shaded woodland, we saw several stands of the **large yellow lady's-slipper** (*Cypripedium parviflorum var. pubescens*), which almost assumes the character of a roadside weed in many parts of the island.

4-16 **Roadside Plants**: Typical of the Upper Great Lakes, colonies of the **large yellow ladies'-slipper** (*Cypripedium parviflorum var. pubescens*) abound in roadside wet spots and shady woodlands. The **small yellow lady's-slipper** (*C. parviflorum var. p–E*) is equally abundant.

Up and up we went, now climbing the "cup" part of the trail, one side of which was a steep, white limestone precipice, very conspicuous from a distance. (Perhaps another reason for the "ice" of the Manitoulin creation legend?) As common ravens wheeled slowly above us, we found many rare ferns that are almost exclusively confined to limestone: the **slender cliff-brake** (*Cryptogramma stelleri*) with two types of fronds—sterile and fertile; and three **spleenworts**—the **green** (*Asplenium viride*); the **maidenhair** (*A. trichomanes*), with its leaflets like tiny squares of malachite; and the famous **walking fern** (*A. rhizophyllum*), with its small, narrow, triangular frond ending in a long slender tip that roots in the ground and sends up more fronds that repeat the process. Perhaps this is the only fern in northeast North America that grows in such a manner. Its solitary relative grows in eastern Asia, in a distribution pattern common to plants that once were found all over the Northern Hemisphere (**circumboreals**), but were driven south by the glaciers.

After lunch on our way to Misery Bay, we stopped at a well-known roadside grassland, Foxey Prairie, named after a nearby village and populated by nesting bobolinks and a species of avens, **prairie smoke** (*Geum triflorum*) of the rose family, perhaps 100,000 plants either in bloom (with nodding, half-open, purplish or reddish petals) or in fruit (with long, white, feathery seed heads that looked like smoke from a distance). Next to

4-17 **Prairies**: In west-central Manitoulin, north of Wolsey Lake, near the village of Foxey, acres of **prairie smoke** (*Geum triflorum* of the rose family) dominate **Foxey Prairie**.

4-18 The pink petals of **prairie smoke**, a Western avens, are seldom seen fully opened.

Manitoulin gold, this **avens** is the most typical of the prairie plants that migrated to the Great Lakes region. In imagination I could see how, in former days, Odawa tribesmen, screened by **prairie smoke**, would sneak up on the herds of unsuspecting white-tailed deer and secure enough meat to carry them through the winter.

Not far from the prairie, our six-car caravan turned off the road into a parking area, and I realized that without fanfare we had arrived at the Misery bay alvar. Since we were so close to the main highway, Jim French, the driver of the car I had been assigned to, carefully locked up.

Outwardly, most alvars are not very impressive, but walking on the virtually level pavement near Misery Bay gave me the eerie feeling of walking on the streets and sidewalks of a housing subdivision from the '50s, whose developer had gone bankrupt and abandoned the whole project. I half expected to see street signs at the "intersections" (Prairie Smoke Drive? Hymenoxys Trail?) in the time-honored suburban tradition of commemorating long-gone plants and animals. Actually, developers have had their eye on the alvars of Ontario for a long time, to turn them into limestone quarries and thus break a few more invisible threads.

Since this alvar was much more overgrown with vegetation than others I had seen, it took me several hours to realize its great extent. Many species of stunted woody plants blocked the view, including **red pine** (*Pinus resinosa*); **Canada yew** (*Taxus canadensis*); and **northern white-cedar** (*Thuja occidentalis*–P). These trees did not cast much shade, and the white limestone reflected a lot of heat into our faces. Further, the trees blocked any cool breeze that could have found its way inland from Lake Huron. Like the alvar on the Bruce Peninsula and the quarry at Marblehead, Ohio, this place was uncomfortably hot.

4-19 When the flowers of **prairie smoke** go to seed, long, silky plumes develop to carry away the seeds in the wind. The masses of white seedheads look like smoke from a distance.

It wasn't long before we saw our first specimens of Manitoulin gold. Where the pavements, were open, level, and free of woody plants, *H. herbacea* appeared in vast numbers, as trim and neat-looking as ever. Although no signs indicated that this location was being protected, we found out later that the government of Ontario was moving quietly to preserve this and other alvars within the province, including the Bruce Peninsula site of *H. herbacea*.

In the United States environmentalists have also been active, but they were too late in the case of the two Illinois counties where *H. herbacea* once thrived. In Will County I myself had seen mile after mile of prairies pockmarked with abandoned strip mines, a few of them transformed into pathetic-looking fishing lakes. Fortunately a few remaining specimens of the Illinois population of *H. herbacea* had been transplanted into a new Wisconsin nature preserve called Chiwaukee Prairie (because it is halfway between Chicago and Milwaukee) on the shore of Lake Michigan. The last I heard, the new plantings were doing well.

4-20 **The Alvars**: The natural limestone pavement, or **alvar,** at Misery Bay, looks very much like an abandoned street, with cracks at right angles, each holding a population of Manitoulin gold. *Alvar*, first used as a habitat term by Swedish ecologists exploring the shores of the Baltic Sea, is one of the few English words borrowed from the Estonian language.

4-23 A close-up of the **Lakeside daisy**.

4-21 The famous **limestone quarry at Marblehead**, Ohio, now a state nature preserve, showing many clumps of **Lakeside daisy**, the Ohio name for **Manitoulin gold** (*Hymenoxys herbacea*–E), a nationally threatened species.

4-22 The **Lakeside daisy** grows somewhat like an Arctic or alpine plant, with clusters of flowers, much larger than the leaves, in bloom close to the ground.

65

4-24 A lavender-flowered vine common to the alvars, the **purple virgin's-bower** (*Clematis occidentalis*–X) climbs over bushes and small trees, such as the Canada yew (*Taxus canadensis*) shown here.

4-25 The odd, half-opened flower of the **purple virgin's-bower** hangs vertically like a Christmas-tree ornament.

4-26 Pink **bird's-eye primroses** (*Primula mistassinica*), found on the muddy shore of Misery Bay beyond the alvar area, bear a yellow collar, the "bird's-eye" of the common name, at the center of the flower to attract pollinating insects.

In Ohio, it took the 40-year efforts of a determined Cleveland woman, Ruth Fiscus, to persuade the owners of the limestone quarry at Marblehead to set aside a small portion as a state nature preserve. In 1996, the Lakeside Daisy Preserve was rededicated to honor Ruth and the late Colleen "Casey" Taylor, a Marblehead businesswoman, who joined forces with her to carry the conservation message from garden clubs all the way to the Governor's desk in Columbus.

Just to be on the safe side, Ohio governmental agencies have planted a small colony of *H. herbacea* on nearby Kelleys Island in Lake Erie. Since the island is almost pure limestone, there is little doubt that the project will succeed.

As we hiked around the alvar, we little expected to see orchids on such a dry habitat, but lo and behold, we found several colonies of the curious **ram's-head lady's-slipper** (*Cypripedium arietinum*), a species more commonly occurring in wet woods or bogs. Unlike other lady's-slippers, the lower petal of which swells out into the familiar rounded "slipper" to trap bees, the ram's head has a very modest-looking, purplish-veined pouch which droops in such a fashion that early botanists were reminded of the head of a sheep.

However, the other orchid of the alvars—the **fairy slipper** or **calypso** (*Calypso bulbosa*)—eluded us. This small orchid, one of the most beautiful in form of any in its large family, something like a shoe made of purple, white, and yellow parts, surmounted by lavender ribbons, was reputed to choose for its habitat on the alvars the roots of northern white-cedars.

4-27 The **red anemone** (*A. multifida forma sanguinea*) is really yellowish-white, but one color variant is bright red. A rock-loving anemone.

4-28 Two unusual orchids frequent the alvars. The strange-looking **ram's-head lady's-slipper** (*Cypripedium arietinum*) bears a white slipper-shaped **lip** petal, blotched with purple, perhaps to attract pollinators. It has the smallest flower (shaped somewhat like the head of a sheep, when viewed from the side) of any of the Eastern lady's-slippers.

Soon other unfamiliar plants clamored for attention. I had never before seen **purple virgin's-bower** (*Clematis occidentalis*–X), a limestone-loving plant originating in the West, but here this vine seemed quite common, clinging to bushes and yew trees, with its very large purple flowers hanging down in a sort of half-opened globular shape. One wonders what sort of insect has evolved to pollinate it.

Bicknell's geranium (*Geranium bicknellii*–E) with its small rosy petals was another oddity. Nearby was the **rock-harlequin** (*Corydalis sempervirens*–P) with its **dissected** foliage (leaves in many parts) and unsymmetrical tubelike flowers, each pink with a yellow lip. Related to bleeding-heart and Dutchman's-breeches, most plants in the genus *Corydalis* prefer dry, rocky habitats. Also present were **wild chives** (*Allium schoenoprasum*), a pink-flowered wild onion, occupying a huge transcontinental northern range extending into Asia; and the **early buttercup** (*Ranunculus fascicularis*–P) with its lace-like leaves.

When we reached the muddy shore around Misery Bay, the limestone-loving plants of the alvar had given way to species that "liked to keep their feet wet," such as the **bird's-eye primroses** (*Primula mistassinica*), pink or light lavender Arctic wildflowers, seldom seen south of the tip of Lower Michigan. These cheerful-looking flowers each contained a yellow "eye" in the center, probably to attract pollinators, and although not as large or showy as the Eurasian cultivated primroses in our gardens, they projected a great deal of charm.

But it was time to return to our cars. Where was Trudy, the photographer? Probably at the parking lot, waiting for us. But at the parking lot—no Trudy. Ann came rushing up, out of breath, with the news that Trudy had just found a great colony of calypso orchids underneath some cedars on the alvars. Too late. We had to get back to the lodge. Supper was waiting. American plan, you know.

4-29 The nymph Calypso of Homer's *Odyssey* has her namesake in the **fairy-slipper orchid** (*Calypso bulbosa*) of the alvars. Pictured here is the white color form **candida**. (See Chapter 10)

4-30 **Two Upper Great Lakes Disjuncts**: **Devil's club** (*Oplopanax horridus*), with its huge leaves and thorny leaf-stalks, is as much at home on Ile Royale as it is on the Pacific Coast of Alaska, 2,000 miles away. Related to ginseng and wild sarsaparilla, but has no known economic value. Photo taken on Ile Royale near the National Park Visitor's Center.

Why was Jim French looking so disgusted? His car keys were locked inside the car, and he had brought no duplicates. This was strange. He hadn't done anything like this before. Just then, Trudy arrived, offering to show us the calypsos. Did we have time? All we needed was another fifteen minutes.

Jim shrugged his shoulders. "Might as well see the orchids. We could be stranded here for a long time."

What a piece of luck! We followed Trudy back to the alvars, where she pointed out a colony of the rare white color form called *candida* very near the ram's-head lady's-slippers. I had seen the ordinary purple form of the calypso, but never the white. And what a great way to end the weekend! Tomorrow morning, we would have to leave for home. No time then to go back and look for tiny orchids. The schedule of the *Chi-Cheemaun* waits for no man.

After all of us had taken our photos, we quickly returned to the parking lot. A friendly truck driver, who just happened to carry one of those notched metal gizmos useful in unlocking car doors, had come and gone. The car was open, ready to take us back. Also, Hideaway Lodge was still holding supper for us. One of our other drivers had called in on her cell phone.

How did all of this happen so fast? Many years later, I look at the little Canada goose made from bent cedar twigs and wonder. Did some benign spirit of nature hear a quickly murmured prayer for help and take pity on us? Manitou only knows.

4-31 On the Upper Peninsula of Michigan along the dunes of Lake Superior near Copper Harbor, I came across this large stand of **Huron tansy** (*Tanacetum huronensis*), a yellow **composite**, or member of the aster family, that has a button-like flower-head. This species belongs to a sub-family that includes **chamomile**, with strong-scented leaves, often used in medicine.

4-32 The **Huron tansy** close up. The typical variety is found on the Upper Great Lakes on sandy beaches, and is isolated by hundreds of miles from other varieties on various Atlantic islands, such as Newfoundland, and on the shores of Hudson Bay.

4-33 **Symbol of the Fragility of Habitats**: The toy Canada goose made from evergreen twigs, perhaps **northern white-cedar**, at West Bay, Ontario, Manitoulin Island, symbolizes with its almost invisible threads how habitats can "unravel" if one of the elements is missing.

The Halophytes Are Coming?

"Why do you keep that awful-looking weed?" asked one of our more outspoken neighbors a few years ago. The plant in question, growing next to our front steps, was over six feet tall, with many thick stalks, bearing long drooping leaves and topped with spikes of small, golden-yellow flowers.

I was not offended by the remark. In fact, I was rather pleased she had noticed. After all, who else has a genuine **seaside goldenrod** in their front yard, and in such thriving condition? Seaside goldenrods are one of a small group of plants called **halophytes** that tolerate salt water in the soil or salt spray in the air. For this reason they are usually found on ocean beaches, salt meadows, and salt marshes, or in specialized inland habitats such as alkali deserts. The seaside goldenrod (*Solidago sempervirens*) can be found growing among dunes on the Atlantic coast from Newfoundland to Mexico—and also along a road a few miles north of Painesville, Ohio, where I obtained my specimen.

I felt no qualms about disturbing the environment by digging up my plant. In fact, there was not much environment to disturb. The clumps of goldenrod lined a weedy strip between the road and the railroad tracks serving a large chemical factory. On the other side of the road I had an unobstructed view of several dismal bodies of water called **settling ponds**. In this blighted landscape, accompanied by the roar of trucks and an occasional fright train, I set about selecting and digging up a small clump of goldenrod, which was still in bloom despite the cold wind and sleety rain typical of the end of October.

After I brought the plant home, I waited for the first warm, sunny day and transplanted it to the part of my garden with the worst soil, a sandy, gravelly patch, probably part of the rubble left behind when the builders finished the house years ago. In my ignorance I even mixed a pinch of table salt into the soil around the roots. Later I learned that very few halophytes actually require salt; they are adapted to tolerating it, but do very well without it. In fact, seaside goldenrods grow only 2 to 3 feet tall in the Atlantic coastal dunes but soar to over seven feet in a freshwater habitat.

At any rate, my plant has adapted itself to its new home almost too well (to the extent of partly blocking the path to the front door), but with its evergreen leaves, as indicated by its Latin name *sempervirens*, and its masses of golden flowers, it adds a touch of color to the garden in late fall. Best of all, since it resists diseases and insect pests, it requires absolutely no care.

The Halophytes Are Here!

According to Jim Bissell, curator of botany of the Cleveland Museum of Natural History, who has discovered many recent halophyte immigrants to Ohio, it is this very toughness and adaptability that characterizes the halophytes and explains their presence here. Since halophytes have been observed in Ohio mainly after 1950, it is safe to assume that the construction of the interstate highway system and the heavy salting of the roads have helped the spread of salt-tolerant plants. Although the actually mechanism of their dispersal is yet unknown, perhaps for years seeds of halophytes from the Atlantic coast have been "hitching a ride" on trucks, trailers, campers, and other vehicles going west, without surviving in significant numbers. But heavy concentrations of salt on the road shoulders and at entrance and exit ramps have opened up new opportunities. Certain side roads off the interstates leading to chemical factories, salt mines, brine pools, and similar industrial developments are now lined with plant species never seen until recent years. This is probably how my seaside goldenrod found its way to the industrial Lake Erie shore north of Painesville.

Other halophytes took different routes. A few from the salt flats of the Far West, such as **Western sea-blite**, or **pahute-weed** (*Suaeda calceoliformis*), have obviously arrived by freight train, since they have seldom been observed growing far from railroad tracks. Aquatic halophytes present another problem. **Ditch-grass** (*Ruppia maritima*), a flowering plant that spends nearly its whole life cycle submerged in salt water and somewhat resembles one of the algae, has recently been discovered inhabiting Northern Ohio brine pools. Since the seeds of ditch-grass survive in damp mud, it is thought that perhaps they are transported on the feet of migratory birds, such as ducks and geese.

One of the greatest cosmopolites of the plant kingdom—**reed grass** (*Phragmites australis*), found from Canada through Mexico in North America and also in large areas of Eurasia, South America, Africa, and Australia—likewise attained its great range on the feet of birds. It too is a halophyte and before the 1950s was found in a limited area of Ohio, mainly along the Lake Erie shore and around inland lakes and swamps, the usual areas where migratory shore birds and waterfowl would put down to rest. It seldom occupied roadside ditches and was rather scarce even in Mentor Marsh. In those places it had to compete with **common** and **narrow-leaved cat-tails** (*Typha latifolia* and *T. angustifolia*).

The picture has changed drastically. All along the interstates reed grass has ousted cat-tails. Mentor Marsh is a sea of *Phragmites*, its plumes up to twelve feet high (occasionally to eighteen feet), presenting a solid green wall, like a forest of bamboo, frustrating to birdwatchers and other would-be observers of wildlife. The reed grass has obviously taken advantage of the great increase in the salinity of Mentor Marsh, documented since the 1950s, when large quantities of low-grade salt **tailings** accumulated from the nearby Lake Erie salt mines. At that time it was still legal to dump salt into the marsh and its tributaries, with the result that we can see today: the largest habitat for halophytes in Ohio.

While it is fairly clear how and why halophytes spread to Ohio, plant physiologists are still puzzled how they can survive in their own habitat. This is strange when we consider that the original land plants, primitive ancestors of all of today's higher plants, developed from green algae that emerged from the sea in Silurian times, 360 million years ago—and were all halophytes. Since then, geologists believe that the sea has become more saline and the present-day plants have lost their genetic adaptability to salt water.

5-2 Close-up of a **seaside goldenrod** planted next to the author's house.

Listing the various Atlantic coastal halophytes reveals that they have little in common. First of all, they differ in ancestry. Among the monocots are a great many grasses, sedges, rushes, and members of obscure aquatic families. Among the dicots are **salt sand spurrey** among the pinks; seaside goldenrod, **salt-water asters**, and woody species (**marsh elder, high-water bush**) from the composites; and **orach, glassworts**, and **seablite** from the **goosefoot**, or **chenopod**, family. Other halophytes belong to the mallow, primrose, gentian, leadwort, and plantain families.

If any single family deserves the name halophyte, the **chenopods** probably have the greatest claim. Most of the weedy, colorless members of this group grew originally by the seashore or in salt deserts and bear such names as lamb's-quarters, pigweed, Russian thistle, greasewood, bugseed, winterfat, and poverty-weed, testifying to their hardiness and humble appearance. (In all fairness, the cultivated members of this family should be mentioned: spinach and beets.)

Secondly, halophytes certainly differ in appearance. Some are prostrate; others, upright. A few are woody; most are **herbaceous**. Some are broad-leaved, others narrow-leaved, and still others leafless. Quite a few have **succulent**, or fleshy, leaves. Most of them have imperfect or colorless flowers, but a few, such as the seaside goldenrod, the perennial salt-marsh aster, the seashore- and rose-mallows, and the sea-pinks, are attractive exceptions. In size we have the greatest variation within the grass family, from the tiny **alkali grass** of less than four inches to the giant *Phragmites*.

The quality that distinguishes halophytes is the ability to control the flow of soil water in and out of the root tissues to a finer degree than most other plants are capable of. In the process called **osmosis**, a normal plant will absorb water from the soil through tiny structures called **root hairs**, one cell in width, found on the growing tips of roots. The root hairs pass the water along to conducting cells in the roots and eventually to every cell in the plant.

Through this conducting, or **vascular**, system, water will reach the leaves, where it combines with gases to create food for the plant in another process called **photosynthesis**. Eventually the leaves discharge much of the water to the outside in the form of vapor. The whole cycle thus depends on the cell structure of the root hairs.

In freshwater habitats water will flow *into* the root hairs because their cells contain a higher concentration of salts and sugars than is present in the surrounding soil. This follows a law of physics which states, in effect, that water molecules tend to flow from a weaker solution to a stronger solution. However, in soils inundated by salt water, the reverse process takes place. The soil water flows *out* of the root hairs. Eventually, in a drying-out process, called **plasmolysis**, the whole plant loses water. First, the leaves droop, and then the stem. If the process is not arrested, the plant dies.

5-3 Close-up of the flowers of a **seaside goldenrod**, showing their large size, compared to other species of *Solidago*.

Halophytes act differently. By means of special devices on the molecular level, still not understood by plant physiologists, halophytes are able to withstand indefinitely above-normal concentrations of salt next to the root hairs. Some halophytes have actually developed special glands in the leaves that excrete salt water. These roughly correspond to kidneys in a human being. Other halophytes appear to be protected by special substances within the cells, such as the amino acid **proline**. Apparently each group of halophytes has its own range of tolerance to salt water and its own method of coping with the salt-water problem and thus can exploit successfully a habitat "off-limits" to ordinary plants.

Success, however, has its costs. As evolution has taken its course, most halophytes with their associated animals are found in salt-water habitats and nowhere else. They have become specialized and usually cannot flourish over a long period in any other habitat. A sudden environmental change can be fatal. For instance, if a salt-water inlet is cut off from the sea by a barrier beach and is flooded with fresh water, the fringe of halophytes surrounding the inlet will not be killed off. Instead, by a process called **ecological succession**, they may be slowly crowded out by the fresh-water aquatic plants that will eventually arrive by seed and compete more strongly for the new habitat.

A tidal flat may thus turn into a freshwater meadow and later become a swamp forest, with its own plants and associated animals.

5-4 Acres of **reed grass** at Mentor Marsh on Lake Erie. It is now classified as *Phragmites australis*. Some of the populations are considered native to Ohio.

5-5 The seed-head of **reed grass** close up.

5-6 The **narrow-leaved cat-tail** (*Typha angustifolia*), a halophyte like reed grass, but not a native to Ohio. Not only are its leaves narrower than those of the **common cat-tail** (*T. latifolia*), but the seed-heads (male at the top, separated by a small space from female at the bottom) are also narrower.

At present the reverse process is taking place in Ohio on a small scale. Salt pollution is attracting halophytes and also their animal associates. A former brine settling pond in Painesville's industrial section has attracted a bushy ground cover of **seablite**. Underneath have been found two species of harmless ground beetles, of the genus *Bembidion*, which are common in saline areas of the West but have never before been reported from Ohio.

Similarly, the salt conditions of Mentor Marsh have attracted two Atlantic coastal species of mosquito as an unwelcome addition to the twenty-five species already present. Most notorious is the **salt-water mosquito**, *Aedes sollicitans*. While it has not been proven that it breeds in Mentor Marsh itself, it has caused concern in the surrounding area since its first appearance in 1973. On the East Coast it has a bad reputation as an aggressive biter and potential carrier of encephalitis. However, in Mentor the salt-water mosquito has been found breeding only in holding ponds near salt wells, restricted areas which can be easily controlled by pesticides. Also, no cases of encephalitis in Northern Ohio have been traced to this cause. The other new mosquito, *Culex salinarus*, is a night biter but not a disease vector.

The late Dr. Sonja Teraguchi, curator of entomology of the Cleveland Museum of Natural History, believed that one of the ways saltwater insects arrive in Northern Ohio is by riding wind currents from the Atlantic or Gulf Coasts. A stationary front can bring Gulf Coast air to Northeast Ohio in two or three days. Insects can also migrate long distances under their own power, twenty miles at a stretch in certain cases, as has been proved by **tagging** insects with **radioisotopes**. As in the case of plant seeds, trucks and other vehicles can transport adult insects or soil containing eggs. Lastly, mud on the feet of ducks and other migrating water birds may hold saltwater insect eggs, which, if released in a suitable environment, will hatch into larvae.

In the case of another salt-tolerant newcomer, the **brine fly** or **shore fly** (*Ephydra cinerea*), lack of predators in Mentor Marsh enable its larvae to survive into adulthood. Found in very saline water all over North America, including Great Salt Lake, the brine fly is now found in the saltiest part of Mentor Marsh, Black Brook, an inlet which has suffered heavily from dumping of saline water from salt mines. Resembling a halophyte in its ability to cope with water loss, the brine fly is able to drink salt water and keep its cell contents in balance with the salty water it swims in. Fortunately, despite its great numbers and omnivorous habits, the fly has not yet caused detectable damage to the environment.

As we go up the food chain to the creatures that eat these insects, we may expect to see in the near future Atlantic coastal species of birds making longer stops in Mentor Marsh and other areas where halophytes flourish. In recent decades at Mentor Marsh or nearby, the **first black rail** (*Laterallus jamaicensis*) was seen, in 1965; the first **tricolored**, or **Louisiana**, **heron** (*Egretta tricolor*), in 1976; and the first **snowy egret** (*Egretta thula*), in 1977. Although these sightings may be coincidences or the result of more thorough bird-watching than before, they do suggest that bird species almost exclusively associated with the Atlantic Coast are being seen more often in Northeastern Ohio.

As Ohio goes, so go the Great Lakes states from New York to Wisconsin, as well as southern Ontario. In 1978 a Michigan botanist discovered that of the 122 plant species identified along one stretch of interstate, 20 per cent were halophytes, including six species new to the state. (**Seaside goldenrod** was one of these.) Searching through the records, he found that only two halophytes had originally been native to Michigan. These had lived around salt springs. The rest were immigrants thriving on man-made disturbances.

West of the Mississippi **salt pollution** in a much more drastic form has also attracted halophytes. This is the age-old problem of creating a man-made desert out of agricultural land underlain by impermeable clay soils. Because all ground water contains some salts in solution, irrigation of crops without proper drainage will cause permanent damage, even with water that is hardly measurable as saline. A destructive buildup of salts in the soil around the roots will occur, stunting or killing the crop plants.

5-7 A member of the pink family, **salt sand spurry** (*Spergularia media*) has very inconspicuous flowers like most halophytes, but under magnification, the petals have an attractive pink tinge. This and the following two halophytes were found near Shipman Pond at Mentor Headlands, near the "Chemical Coast" in Lake County.

This situation has caused the decline of many Old World regions famous for intensive farming, such as in the Middle East, because the impermeable soils allowed salts to collect. At present, salt pollution threatens prime food-producing areas in the American West, including the Central and Imperial Valleys of California. Roadside salt pollution in the Midwest pales in comparison to the magnitude of this problem, but in both cases the presence of halophytes clearly reveals the underlying chemical imbalance.

What is the future outlook for halophytes in Ohio? For one thing, they will increase in numbers and diversity. Just in the recent past a homely new plant, giving off a foul odor, the **fetid marigold** (*Dyssodia papposa*), a composite from the Great Plains states, has appeared on the interstate between Cleveland and Columbus. It may prove to be a halophyte, for it grows with **Western annual aster** (*Aster brachyactis*), an Atlantic halophyte already well established on the interstate.

Secondly, the increase of gas and oil wells throughout the state has necessitated huge quantities of brine as a waste product. Since building settling ponds to collect the brine is expensive, it is often pumped into trucks and dumped illegally at night along back roads and into streams. We now have salt pollution affecting many local wells and drinking-water sources. In some cases researchers have found poisonous hydrocarbons—benzene, toluene, xylene, and others—in the brine, to further complicate the job of water-purification systems. Bringing illegal brine dumpers to court may be difficult, but public prosecutors should become aware of a surefire test for the presence of brine—halophytes. As an example, there is a sealed-off salt well in an industrial area near Barberton, Ohio, that is surrounded by concentric zones of a grass called **sprangletop** (*Diplachne fascicularis*) and a chenopod called **orach** (*Atriplex patula*). The owners of the property might just as well have put up a sign, stating in big letters, "DANGEROUS SALT LEAK," for the above-named plants are halophytes. Thus, the day may come when halophytes will be used regularly as "stool pigeons" against brine dumpers.

Lastly, if the interstates get too salty, as is likely, nothing will be able to grow on the road shoulders and median strips except halophytes. If state highway officials are in the market for an attractive halophyte to prevent soil erosion, I would like to nominate seaside goldenrod. It is a perennial and thus does not need replanting every year. It is insect and disease resistant. Its leaves never turn brown in the summer. It has a colorful appearance in the fall, and despite what the neighbors say, I like it.

5-8 Tiny flower of the **annual salt-marsh aster** (*Aster subulatus*).

5-9 The flowers of the **western annual aster** (*A. brachyactis*) are folded up, even in bright sunlight.

Mallows

6-1 The **Shrubby Hibiscus**: A typical mallow—five big, colorful petals with rounded edges and a central column of contrasting color—here represented by the shrubby hibiscus (*H. rosa-sinensis*), a universal house plant.

The scene is the fifth-grade class in Mt. Royal Elementary School, in Cumberland, a medium-sized industrial town in the Allegany Mountains of western Maryland. The time: a balmy spring afternoon in 1939. The instructor: Miss Fuller—tall, with gray hair in a bun; the science specialist of Mt. Royal, also the sixth-grade teacher, the principal, and a tyrant. The subject: the weekly nature-study class (probably mandated by the State Board of Education), which today is to be devoted to the wildflowers of Maryland. We have had "drill," and now we have "recitation."

"Perry Peskin, are you paying attention?"

"Yes, Miss Fuller."

"Very well. What's this plant?" She holds up a flashcard depicting some gaudy white and pink flowers, each about the size of a coffee cup and of a type I have never seen before. In fact, as I look back, most of the pictures she has been showing us have been of unfamiliar plants, more common around Chesapeake Bay and the Atlantic seaboard of eastern Maryland than in the mountains around Cumberland. From personal experience in tramping through the hills behind our house, I know only two wildflowers by name—**Johnny-jump-ups** and **moccasins**, and the state of Maryland hasn't seen fit to put these on a flashcard. However, since this is recitation, and everybody has to be tested and given a grade, in these rote-memory days, I make a wild guess.

"I think it's a mallow."

"Right, but what kind?"

Even at the age of ten, I have a healthy appreciation of the absurd and can never resist a good pun. I decide to play dumb and put it in the form of a question.

"Marsh mallow?" There is a pregnant pause, followed by a slight restless stirring in the class. Even some sixty years later I can still hear it.

Evidently Miss Fuller hears it too because she quickly says, "That's right. **Swamp rose-mallow**," and holds up the next picture. But it's too late.

In defiance of Miss Fuller's rule about talking out of turn, my good friend Jennings blurts out, "He said marshmallow!" In a split second I can hear the word *marshmallow* being taken up by the other thirty pupils in the class. I have committed

the unforgivable. I have brought laughter and merriment into Miss Fuller's nature-study class.

As a result of this incident, Miss Fuller, who always practiced strict mirth control, remembered me very well the following year when I entered the sixth grade, and she and I...

But let's not dwell on the past. Suffice it to say, she never forgot me, and I never forgot mallows.

6-2 Close-up of the **column of shrubby hibiscus**, showing pollen-receiving stigmas at the end (in orange) with pollen-producing anthers below (in yellow).

6-4 Close-up of the flower of **swamp rose-mallow**. Note the white column.

6-3 **Mallows of the Continental US:** **Swamp rose-mallow** (*Hibiscus palustris*) in a salt marsh on Chincoteague Island, Virginia, on the Atlantic coast. This is the pink-petaled variety.

* * * * * * *

Eight years later, as a sophomore at Case Western Reserve University, in Cleveland, Ohio, where my family had been living since 1943, I had just chosen my major as English with biology as a minor, in preparation for a career as a high-school teacher. In the required botany classes, conducted mostly by the learned and affable Benjamin ("Pat") Bole, I learned about the families and evolution of the flowering plants, as well as the importance of their scientific names. For instance, I found out for the first time that the Johnny-jump-ups and moccasins in the Cumberland woods should really be called **birdfoot violets** (*Viola pedata*) and **pink lady's-slippers** (*Cypripedium acaule*).

I also learned that the **mallows** were among the most distinctive and important of the major plant families in North America. If it weren't for the mallows of the genus *Gossypium* (especially the tropical American species *G. hirsutum*, still found wild in southern Florida and the Keys), we wouldn't have any cotton fiber for clothing and textiles. Other mallows like the **hollyhocks** and **rose-of-Sharon** provide beautiful garden ornamentals. The largest genus, *Hibiscus*, supplies the familiar **shrubby hibiscus**, or **rose-of-China** (*H. rosa-sinensis*), an indoor plant inhabiting every hotel lobby from Florida to Patagonia. Hibiscus also gives us the vegetable **okra**, the main ingredient in chicken gumbo soup.

Mallows look different, too. Their leaves are usually lobed, recalling those of maples, and their flowers are often large and brightly colored, with five semicircular petals arranged like a bowl or cup (or a dish antenna in certain of the *Hibiscus* clan).

The numerous male, pollen-bearing **stamens** give off a fragrance attractive to insects and are combined, within a structure called the **column**, with the pollen-receiving **pistils,** where the seeds will eventually be produced. Like the orchids, which are considered the most advanced plant family and have a similar structure, the mallows are designed to be **cross-pollinated** (pistil of one plant receiving pollen from another) by insects and produce a high percentage of fertile seeds. The conspicuous column in the middle of the flower, a sort of trademark, enabled students like myself to recognize mallows whenever I saw them.

And I began to see them everywhere. *Gray's Manual of Botany* lists thirty-three well-established mallow species from twelve genera for northeastern US and Canada alone. Some, like the **common mallow** (*Malva neglecta*), had small white or lavender flowers and crawled along the ground; others, like the **musk mallow** (*M. moschata*), were medium-sized upright plants with fairly large pink or white flowers and grew in open fields. But these were European invaders, accustomed to living in dry, disturbed areas.

The native American mallows of the genus *Hibiscus* were tall, conspicuous plants with huge flowers, like those of hollyhocks, and preferred salt- or fresh-water marshes. In the Lake Erie marshes between Toledo and Sandusky, Ohio, I finally found Miss Fuller's swamp-rose mallow (*H. moscheutos*) in its natural habitat. It grows up to seven feet tall and has showy pink flowers, sometimes as wide as eight inches across—dinner-plate size. (A color variation on the Atlantic coast has white flowers with a red center.)

6-5 Color variety of the **swamp rose-mallow**, all white with a red center and a white column.

6-6 A field of **musk mallows** (*Malva moschata*), a common European invasive plant that most likely escaped from gardens. Found throughout northern US and Canada.

A shorter plant related to the rose-mallows, the **seashore mallow** (*Kosteletzkya virginica*), has smaller, more lavender-colored petals and grows in **brackish marshes** and on sandy shores of the Atlantic and Gulf Coasts from Long Island to Texas. I first saw it on Chincoteague Island, Virginia, at the National Wildlife Refuge.

Wherever I have traveled in the past twenty years looking for endangered plants, it seems as if I am always bumping into new species of mallows. Partly because they have big, colorful flowers and partly because they prefer to grow out in the open in disturbed areas like **roadsides, meadows, river banks, flood plains,** and **railroad rights-of-way,** they tend to stand out more than plants in other families.

Basically a tropical, Mediterranean, and warm temperate group, mallows are much commoner in southern latitudes than in northern, with virtually none on high mountains above timber line or in the Arctic. In the deep South, every grassy stretch beside the road seemingly yields a species of *Sida*, usually *S. rhombifolia*, a mallow that produces a small white flower at every leaf axil. When the roadsides are mowed, this plant becomes a creeper with every new leaf accompanied by a white flower.

In Florida one can easily find the tropical mallow **Caesar weed** (*Urena lobata*) featuring large white flowers with red centers. Like cotton, it is one of many American mallows utilized for their fibers.

South Texas has its gorgeous red mallow, the **Turk's cap** or **sleeping hibiscus** (*Malvaviscus arboreus var. drummondii*), so called because it never opens completely; and the yellow **Rio Grande mallow** (*Abutilon hypoleucum*).

In Georgia I encountered a large roadside hollyhock-type mallow with cream-white petals, the **pineland hibiscus** or **comfort root** (*Hibiscus aculeatus*).

Even the oases of the Southwestern deserts have their full complement of colorful mallows, such as the apricot-orange **globe mallows** of the genus *Sphaeralcea*; and the **desert five-spot** of the Mohave (*Eremalche rotundifolia*) with its pink cup-shaped flowers marked by a large, dark-red spot at the base of each petal.

Although not North American, the large, colorful native mallows of the Hawaiian Islands certainly qualify under the Endangered Species Act of 1973 as deserving federal protection, for they are among the most endangered plants in the US and in the world. With their best lowland locations taken over by agriculture, urbanization, and the introduction of aggressive foreign trees; and with many of their mountain habitats eaten down to the ground by feral goats, these rain-forest mallows (as well as other endemics, such as the **tree lobelias**) survive only in wildlife refuges and private preserves. In February 1997 I was lucky enough to see one species of native hibiscus in bloom at the Limahuli Botanical Preserve, on Kauai, the least disturbed of the larger islands in the

6-7 The **seashore mallow** (*Kosteletskya virginica*) also at Chincoteague Island, Virginia. Petals are lavender-pink, and the column is yellow.

6-8 This apricot-orange **desert globe mallow**, with its white column (*Sphaeralcea ambigua*), was photographed in Titus Canyon at Death Valley National Park, California.

Hawaiian chain. Limahuli is one of several dozen American arboreta and botanical gardens licensed to propagate endangered native plants for eventual distribution into the wild.

The melodious Polynesian language, as spoken in Hawaii, is like Greek: it has a name for everything, including every plant in the island flora. At Limahuli I saw the bushy hibiscus from the Waimea Canyon area (and only from that area), which the Hawaiians call **koki'o ke'oke'o**. (This sounds something like koh-KEE-oh KAY-oh-KAY-oh.) Botanists have given it the much more prosaic name of *Hibiscus waimeae var hannerae*. It has large white flowers with a long, bright scarlet column. Its future is uncertain. Many of the Hawaiian native plants, perhaps including this one, are pollinated by small birds of the **honey-creeper family**, found only on the Hawaiian Islands and in decreasing numbers, and their future is uncertain too.

* * * * * * *

All the time that I was seeking out new plants, including mallows, in the South and West, I had not forgotten a pet project of mine—to find the four very rare Eastern mallows listed in the 1950 *Gray's Manual*. These were sturdy plants well adapted to withstand the bitter winters and short growing seasons of the Midwest and the Appalachians, yet extremely local in distribution, suggesting a pattern of slow decline to extinction. The four species consisted of the **Virginia mallow** (*Sida hermaphrodita–P*) the **glade mallow** (*Napaea dioica*), the **Kankakee mallow** (*Iliamna remota*), and the **Peters Mountain mallow** (*I. corei*).

The first of these should be renamed the *West* Virginia mallow since most of the populations are in a narrow band across that state (basically the Kanawha River Valley) and in the Ohio valley of neighboring Kentucky and Ohio. There is also a widespread but declining population in the Potomac river drainages of Maryland and Virginia and the Susquehanna drainages of Pennsylvania. A few outlying locations in northeast Indiana (discovered in the 1980s by State of Ohio botanist Allison W. Cusick); northwest Ohio; and formerly in Michigan, Tennessee, and Virginia add to the confusion as to the exact extent of the original range of this rare plant.

In late July 1986, I spent a week in southern Ohio trying to locate and photograph all the great rare Ohio plants I had heard about for so long, including

6-9 Another **Mohave mallow**, this **desert five-spot** was found growing along the edge of the Amargosa River in Tecopa, California. The five red spots at the base of the petals are **honey guides,** signaling nectar to bees and other pollinators. Known scientifically as *Eremalche rotundifolia*.

6-10 The **Turk's cap** (*Malvaviscus arboreus var. drummondii*) is also known as the sleeping hibiscus because its bright scarlet petals never open completely. Perhaps pollinated by hummingbirds, it is a tropical American mallow barely reaching southern US.

the Virginia mallow. Without the help of members of the Ohio chapter of the Nature Conservancy, especially Marilyn Ortt of Marietta, I doubt if I would have found one-tenth of those species on my own, especially the mallow, which is abundant but in very scattered locations on the wide flood plain of the Ohio River.

Using Marilyn's directions, I followed Ohio 7, the twisty road that parallels the meanderings of the Ohio River in the southeastern part of the state, from Marietta to beyond Gallipolis (pronounced GAL-la-po-LEECE), an old town founded by French settlers. I was told to look for the village of Clipper Mills, just a wide spot on Ohio 7 and not even on the road maps. Approaching Clipper Mills, I could see the big barges slowly moving down the river, and the fertile flood plains occupied either by farms or giant factories and power plants. Very little appeared in a natural state, either in Ohio or across the river in West Virginia.

Gradually the roadside vegetation changed from short grass to a dense curtain of **Johnson grass** (*Sorghum halepense*), an invasive plant of Mediterranean origin, growing over ten feet tall. Interspersed with these giants were unfamiliar hairy, mullein-like plants with spikes of large yellow flowers resembling those of snapdragons. These proved to be **mullein foxgloves** (now classified as *Dasistoma macrophylla*) found in oak woodlands. The mullein-foxgloves must be of an ancient lineage of plants because their present-day distribution includes only North America and Madagascar, an unlikely combination of geographical areas and probably dating back to the Cretaceous Period, over sixty million years ago, when all the world's continents were connected for the last time.

As I approached the sign proclaiming the town limits of Clipper Mills, I again felt the road hemmed in by tall plant growth, not Johnson grass, but a ten-foot-high hedge of a skinny, leafy plant with scattered bunches of small white flowers, so insignificant that they hardly registered from a distance. Could this modest, colorless plant be the rare Virginia mallow?

Parking off the road, I got out to inspect its features close up. The toothed leaves were lobed something like a maple—well, that would fit the mallow family. But the umbels of white flowers with notched petals about a half-inch long—what self-respecting mallow would have flowers so small and inconspicuous? What gave the whole puzzle away, however, was the light lavender mass of **stamens** wrapped around **pistils**—small, to be sure, but a genuine **column** just the same.

Also the habitat was right: in an **open field** or **flood plain**; with no trees; in a sunny, dry, and disturbed area; on poor soil. For most members of the mallow family, these conditions would fit, plus a railroad track somewhere in the picture, because railroads typically were built on flood plains—the land is cheaper and more level—and they were often elevated on a roadbed of rocks or cinders, providing the necessary drainage most mallows require.

A day or so later, I happened to be driving through West Virginia on I-77 to make better time from Marietta to the southernmost counties of Ohio, because following the river on Ohio 7 can be maddeningly slow. As I exited from the interstate, I must have made a wrong turn because I was now driving along a quiet back road beside the Kanawha River near the town of Leon. As the road made a sharp turn following a bend in the river, I came face to face with an extensive colony of Virginia mallow on the banks of the Kanawha, just where the books say is the largest concentration of the plant in the country.

Several experts on plant distribution within Ohio believe that the Kanawha was part of a pre-glacial river system that originated in western North Carolina, where the New River flows today. From there it made its way north into the valley of the present Kanawha, then west for a short distance in the present valley of the Ohio before heading north again through western Ohio, northern Indiana, and northern Illinois. This large river, called the **Teays** (pronounced "taze") after a town in West Virginia, finally emptied into a salt-water extension of the Gulf of Mexico where the Mississippi Valley exists today.

After the last glacial period up to the present time, a period of about 12,000 years, all the water that has drained off the western slopes of the Appalachians has flowed into a new outlet—the Ohio River—because the original bed of the Teays through the Midwest has been buried under gravel and glacial deposits. However, the distribution of plants, fish, and aquatic invertebrates like crayfish still indicates the outlines of the ancient river system. The western localities of the Virginia mallow from Indiana to West Virginia fit the pattern to a considerable degree.

*　　　*　　　*　　　*　　　*　　　*　　　*

Mallow number two on my wish list—the glade mallow (*Napaea dioica*)—differs from the Virginia mallow in two respects: it is a one-species genus, that is, without any close living relatives; and is most abundant in the states of the Old Northwest, bounded by the Ohio and Mississippi Rivers (Ohio, Indiana, Illinois, Michigan, and Wisconsin), where it was first discovered in **glades**, an old word meaning meadows and grasslands, now superseded by *prairies*. Since the genus probably didn't evolve in the Old Northwest, which was mostly under ice during the last glaciation, plant geographer have looked for its origins in the bordering states, where it has also been reported: Pennsylvania, Minnesota, and Iowa. In the last two states, a **Driftless Area** has been

6-11 **A Mallow of Hawaii**: A very rare shrub, the **Waimea Canyon hibiscus** (*H. waimeae var. hannerae*) is known in Hawaiian as koki'o ke'oke'o. Specimen here blooms in the Limahuli Garden on the island of Kauai. Note the long scarlet column. A high percentage of native Hawaiian plants, including this one, are in danger of extinction.

discovered in the upper Mississippi Valley which apparently was shielded during the last glaciation from the advance of the ice sheet from Canada. It was like an island of refuge for plants surrounded by a sea of ice. Several rare plants of the Midwest, such as the northern monkshood (*Aconitum novaboracense—E*), supposedly originated in the Driftless Area during glacial times. (See Chapter 7 for more on the Driftless Area.)

However, a recent report (March, 1998) of a new location for the glade mallow in southwest Virginia, near the valley of the New River, ties it more closely to the Southern Appalachians and the ancient Teays River system. At all events, the original range of this species will have to be reevaluated.

Nevertheless, all of these topics were far from my mind when one day in late August of 1989, I received a map I had requested from a friend working in the Ohio Department of Natural Resources in Columbus. I had heard that there were glade-mallow sites within a few hours of driving time from Cleveland, and since I report all the rare plants I find to ODNR, they were happy to send me the map on condition that I would report my findings.

The site turned out to be on a railroad track about eighty miles south of Cleveland in a rolling plateau area not far from the old religious colony of Zoar, now a picturesque restored village.

When I arrived at the designated spot, I recognized the same unfavorable environmental conditions that discourage most plant families but seem to favor the mallows: a heavily trafficked highway, on one side of which was a large truck depot and on the other a high railroad embankment.

Scrambling up to the top of the steep bank on hands and knees wasn't exactly easy, especially with the loose, rocky soil, the many clumps of thorny blackberry canes, and a colony of **tall nettles** (*Urtica procera*) to navigate around. Finally up on top, I looked down on the other side and beheld a lush, green golf course. Nestled between it and the railroad tracks was the Tuscarawas River. The whole mallow pattern was there.

I didn't walk very far along the tracks before I sighted a long line of unfamiliar, bushy plants over six feet high, very leafy with a scattering of small flowers and broad, many-lobed lower leaves. This proved to be the **glade mallows.** I counted at least fifty plants.

Although the white flowers of the glade mallow resembled those of the Virginia mallow in size and in the pale lavender columns, there were subtle differences. The petals of the glade mallow were typically rounded, almost semicircular in form, and lay fairly flat, with a relatively small column. In contrast, the petals of the Virginia mallow were more oval-shaped and longer, with a short split in each one, and were drastically swept back from the longer column, instead of enclosing it.

6-12 **Rare Ohio Mallows: Virginia Mallow:** The Ohio River with its characteristic barge traffic. Extensive agricultural and commercial use of the flood plain create a constantly disturbed habitat.

The most obvious difference between the two species, both of which can reach ten feet in height, lies in the basal leaves of the glade mallow. I couldn't recall any North American plant that has leaves similar in size and shape. One would have to go to the tropical rain forest to find trees of the **fig family**, such as the **cecropia** of Latin America, with the huge, dissected circular leaves, each with multiple large-toothed lobes, nine to eleven in all, that distinguish the glade mallow. How this coarse, bristly, weedy plant got the name *Napaea*, literally, "a nymph of the glades," can be attributed only to the ironic sense of humor of the early botanists.

One wonders what the function of these giant, umbrella-like leaves could have been originally—perhaps to shade out seedlings of any plant, including its own offspring, that might compete for space in its habitat.

The small population of glade mallows in Ohio received a big boost in 1991 when well over 100 plants were found growing at Wright-Patterson Air Force Base on the site of a proposed water-treatment plant. They were removed and transplanted to a nearby ODNR preserve, called Huffman Prairie, which already had a stand of glade mallows. With these and other sites, Ohio has probably one of the most stable and least endangered populations of glade mallows in the country.

Although the history of these two mallows in pre-settlement times can never be fully known, they probably were always rare because of their adaptation to wetlands, the only large areas free of a forest canopy. The last glacier apparently drove them to **refuges**, especially in the Southern Appalachians, and when the ice receded, they came back to the Midwest via the ancient Teays River system. When a hot, dry climate change, called the Xerothermic Period, occurred around 6,000 to 2,000 years ago, these two species probably had their heyday, because prairies succeeded forests in many parts of the Midwest. Later the pendulum swung the other way when the forests reclaimed the grasslands, and now agriculture and urbanization are taking their toll of both habitats. However, these two mallow species are survivors. Russian scientists during the Cold War period researched the Virginia mallow intensively for possible economic uses and discovered that each plant could produce an annual crop of 10,000 seeds, a sort of "disaster insurance" that comes into play when their habitat changes. Their story is not finished by a long shot.

❋   ❋   ❋   ❋   ❋   ❋   ❋

6-13 The yellow flowers of the **mullein foxglove** (*Dasystoma macrophylla*) of the snapdragon family resemble those of its close relatives, the **false foxgloves** (*Aureolaria*), also parasitic.

While the origins of the Virginia and glade mallows remain partly obscure, the Kankakee mallow's ancestors definitely came from the Rocky Mountains, the only place in the world where the genus *Iliamna* occurs. The **mountain hollyhocks**, as they are called, flourish in the Rockies from the foothills up to 9,000 feet, and from British Columbia to Arizona—perhaps enduring the harshest weather and terrain of any mallows in North America. Though on the average smaller than the garden hollyhock (*Althaea rosea*), which was brought over from Eurasia, the dense pinkish-white to rose-purple spikes of the mountain hollyhocks, with their cup-shaped flowers up to two inches in width, rank among the showiest of the Rocky Mountain flora. Since they prefer, like almost all mallows, to live in open areas, such as streambanks, roadcuts, and rocky hillsides, visitors to Glacier or Yellowstone National Parks can spot them almost from the first day.

When the 1950 *Gray's Botany* was published, the Kankakee mallow's only known residence was Altdorf Island in the Kankakee River of Illinois—a remarkably limited habitat for any species. Apparently it was one of many western plants that migrated eastward in response to the Xerothermic Period and evolved into a separate species. (The **eastern prickly-pear** cactus, now known as *Opuntia humifusa*, is perhaps the most famous example.) Later the Kankakee mallow was found in northern Indiana on or near a railroad bridge that crossed the Elkhart River, not far from the headwaters of the Kankakee, although in a different drainage system. Later still, botanists found a third location in the James River Gorge of southwestern Virginia.

6-14 Close-up of a cluster of white flowers of the **Virginia mallow** (*Sida hermaphrodita*–P) with swept-back petals and a conspicuous column.

It is entirely possible that intense exploration of other river systems will reveal hitherto unknown populations of the Kankakee mallows. Less than ten years ago, Ohio botanists were amazed when a riverbank species in the rose family, the **Virginia spiraea** (*Spiraea virginiana*–E), a conspicuous shrub with large showy clusters of white flowers, was discovered in the flood plain of the Scioto Brush Creek, near where it meets the Scioto River. Up to that time, this federally endangered plant had never been found outside of deep valleys of the Appalachians from West Virginia to Tennessee and North Carolina.

Will the Kankakee mallow ever pop up in southern Ohio? It is roughly halfway between Indiana and southwestern Virginia and has many river valleys to provide suitable habitat, without many people nearby to notice a colony of mallows. The sad truth about this type of disturbed terrain is that it is often impassable, either on foot or by boat. Immense quantities of boulders, fallen trees, mud, and quicksand deposits, not to mention man-made debris, create insuperable barriers to plant investigation and at the same time

6-16 The small flowers of the **glade mallow** have the typical mallow-like rounded petals, unlike the oblong, split petals of the Virginia mallow.

6-15 **Glade Mallow**: Huge lobed basal leaves and small white flowers characterize the **glade mallow** (*Napaea dioica*).

form the underpinnings of new forests, which will be swept away in floodtime. Islands that have enlarged and elongated after one flood can be eroded away overnight from the next. Only plants like the mallows that sink deep roots and disperse large numbers of waterproof, long-lived seeds can survive under these constantly changing conditions.

My first experience at a Kankakee mallow site was a disappointment but could have been a disaster. In the third week of July 1979, I had just driven my young daughter to a summer camp in Indiana. I had been reading that the Kankakee mallow could be found on Altdorf Island in Kankakee River State Park near Bourbonnais, Illinois, about fifty-six miles southwest of Chicago and about twenty-five miles from the Indiana border. It seemed a simple side-trip to take before returning home.

I really should have written to the park naturalists at Kankakee River before setting off, because when I arrived at the visitor's center, one of the staff members was very discouraging: "Yes, that's the famous island that is still the home of the Kankakee mallow, first discovered there in 1872," and "No, the mallow probably isn't in flower yet," and "No, there are no boat trips to take visitors to the island, but you can rent a canoe at the campground," and "Before you leave, take a look at the picture of the mallow on the wall by the door."

I looked longingly at the picture, which showed a dense stand of the mallow in bloom, much like a bed of hollyhocks in an English garden. I didn't tell the naturalist that I had never rowed a canoe in my life, but I drove over to the campground anyway. Perhaps I could hire the services of someone with that skill.

The young woman managing the campground was very friendly: "No, there isn't anyone around here who has time to row you over right now, but maybe you won't need a boat."

6-17 **A Rare Flood Plain Species**: The **Virginia spiraea** of the rose family (*S. virginiana–E*) was once thought to be confined entirely to river bottoms in the southern Appalachians. In the past decade it has been found in southern Ohio. For sheer attractiveness, it equals the Asiatic spiraeas of our garden ornamentals.

"How's that?"

"Actually the river's very shallow. Probably not above your knees. You could easily wade over there and back."

I looked at the island, only about a tenth of a mile away, and then at the river, flowing at a fast clip and probably cold. Yet this idea sounded very tempting. It wouldn't take too long to wade over, and since I might not be able to come back here again...

"Of course," the young woman continued, "you'll have to watch out for any deep holes."

"How deep?"

"Five or six feet."

I looked at the island again and then at the smooth-flowing river and then at a preview of tomorrow's headlines in the Kankakee, Illinois, newspaper: PARK POLICE DRAG RIVER IN SEARCH OF OHIO VISITOR. After studying that image, I thanked the friendly campground manager and departed. For the next ten years, having given up exploring river bottoms and flood plains, I put the Kankakee mallow out of my mind.

In early 1989 my wife Carol and I attended a three-day Spring Wildflower Symposium at Wintergreen, a resort-condominium complex in the Blue Ridge Mountains of southwestern Virginia, on our way home from a visit to Williamsburg. The lectures and field trips were very enlightening. One of the speakers was a professor of botany from nearby Lynchburg College, Dr. Gwynn Ramsey, who showed us his slides of the flora of the James River Gorge, including, in all its glory—the Kankakee mallow! Up to that time, I wasn't aware of the James River population at all, so after the lecture, I asked Prof. Ramsey if I could accompany him on his next walking trip up the Gorge, and he agreed. We would meet around August first, when the mallows would be in good bloom.

The end of July found me again in the Southern Appalachians, by now my favorite stamping grounds. On the morning of August first, near the bridge where the main highway crosses the Gorge below the Cashaw Dam, at Snowden, Virginia, Dr. Ramsey was waiting for me with one of his graduate students. We descended cautiously into the rocky gorge on a gentle slope until we found a railroad track that provided easier walking. I smiled to myself as I recognized all the familiar conditions here that were ideal for mallows: rock-strewn river bottoms, railroad track, and open woodlands, although with the dam controlling the periodic floods, perhaps the woodlands would become denser and less disturbed as time went by, thereby limiting the population of the mallow.

Prof. Ramsey was pointing out some small plants growing along the track: the **forked chickweed** (*Paronychia fastigiata*), a tiny-leaved mat-like plant of the pink family, native to disturbed areas of the South, such as **shale barrens**; an introduced composite, the **annual wormwood** (*Artemisia annua*), which may some day replace quinine as a cure for malaria;

6-18 The **Kankakee Mallow**: The James River Gorge in western Virginia has steep wooded slopes.

and—"Uh, oh, I feel a train coming!" Prof. Ramsey pointed to the rail he was standing on, which carried tiny vibrations. He was correct: the train came roaring through shortly after we scrambled off the tracks.

Reaching a clearing, we discovered among the rocks between the railroad tracks and the river the object of our search: three green-stemmed plants about five feet tall with ascending branches and large maple-like leaves, each stem topped with a few large, handsome lavender-pink flowers, about two inches across. Outside of the rose-mallows I couldn't recall a more striking member of the family, certainly a far cry from the Virginia and glade mallows.

As its name indicates, this Virginia population of *Iliamna remota* is far removed from its Rocky Mountain homeland, by about two thousand miles, and grows in a more scattered fashion than in the picture of the Altdorf Island colony I had seen ten years before, but it was the Kankakee mallow just the same. Face to face with one of the rarest plants in the East, I felt very fortunate to have met one of the few people in the country who knew its location.

✳   ✳   ✳   ✳   ✳   ✳   ✳

6-19 **Dr. Gwynn Ramsey** at the James River Gorge where he discovered the Kankakee mallow site.

This still leaves, among the four rare Eastern mallows, the Peters Mountain mallow (*Iliamna corei*) unaccounted for, and I doubt if I will ever see it. Ever since the colony took a population nosedive in 1986, its site on a sandstone outcrop on one mountain in southwestern Virginia is strictly off limits to visitors.

The near-extinction of this species and its gradual resurrection present a case-history of the stresses that endangered plants face all over the world. Discovered in 1927 by Dr. Earl Core, considered in his time the greatest authority on Southern Appalachian plants, it was at first considered a geographical subspecies of the Kankakee mallow until several "splitters," including M.L. Fernald, editor of the 1950 *Gray's Botany*, noticed many differences. Compared to the Illinois population of the species (Fernald didn't know of the Indiana and James River colonies), this mountain mallow was shorter, had a different leaf shape, and lacked fragrance, among other traits. Therefore, it was distinct enough to rate as a separate species.

Whatever the cause—the unavailability of ground water on the sandstone outcrops, or the extreme surface temperatures in summer—evolving as a separate species inadvertently qualified the Peters Mountain mallow for protection under the Endangered

Species Act of 1973—and it really needed it. Constituting originally about fifty individuals when discovered, the population of the mallow declined to three in 1986, due partly to browsing by deer and feral goats and partly to competition with a tall sunflower-like composite, **leafcup** (*Polymnia canadensis*), never known from this area of western Virginia until logging had thinned out the forest cover.

Worse yet, the population had reached such a critically small size that it was no longer cross-pollinating. **Self-pollination** produced infertile fruits that fell off before setting seed, and thus no new plants were seen sprouting nearby. This is the fate of many plant populations on islands, such as the numerous species of native trees in the Hawaiian archipelago, and is a condition that usually precedes extinction.

However, under the terms of the Act of 1973, the government was empowered to step in and fund public or private agencies to save the mallow, once a **recovery plan** was in place. First, botanists at Virginia Polytechnic Institute and State University at nearby Blacksburg, by sifting through the leaf litter in the area where the surviving mallows were growing, found over ninety-five seeds. Why hadn't they germinated? Tests revealed that the seeds were fertile, but the tough seed coat had to be nicked with a razorblade to allow the embryos to sprout.

Tough seed coats are a natural characteristic of plants living in the open, such as in grasslands. When these habitats are invaded by tall or densely bushy woody plants that would shade out the native grassland species, the seeds of these plants remain dormant and cease to germinate until a natural or man-made fire removes the competing intruders from the habitat. The heat from the fire also weakens the seed coat and allows germination to proceed at a rapid pace.

The Virginia botanists found that nicking the seed coat produced many healthy mallow seedlings, which grew to maturity in the greenhouses of the university. Through cross-pollination, thousands of fertile seeds resulted, and their offspring were ready to be returned to the wild. However, the National Forest Service policy of fire suppression had to be relaxed on Peters Mountain.

In 1992, the Nature Conservancy, a private conservation organization that specializes in protecting habitats of rare species worldwide (It currently protects the Elkhart River site of *I. remota*.), acquired the mallow site on Peters Mountain and has been managing it ever since. The major management tools have been fences to keep out deer and goats; removing the leafcup and other aggressive plants; and strategic burning of the area (called **prescribed fires**) every spring.

6-20 The **Kankakee mallow** (*Iliamna remota*) in the James River Gorge was first discovered in 1964.

6-21 With its large pink-violet blooms resembling those of hollyhocks, the **Kankakee mallow** has one of the most attractive flowers in its family.

After the 1992 burn only four out of twelve mallow seedlings survived their first year, but after the 1993 burn, 400 seedlings appeared! Even if only 20% survived, the species was figuratively (and literally) out of the woods.

Since trampling of plants by unauthorized visitors is a very real threat to the mallows atop Peters Mountain, I doubt if I'll ever get a chance to see this species in the wild until laboratory- germinated and greenhouse-grown seedlings are transplanted to other suitable habitats in the area. This seems to be a successful trend, especially with low populations of animals. Just in the past decade the Fish and Wildlife Service has introduced California condors into Arizona, an area where the species once existed, in the hope that a new population will thrive.

✳   ✳   ✳   ✳   ✳   ✳   ✳

6-22 Note the dark red and light yellow column of the **Kankakee mallow** and the truncated petals rather than those of semicircular form.

However, I don't mind waiting until a rare species has made a real comeback. I've seen more than my share of mallows already, including many of the native species in eastern North America in *Gray's Manual.*

There are still a few foreign invaders that have eluded me. Paging through the mallow family in *Gray* just the other day, I noticed that I've never seen the European *Althaea officinalis*, close relative of the **garden hollyhock** (*A. rosea*). *A. officinalis* has a very local distribution, bordering marshes from Quebec south to Virginia and westward to Michigan and Arkansas. With its many whitish or pink flowers, blooming from August to October; deep scarlet column; and erect stem up to four feet in height, it is quite attractive. Like many other mallows, it is also a useful plant. The bark of its perennial root yields a sweet mucilaginous paste formerly employed in medicine and in making a type of spongy candy, before the modern ingredients of corn starch, cane sugar, and gelatin replaced it.

You guessed it. *Althaea officinalis* is the **marsh mallow**. As I sit back in my easy chair, sipping a cup of herbal tea flavored with hibiscus flowers, I imagine I hear a ghostly chuckle—the spirit of Miss Fuller having the last laugh.

Faribault Diary:

an Ohioan's Search for the Dwarf Trout-Lily

Before I visited the home of the **dwarf-trout lily** (*Erythronium propullans*)—southeastern Minnesota—in early May of 1995, I had the conventional idea that it was just an ordinary spring wildflower that happened to be rare, and that its location was just a typical slice of the Midwest. However, at that time I didn't know that over the past quarter-century plant geneticists, evolutionists, and conservationists have discovered that there is nothing typical about the trout-lily or its location, and that, in fact, it is likely to face extinction in the wild, perhaps in the near future.

The genus of the dwarf trout-lily, *Erythronium*, consists of about thirty Northern Hemisphere species of small lily, named by the founder of systematic botany, Linnaeus, from the Greek *erythros*, meaning red, referring to the red-purple or pink-violet petals of the European species *E. dens-canis*. The Chinese, Japanese, and Korean species are also red or pink, but in North America the greatest number are yellow or white. These include the common adder's-tongues (also called trout-lilies because their speckled leaves resemble the pattern on a trout's scales) of the Eastern, Southern, and Midwestern forests, which bloom profusely in the early spring before the leaves of the canopy trees develop and shade them out.

7-1 In eastern North America, the most common adder's-tongue lily, now usually called **fawn-lily or trout-lily** (*Erythronium*), is the **yellow** species (*E. americanum*). Note the spotted leaves; the six **recurved** petals (turning backward so far that they touch); the long, brick-red, paddle-shaped anthers, and the long flower stalk that raises the flower above the leaves.

7-2 **Straight River Bottomlands: The reflexed petals of the white trout-lily** (*E. albidum*) are twice as large as those of the dwarf plant. Note the yellowish, paddle-shaped **anthers**.

7-3 My first view of the **dwarf trout-lily** (*Erythronium propullans*), the most unusual member of its genus in North America. Note that the nodding petals spread into a bell shape, but are not recurved. Also, they are pink, tiny, and overtopped by the spotted leaves.

7-4 From underneath, a **dwarf trout-lily** reveals tiny golden, globe-shaped anthers, which do not protrude. Petals vary in number: this specimen reveals the normal number of six petals, but many others have four or five.

96

The Rockies and Pacific Northwest have over twenty species, making this area the world's center of variety for the genus *Erythronium*. New species are still being discovered, the latest one having been found in 1996 close to Yosemite National Park. A white-petaled species with a yellow center, it is the only North American trout-lily with fragrant flowers. It has not yet received a scientific name at the time of this writing (1999).

Most of the New World trout-lilies have yellow or white petals, including the tall glacier lily (*E. grandiflorum*), whose spectacular colonies of yellow flowers clothe Western peaks below timberline just after the snow melts. However, three Northwest species are pinkish or red, recalling the Old World trout lilies. Only in the late nineteenth century was another pink trout-lily discovered—in the small town of Faribault, Minnesota, and surrounding Rice County; and in neighboring Goodhue County—and it also had the smallest flower in its genus.

Curious about this Minnesota **endemic** (species with a very limited range), which was on the federal **endangered** list, a term that follows the guidelines set up by the Endangered Species Act of 1973 and means "close to extinction," I sent away for a pamphlet entitled "Minnesota Dwarf Trout-Lily," by Nancy Sather, a botanist with the Minnesota Natural Heritage Program. As part of the state Department of Natural Resources (DNR), this program maintains a computerized inventory of every rare plant, animal, and habitat in Minnesota. (All fifty states have a similar agency.)

When the short pamphlet arrived, I discovered another unique feature of the dwarf trout-lily: sterile flowers. Addressing the question why the species is so rare, the author writes: "Unlike many flowering plants, the dwarf trout-lily almost never produces seed. Instead it grows from an underground bulb that renews itself annually. Population size is only increased when the underground stem of a flowering plant produces a single offshoot runner bearing a new bulb."

Additional sources revealed yet another oddity: although the southeast corner of Minnesota now looks similar to other parts of the Midwest, it has a totally different geological history. While other parts of North America were covered by the last of the four glaciers, called the Wisconsinan, 35,000 to 12,000 years ago, the southeastern counties of Minnesota were free of ice, as shown by the lack of layers of **glacial drift** (sand, gravel, pebbles, and boulders) in the top soil. Along with parts of northeast Iowa, southwest Wisconsin, and northwest Illinois—all areas now adjacent to the upper Mississippi River, the southeastern corner of Minnesota became part of the **Driftless Area**, an island of living plants and animals, completely surrounded by lobes of the last glacier that somehow separated from each other north of the area and then merged in the south.

What was life like for 23,000 years inside the Driftless Area? No one knows for sure, but comparisons can be made with areas next to glaciers in Alaska and northern Canada that have a **tundra** type of habitat. This term refers to a virtually treeless area of rocky or gravelly soil, supporting a sparse vegetation. It must have been extremely dry, since the glaciers had tied up most of the world's water and created an arctic desert. (Nome, Alaska, even today has only four inches of rain during its short but very sunny growing season.) As in the Arctic, **permafrost**, a rocklike, permanently frozen condition of the subsoil, probably supported only shallow-rooted plants, certainly not trees, except along rivers and streams, and in marshlands.

Except for the dwarf trout-lily, the few plants whose present populations seem to be linked to the Driftless Area give some hints of their tundra ancestry. Most dwell on rocky slopes or ledges and are considered **disjuncts**, that is, plants formerly occupying a large continuous range but now confined to widely scattered locations, due to changes in climate. The **northern monkshood** (*Aconitum novaboracense*) of the crowfoot family, for example, evolved in the Driftless Area as a hybrid derived from Arctic, Rocky Mountain, and Appalachian species, according to the theories of the late Wisconsin botanist Dr. James H. Zimmerman. After the glaciers receded 12,000 years ago, this fertile hybrid spread through the northern Midwest and Northeast to establish colonies in habitats its Arctic ancestors preferred: porous sandstone or damp gravelly slopes that are like "natural air conditioning," giving off a constant stream of cool air even in the heat of summer.

When the climate changed again during the hot, dry spell known as the Xerothermic Period, 6,000 to 2,000 years ago, many forested areas became prairies, filled with invading Western grasses and flowering plants, and northern monkshood became a disjunct, found only in the Catskills of New York, two sandstone ledges in northeast Ohio, one of which I have visited, and the rest in the Driftless Area of Wisconsin and Iowa.

Since I had never visited the Driftless Area, I decided to take a few days in May, to see the dwarf trout-lily and any other unusual plants I might stumble across. These would include forest plants, Driftless Area types adapted to rocky ledges, and early blooming prairie species, such as *Anemone patens*, a glamorous, blue-flowered anemone called the **pasque-flower.**

I would need help in setting up headquarters and finding guides, so I called up the Minneapolis Chapter of the Nature Conservancy, a national organization that specializes in saving habitats and that has given me a lot of help in the past. By great good fortune, Julie Muehlberg, the public-relations manager of the chapter, offered to help me out when I told her I'd like to write an article on the rare plants of the Driftless Area, especially the dwarf trout-lily, from an amateur's point of view.

She explained that Faribault (pronounced FAIR-a-BOH), about sixty miles south of the Twin Cities, would be the ideal place to work from, since it sits in the middle of the dwarf trout-lily range, where the Straight River flows into the Cannon. These two rivers, plus the Zumbro, are the only drainage areas within which the plant has ever been found. Also, two of the best sites for studying the rare plant—River Bend Nature Center inside Faribault itself, and Nerstrand Big Woods State Park, northeast of town—would be close by.

Finally Julie gave me a list of motels in Faribault and asked me to call her back after I had decided where I would be staying and when I knew my plane schedule. With this kind of help, it was now easy to plan the trip. The following account in diary form recalls some of the major events and impressions of a long, but rewarding, five days.

Tuesday, May 2, 1995

"Y'ready t'order?"

"Yes, I'll take the roast chicken with mashed potatoes on a bed of rice,"

(This sounds a little heavy on the calories, but I'm really starved.)

"D'y'want white or dark meat?"

"White's fine."

Loud voice from the kitchen: "We're outta white!"

"That's okay, I'll take dark."

As I sit in the small but busy restaurant in downtown Faribault, it feels good to relax in congenial surroundings before a heavy day of plant hunting tomorrow. Somehow it seems out of keeping that such an ordinary-looking part of the northern Midwest could harbor any wildlife at all, let alone botanical rarities. It's all rich, flat farm country—corn fields, hay fields, and pasture—with a few woods and small towns scattered here and there. Take Faribault itself, where the dwarf trout-lily was first found, not far from downtown: founded by a nineteenth-century fur trader, Alexander Faribault, it's just a typical small Midwestern town of around 17,000, known mainly for its blue-cheese industry and woolen mill.

And this restaurant itself—located, according to the sign outside, in "Historic Downtown Faribault," which usually means "no business"—it's packed full of people, so much so that I have to take a seat next to the kitchen counter, where the waitresses pick up their orders.

In the small town where I grew up, I remember restaurants very much like this: all the customers knew each other and called the staff, who were frequently the owners, by their first names; all the waitresses were over fifty and wore white aprons with frills

7-5 **Jay Hutchinson**, my mentor during my stay in Minnesota.

7-6 **Nerstrand-Big Woods State Park:** Although this beech-maple forest harbors a large population of the trout-lily, they were not yet in bloom, perhaps due to the deep shade cast by the trees. However, there were many specimens of the pink-petaled form of the normally cream-colored **Dutchman's breeches** (*Dicentra cucullaria*). This may be a rare color form called *purpuritincta*.

along the edges; the mimeographed menus got changed once a week and nestled inside clear plastic covers that were turning faintly yellow; and the customers were of mixed ages that included family groups, business people, old-timers, and lots of teenagers. For instance, at the next table that red-haired kid with the freckles and turned-up nose looks so familiar, but where have I seen him before? Then it dawns on me: this place is straight out of a Norman Rockwell cover on the old *Saturday Evening Post*. Even if I never see the dwarf trout-lily, reliving my small-town childhood of some fifty years ago will be worth the trip.

As I wolf down my supper, I think over the happenings of the day. Although the plane ride from Cleveland was uneventful, I noticed a number of bullet holes in the windows of the main concourse of the Twin Cities Airport when I arrived. As I passed by on my way to the baggage-claim area, some of the airport employees were explaining to groups of travelers that a demented man had pumped the place full of lead a few hours earlier, but luckily no one was hurt.

Not exactly the most auspicious way to begin a five-day stay, but a half hour later I was rolling along the interstate in a rental car in glorious sunshine, oblivious to the cares of the world and really feeling at home among the corn fields and dairy farms of southeast Minnesota, so much like the scenery along the Lake Erie plain between Cleveland and Toledo, at least where urban sprawl has not laid down its heavy hand.

Arriving at the Faribault exit in less than an hour, I passed the typical crowded, noisy, treeless shopping malls and motel strips, with their chain stores and fast-food places, which to many eyes mark the decline of Main Streets all over America. My own motel, however, was in a quieter, more secluded neighborhood, literally on a backwater, since a wide stretch of the Straight River flowed behind the buildings. The balcony off my room overlooked a small island, where a family of wood ducks was taking up residence. This was a better beginning.

After I had gotten settled, I received a telephone call from Nancy Sather, in St. Paul, the author of the trout-lily pamphlet. She had heard from Julie that I was coming to Faribault, and wanted to know if I was free to join a "search group" Thursday to look for new populations of the dwarf trout-lily at a farm near Cannon Falls in Goodhue County. She also gave me the number of a Faribault plant enthusiast named Alden "Mack" McCutcheon, whom I should call for the meeting time and directions to the site.

It's now evening, supper is over, and I'm back at my motel, looking over road maps and schedules for the next few days, when I notice on the desk that there is a note to call Julie at her home. She asks me about my trip and if the motel is satisfactory, and then tells me that a friend of Nancy's, Jay Hutchinson, a free-lance writer and nature photographer,

will be driving through Faribault tomorrow morning to take me to a newly discovered trout-lily site south of town. If I would like to join him, I should be able to reach him at his St. Paul telephone number.

When I call Jay, he is very agreeable and says he will be here tomorrow after breakfast. After hanging up, I realize that though I've been in Faribault only about six hours, I already have a personal guide, and my schedule for tomorrow and Thursday is set. I can't get luckier than this.

7-7 The **false anemone** (*Isopyrum biternatum*). This relative of the wood anemone with fern-like foliage and colonial habit is rarely seen in northeast Ohio except on limestone soil.

Wednesday, May 3, 1995

Jay, a tall, gray-haired, ruddy-complexioned, outdoors-looking man with a friendly manner, arrives, and on the way to the trout-lily site he explains about himself and where we are going. Since he is not tied down to a single employer, during one year he can be visiting Ellesmere Island in the Canadian Arctic to photograph wolves, and the next year he may find himself on an assignment to photograph trees of medicinal value in the Amazonian rain forest of Peru. He also is a retired forester, writer, and public-information man with the US Forest Service. In his spare time he goes around Minnesota looking for new locations of rare plants to keep the Natural Heritage inventory up to date, an activity similar to my own sporadic travels around Ohio, but much more successful.

For instance, after hearing for many years that the dwarf trout-lilies were to be found only in the Straight River watershed of Rice County, where Faribault is located, and in the Cannon River watershed of Goodhue County, next county to the east, Jay started exploring Steele County, south of Faribault, a few years ago to see if the Straight River bottomlands there would yield new sites of the rare plant. Surprisingly enough, they did, and so a third county was added to the trout-lily's range.

Soon we turn off the main highway onto a private road, whose owner has given Jay permission to enter, and park the car near a woods. Jay indicates that a streamside area within these woods is part of the Straight River drainage system, and with luck we will find the plant we're looking for in bloom.

The woods look like the typical second-growth beech-maple forests I'm familiar with in Ohio except hardly anything is in bloom on the forest floor. None of the trees are in leaf, either. As we near the stream, the ground becomes more open and muddier. Large clumps of the **white trout-lily** (*Erythronium albidum*), familiar in Ohio, appear in full bloom. As usual, the clump consists of many plants, each with two basal leaves, but only a small number actually send up a flower stalk. I have read that the plants have to wait for many years before enough nutrients accumulate in the bulb to supply energy for flowering and setting seed.

As in all the other trout-lilies I have seen, its six petals are recurved to such a degree that they look like a nickel-sized cluster of sharp teeth sticking up. In this way they reveal the six yellow, paddle-shaped **anthers** (producing the pollen) and the inconspicuous white, three-parted **stigma** (receiving the pollen from another plant by way of an insect, usually a bee). As in other members of the lily family, and in **monocots** in general (one of the two great divisions of flowering plants), all the flowering parts are in threes and sixes, whereas the **dicots** have parts in fours or fives.

7-8 **Cannon Falls Prairie:** The prairie at Cannon Falls has a few low shrubs and trees, notably the **cork elm or rock elm** (*Ulmus thomasi*–T). Note the corky ridges on the branches.

"We're very close to the colony of the dwarf trout-lily," Jay announces. "Look sharp or you might miss it." I look on the edges of the colonies of the white trout-lily, but eventually I discover numbers of dime-sized pink flowers *within* the colonies. These look so wilted that they could almost be dismissed as faded white trout-lilies or even spring-beauties: they have four or five petals, occasionally six; the two spotted basal leaves are narrower than those of *E. albidum* and are much higher than the flower, not at the same level; the nodding petals assume a bell shape and are somewhat spreading but not recurved; the golden anthers are fuzzy and globular, not smooth and paddle-shaped, and they don't protrude beneath the petals. Despite all these differences, this plant hardly looks like a separate species, and yet it is—and one of the great rarities of the Midwest flora, to boot. All I know is that I could never have found *E. propullans* without Jay's help.

"Well, that's one down," Jay says on our way back to Faribault. "Anything else you want to find?"

I tell him that I'd like very much to see plants that are adapted to rocky ledges and to prairies, including the pasque-flower, but that I'll probably have to drive to some of the prairies in state parks near the South Dakota border.

"Not necessarily. There's a colony of pasque-flowers in a prairie next to a bicycle trail near Cannon Falls, less than fifty miles away."

7-9 A half-wilted **pasque-flower** (*Anemone patens*). This large, blue prairie anemone with many stamens often blooms around Easter in many grasslands of the Northern Hemisphere.

7-10 **The Rocky Highlands near the Upper Mississippi: At the Whitewater Wildlife Area. Bloodroot** (*Sanguinaria canadensis*) of the poppy family bursts into bloom in huge clumps, perhaps due to limestone in the soil. This colony has at least 17 flowers.

I tell Jay about the search group that I will join tomorrow, which will be near Cannon Falls, and he says that Mack McCutcheon can probably show me where the bicycle trail is located. He also explains that everybody thinks that Minnesota originally had forests in the eastern half and prairies in the west, but that's oversimplifying.

"Just imagine a slanted line drawn roughly from the southeast corner of the state next to Iowa to the northwest corner next to North Dakota. East of that line are the forests by the Upper Mississippi and Lake Superior; west are the prairies. Cannon Falls sits practically on that line, so it has (or had) both prairies and forests."

By now we're back in Faribault, and Jay drops me off at the motel, mentioning if I'm not busy Friday, he is free to show me some more rare species. I readily agree.

Shortly after lunch I'm off on my own along some county roads to Nerstrand Big Woods State Park, watered by a tributary of the Cannon River. For an agricultural state, Minnesota has a gem of a park with impressively tall trees, perhaps some from the original undisturbed forest, but the majority probably second-growth, resulting from the timber operations around the turn of the century, very much like the few large forests left in Ohio.

The river has a large falls, and lots of spring wildflowers grow by the boardwalk, where I'm supposed to find an extensive colony of dwarf trout-lilies. But I'm apparently too early.

However, it's nice to see the golden marsh-marigolds, blue and white hepaticas, and many clumps of bloodroot, with their white, eight-petaled blossoms. The white trout-lily grows abundantly here, along with the cream-colored **Dutchman's-breeches** (*Dicentra cucullaria*). But it's very curious: there are also two other forms of the *Dicentra* here that I've never seen before: one with very small, white flowers; and another with normal-sized pink flowers (perhaps of the color form *Gray* calls *purpuritincta*). Is there something in the soil or water of Minnesota that encourages dwarf or pink-flowered blossoms? Probably just a coincidence.

Back at my motel, I will have no trouble falling asleep after a full day like this. But first I'll call Mack for directions for the search group.

Thursday, May 4, 1995

The search is on! This morning I'm with eight to ten friendly Minnesotans—amateur botanists like myself—on a large farm property near Sogn in Goodhue County, about eight miles south of Cannon Falls. With all the new housing going up, this area will soon be part of Greater Twin Cities, if it isn't already. Before urbanization takes hold, we're here to investigate the few natural wetlands left. Mack's directions to the farm were good, and I have arrived in time to get acquainted with the group. We cross a few fallow fields to a stream.

As we explore the Little Cannon River bottomlands, I mention my interest in prairies to Mack, and he agrees to guide me around the Cannon Falls bicycle trail this afternoon.

The bottomlands look very promising with large numbers of white trout-lilies in bloom, always a good sign in this part of Minnesota that the dwarf species will also show up. But no luck. We will not be able to add to the 500-plus colonies of *E. propullans* already discovered. This sounds like a large population, but each colony consists of only one parent plant surrounded by offshoots, and these in turn have produced a bulb of their own and more offshoots later on. In a way, there are only 500 individual plants if we count the offspring plants in any colony as clones. (As of now, no one can be sure how many parent plants exist in each colony.) To provide genetic variation for one species, in order to cope with future man-made or natural disasters (introduced animal predators, loss of pollinating insects, drastic changes in temperature, flooding, foreign weeds, and many others), 500 individual plants is not a great number.

As we wander back to the farmhouse to pick up our brownbag lunches and thermos bottles, we run into a patch of **false anemone** (*Isopyrum biternatum*), a low, very attractive white-petaled plant with fernlike leaves. Closely related to the wood- and rue-anemones of the Ohio woods, it prefers a limestone soil, commoner in Ohio in the western part of the state than in the northeast, where I live.

After lunch, Mack gives me directions to a parking lot near some baseball diamonds on the outskirts of Cannon Falls. We will meet there in a half hour and walk over to the bicycle trail. Everything goes as planned: I find the baseball diamonds and park my car nearby. But in the course of getting out my camera and binoculars from the back seat,

I unknowingly drop the ignition key on the floor before locking all the doors, thereby locking myself out without a duplicate key. Rather than make Mack wait any longer, I decide to keep this dilemma to myself until we have finished walking the bicycle trail.

The prairie surrounding the bicycle trail consists mostly of grasses and low shrubs, with a scattering of taller trees. Parts of the grassy area are blackened, suggesting that they were burned not long ago in accordance with current ecological practice. To maintain a healthy prairie habitat, park managers burn prairies to keep down trees and shrubs and encourage the fireproof seeds of grasses and herbaceous plants to sprout.

In a patch of disturbed sand near the parking lot, a group of tiny plants, no more than three inches high, are growing in a colony. Each has a basal rosette of leaves and several stalks bearing small white umbels of flowers, conveying a candelabrum effect. I collect one, thinking it may be a rare member of the mustard family called **whitlow grass** (**Draba**), which I almost never see in the wild. However, the clusters of flowers remind me of shooting-stars and primroses. With this clue, I key it down to **western rock-jasmine** (*Androsace occidentalis–T*) of the primrose family—the midget of this rather glamorous group.

Mack tells me that some of the low bushes are really stunted specimens of the cork elm, or rock elm (*Ulmus thomasi-T*), a very rare tree in Ohio. Looking closely at the branches, I see corky ridges extending out from them, serving what purpose I cannot guess. A **calciphile**, or limestone-loving plant, of rich woods, it also seems at home on this prairie.

I find **gray-headed coneflower** (*Ratibida pinnata*) with last year's flowers still present. **Prairie smoke** (*Geum triflorum*) with its three unopened buds is easily recognizable. A member of the rose family, its purplish flowers bloom in late spring, and in the summer its many white, feathery seedheads blowing in the wind look as if the prairie is on fire, thus the common name.

The most unexpected plant I see is the **long-tipped wild ginger** (*Asarum canadense var. acuminatum*), a variety of the common wild ginger, familiar as a shade-loving, ground-hugging plant in every Ohio beech-maple forest. The typical variety has shiny, kidney-shaped leaves, whose stalks bear at their base a single brown-purple, three-sepaled, primitive looking flower without petals. (Along with Dutchman's pipe, it's placed in the birthwort family, which doesn't seem to have close relatives among the flowering plants.) This variety with broad tapering leaves and long, pointed sepals extends into Iowa and Missouri and is apparently well adapted to prairies and other open habitats.

Returning to the parking lot, I notice what seems to be crumpled pieces of blue Kleenex littering the recently burned areas by the bicycle path. Before I start bemoaning the sloppy habits of visitors in nature preserves, I walk over to investigate and am pleasantly surprised to find the large blue blossoms of the **pasque-flower** (*Anemone patens*), nodding and past their prime but still recognizable. This important item on my wish list apparently seeded itself liberally the year before, and when the prairie was burned, the dormant seeds sprouted to produce new plants. The Midwest anemone with the largest flowers, and the only one with blue petals, the pasque-flower traditionally blooms around Easter, called *pasque* in many European countries. Coming from a large group of arctic and alpine anemones in Eurasia and western North America, some of which are poisonous to livestock (perhaps as a response to grazing), *A. patens* is similar in its showy flowers, highly dissected and threadlike leaves, and silky-hairy stems. Like prairie-smoke, it is distinguished by its feathery seedheads, which are a dispersal device.

At the parking lot, I receive a short bulletin on my memory screen: "the keys!" The prairie has been so full of new things that I have forgotten about my own problems. I am really embarrassed by my stupidity, but I have to tell Mack. Luckily he knows the chief of police in Cannon Falls. Together in Mack's car we drive over to the police station, where the chief himself volunteers to help us out. Luckily crime has taken a holiday in Cannon Falls, at least for a while.

With a notched metal gadget, the chief has no trouble unlocking my car. Thanking him and Mack, I drive back to Faribault, full of good feelings about people in small-town America.

Tonight I receive a phone call from Jay, offering to take me on an all-day trip tomorrow to the Mississippi bottomlands to find a rare Minnesota plant called **Leedy's roseroot** (**Sedum integrifolium ssp. leedyi**). Descended from an Arctic-alpine species of eastern Asia and northwestern America belonging to the worldwide *Sedum* genus, it grows on cliffs in only two counties in Minnesota and two in the Finger Lakes region of central New York State, a true Driftless Area disjunct. When I tell Jay that I'm not too good at scaling cliffs, he says, "Not to worry; we're bound to discover some specimens easily visible from a path."

With another rare plant to find, I'm looking forward to tomorrow's adventure.

Friday, May 5, 1995

We have been driving for well over an hour east of Faribault to the tiny lumbering town of Elba, in Olmsted County, about eighty miles away. Jay's friend there, at the headquarters of the Whitewater Wildlife Area, has promised to give us directions to the most accessible sites of Leedy's roseroot. The WWA was set up to preserve one of the least disturbed forested regions of Minnesota's southeast corner in the bottomlands of the Upper Mississippi. Here the Whitewater and its tributaries have created a dissected plateau that from a distance looks very similar to the scenery of Appalachia.

7-11 A colony of limestone-tolerant **walking ferns** (*Asplenium rhizophyllum*) with narrow triangular blades that root at the tips and form other plants.

As we descend toward our destination, the rooftops of the town appear, oddly resembling some community miraculously transported from West Virginia to Minnesota, with long ridgelines dominating the horizon in all directions. Unfortunately Jay's friend, the naturalist at the WWA's headquarters building, has had to depart on important business but has left us an envelope taped to his door, containing his apology and a relief map of the Whitewater tributary we are going to explore. It is complete with trails, parking areas, and sites of the rare roseroot, all highlighted in yellow.

As we journey out of town, I am struck with the contrast between yesterday's walk on the flat prairie at Cannon Falls and today's trek through the hill country, just one county to the east, where we must carefully follow a relief map. Am I ready for all this climbing up and down?

We accomplish the first leg of our trip: driving along county roads, then on to a dead-end dirt road into the wildlife area, parking in what appears to be a dense forest. I scramble out, loaded down with two cameras, a pair of binoculars, and a backpack containing brown-bag lunch, thermos, poncho, compass, and mosquito repellent. As usual, I'm overorganized. Holding the map with yellow highlights, Jay leads me along a fairly wide path that goes up, up, up. Puffing away, I'm glad I can't see the relief map; it would be too discouraging.

Although the branches of most of the hardwood trees are bare, a few **rock elms** with their corky twigs have leaves coming out in big bundles. Also, the **leatherwood** (*Dirca palustris*), an uncommon shrub or small tree in Ohio, is already in flower, with tiny greenish-yellow florets similar in size and color to those of the maples it is remotely related to. As its name suggests, one can easily tie a knot in its very supple branches.

The spring wildflowers are a different story, with large, colorful patches stretching out beneath the trees everywhere we look: acres of white-flowered false anemone; very large clumps of **bloodroot** (*Sanguinaria canadensis* of the poppy family); the white trout-lily fraternizing with the yellow (*E. americanum*), but not any dwarf species visible; and lots of hepatica, toothwort, and Virginia bluebell. A few trilliums and cow parsnips are just coming into leaf. The whole scene reminds me of Ohio about four weeks ago. One of the bloodroots has at least seventeen flowers visible, compared to the measly two or three in Ohio plants. Since each of its flowers lasts only a day or less, I consider myself very lucky to have arrived just at the peak of bloom.

When we reach the top, we have a great view of white limestone ridges and one of the tributaries of the Whitewater down below. I ask Jay where are the cliffs where Leedy's roseroot is located. For an answer, he points down to the creek.

"You mean, we came all the way up here, and now we have to go down to the bottom again?"

"Yep, no other way to do it."

I mutter under my breath, "Able was I ere I saw Elba."

We decide to eat lunch and then follow a narrow path with plenty of switchbacks until we reach the creek. At that point another path going to the left and paralleling the creek should take us directly to the roseroot site.

Now we have to go single file, with Jay leading. I have a tough time keeping up with his long strides, and very often he is out of sight, on one or two switchbacks ahead of me. Some of the plants along the path are unknown to me, including a very slender, delicate fern, which I later key out as **Mackay's brittle fern** (*Cystopteris tenuis*), a species that thrives on limestone ledges. Jay explains that since the bedrock of these slopes is made from a special type of limestone deposited by sea creatures in ancient times, it has more holes and fissures than usual and thus is well adapted to provide the "natural air-conditioning" that Driftless Area plants, such as Leedy's roseroot, require.

I'm getting close to the bottom. Jay is way ahead of me now. **Bitternut hickory** (*Carya cordiformis*) predominates. Another fern, this time the familiar **walking fern** (*Asplenium rhizophyllum*), found only on limestone rock. It "walks" by extending along the ground its triangular fronds, about three inches long, which then take root at their tips and produce another set of fronds, which repeat the process.

Then I reach bottom. I'm facing the creek, my feet practically in the water, with steep white limestone cliffs on either side of me, and no more paths. Are we going to wade through the shallow creek for the rest of the way? I hurriedly shuffle through the backpack: no canvas "wet shoes," not even an extra pair of socks.

"Hey, Jay!" I yell into thin air, since I can't see him. "What are we supposed to do now?"

"Follow the rim trail around the cliffs." The answer seems to come from far away. "It'll get wider; don't worry. I think I see one of the roseroot sites right now."

What rim trail? Does he mean this ledge about six inches wide? By slowly sidling crabwise while hugging the vertical limestone slopes, I manage not to slip into the water and finally make my way into a sort of clearing. Jay is standing about fifty feet ahead of me, examining the cliff at eye level, where there is a red marker made of tape or string. As I approach, he shows me the relief map with a number of yellow X's marking the roseroot locations by the creek. This is the first. His Elba friend didn't leave anything to chance.

Above the red marker and growing right out of the cliff is a six-inch stem with spirals of apple-green, fleshy leaves, forming a dense cluster on top, reminiscent of the European garden plant **hen and chickens** (*Sempervivum tectorum*), which belongs to the same world-wide stonecrop, or orpine, family. The name roseroot was given to a European relative that has fragrant roots. Right now Leedy's roseroot is not very impressive, but later on, it will be topped with a conspicuous cluster of red and yellow star-shaped flowers. In fact, further down the trail we find a plant with reddish buds.

After finding this rare disjunct, we celebrate by taking pictures of the habitat, the plants, and each other. Standing on the rim trail, I have to pose with one foot above the other on the slope since there is nowhere else to put it. I must look as if I'm saying, "I claim this land for America!" All I'm lacking is a flag.

The trail going back doesn't seem so strenuous as coming down, but we're tired and hungry. At Plainview, on our drive back to Faribault, we notice the city fathers have set up picnic tables in the local park and are serving food cafeteria-style—probably as a fund-raiser for a local charity or church. We're among the last customers of the day, but it's a pleasure to stop for a home-made supper in a relaxing small-town atmosphere.

Saturday, May 6, 1995

My last full day in Faribault, and I'm on my own. Wondering where to explore, I start looking at the maps for another nearby prairie when I remember that I haven't yet seen River Bend Nature Center in Faribault itself. Also, I haven't talked to Mr. Orwin Rustad, the local expert on the dwarf trout lily, whom Julie recommended.

I ask my landlady at the motel about the nearest way to reach River Bend, and she not only gives detailed directions but suggests I visit an active beaver pond a mile or so down the road. I thank her, and since the pond is on my way, I stop to have a look.

No beavers visible at the beaver pond, but a great egret, a pied-billed grebe, and plenty of beaver lodges. I'm ready to go on, when I see swimming towards me a large brown animal, shaped like a muskrat but with a whitish face. I've never seen beavers up close before, since they're usually nocturnal, but that's what it is, right in the city limits. Apparently its ancestors somehow evaded Alexander Faribault 150 years ago.

It dives and disappears among the marsh grass before I can get my telephoto lens on it, but I receive a consolation prize. On the shore ahead of me, pawing away at something, is a **thirteen-lined ground squirrel** (*Spermophilus tridecemlineatus*), a rodent that's very rare in my part of Ohio. It looks like a large chipmunk with all those stripes, and it's so busy that I take its picture easily.

To reach River Bend, I have to go through downtown, cross the railroad tracks and the bridge over the Straight River, and drive through more residential neighborhoods till I reach another stretch of the river, where I see a sign for the park. River Bend is the typical town park with playing fields and picnic tables, but it also is a nature preserve with a resident naturalist and long stretches of forest along both sides of the Straight River, where the dwarf trout-lily can be found in many colonies.

Obtaining a map at the naturalist's cabin, I take the path along the river, not finding any rarities but enjoying the pleasant day and the surroundings. So it's more than a little jarring to turn a corner and nearly stumble over a dead body lying prone in the grass. A drowning victim washed ashore? A homicide? I'm ready to call 911 on my cellular phone, if I had a phone, but then I notice a black object pushed into the face of the corpse. A pistol? Maybe the suicide weapon?

No, it's a camera. He's not dead; he's just a nature photographer like myself, assuming the proper position for photographing the dwarf trout-lily, a "belly plant" if there ever was.

I so seldom meet other people in my line of work that I forget to introduce myself and ask the photographer his name and what his interest is in this rare plant. All I can get out of him is that he's from Detroit and has been to Faribault several times before. Then we go our separate ways, and I start looking at the colonies of tiny lilies along the river. They're in excellent bloom, and I'm able to take many pictures, including a good shot of one with its petals reflexed, just like the white trout-lilies nearby.

As I stroll along the lily-bordered path, it hits me like a hammer: that dwarf plant with the reflexed petals might be a hybrid. There is a theory that the dwarf species evolved from the white trout-lily after the glacier receded, but at the same time it lost the power to seed itself and so began sending out only runners to produce new plants. (*Propullans* means *sprouting forth*).

I rush back to the place where I saw the dwarf with the reflexed petals. If I find it, I'll check to see if the anthers are fuzzy and globular, like *propullans*, or smooth and paddle-shaped like *albidum*. But it's like finding a single four-leaf clover in a three-acre lawn. There are dozens of *propullans* here, and they all look bell-shaped, not like a Turk's cap, or reflexed, at all. Perhaps when my photograph is developed, it will show the shape of the anthers.

A bit discouraged, I return to my car by way of the nature center, where the naturalist is kind enough to Xerox for me his only copy of an extensive federally-mandated **recovery plan** for saving the dwarf trout-lily, written by Welby Smith, botanist

7-12 The **yellow trout-lily** (*Erythronium americanum*) fraternizing with the **white trout-lily** (*E. albidum*). The former is at the very northern edge of its range in southeast Minnesota. There were no dwarf trout-lilies in this habitat.

for the state Department of Natural Resources. I'll have to study this when I return home.

The naturalist also hands me some official booklets, all written by Nancy Sather, on various rare plants in the state: Leedy's roseroot; **prairie bush-clover** (*Lespedeza leptostachys*), another Driftless Area endemic; and the **western prairie fringed orchid** (*Platanthera praeclara*), a northern Midwest species threatened in all parts of its range. The last two also bloom in southeast Minnesota, but in the summer. There's an excuse to come back here again.

I return to the motel to call Mr. Rustad from my room. The local authority on the dwarf trout-lily, having explored most of its locations, he also knows a great deal about the requirements needed to complete its life cycle. From his observations, he has concluded that it takes each plant on the average of seven years to flower and produce a new offshoot and bulb. A retired biology teacher at a local private school, Shattuck-St. Mary's, Rustad is delighted to hear that I write for a Canadian quarterly since he is also a free-lance writer for a Canadian magazine himself. I learn much about the history of the discovery of *E. propullans* from this conversation.

It all started at an Episcopal girls' school in Faribault called St. Mary's Hall, which at that time was located in a large house near downtown. Later the school was merged with Shattuck School for boys, and under the name Shattuck- St. Mary's, a new campus was built overlooking the Straight River and has since become the most conspicuous local landmark, somewhat resembling a walled English castle dominating the city.

7-14 Although Leedy's roseroot was not in bloom, this close view of its glamorous northern relative, **common roseroot** (*Sedum rosea*), gives some idea of its color and type of inflorescence. (The flower cluster of *rosea* is much showier than that of *integrifolium*.) Photographed on the coast of Newfoundland's Northern Peninsula, growing with other tundra plants.

In 1870, while the school was still located near the center of town, a young botany teacher, Mrs. Mary Hedges, searching for wildflowers in a woodland behind the school on a tributary stream of the Straight River (at a site that still exists), came upon the original colony of the dwarf trout-lily. Never having seen such a plant before, she consulted with her headmistress, Miss S. P. Darlington, who just happened to be the daughter of the famous botanist William Darlington (for whom the **California pitcher plant**, or *Darlingtonia californica*, is named) and who was an avid botanist herself.

The two women made up a herbarium sheet and sent the specimen to America's preeminent plant authority, Asa Gray of Harvard, the compiler of the first comprehensive flora of the northeast US and eastern Canada, namely, *The Manual of Botany*, which is still the bible of amateur naturalists like myself. In 1871, Gray described and named the dwarf trout-lily in the journal *American Naturalist*, thus making Mrs. Hedges' discovery official.

"But what happened to Mary Hedges later?" I break in. "Did she continue finding new sites for the dwarf trout-lily and other rare plants in Minnesota?"

"That's the mysterious part of it," replies Mr. Rustad. "No one seems to know. She left St. Mary's several years later, and if she did further research in botany, there are no traces in the literature."

I thank Mr. Rustad for this valuable background material. It's time to grab a quick combination lunch and supper, and then I have to come back to pack for tomorrow's plane trip home.

Hurrying off to "Historic Downtown Faribault," I find the restaurant busy as ever. As I sit down near the kitchen counter, I think over all the places I have seen this week, with their varied habitats and plant communities, and all the people who helped me out. Where else have I visited that I received such red-carpet treatment?

At this point, the waitress in her white, frilled apron is inquiring about dessert. She must have acted on the stage earlier because with a dramatic manner, she asks, "How does our special for tonight strike you—luscious, mouth-watering, deep-dish, home-baked apple pie?" I can almost hear the national anthem in the distance.

"Sounds great, but make it a small..."

Loud voice from the kitchen: "We're outta apple!"

" . . . serving of vanilla ice cream."

When in Faribault, go with the flow.

Postscript

After I returned to Cleveland, I had my Minnesota slides developed and discovered that the "hybrid" at River Bend did not reveal any anthers or stigma even with the petals rolled up, so judging from the size of the flower parts alone, it was still a dwarf trout-lily.

*I also read through Welby Smith's **recovery plan**. In it, he notes that there are over 500 colonies (read "clone clusters") at nineteen separate locations. If these colonies are completely monitored and censused regularly; if the locations are made secure from any human disturbance; if their watersheds are protected from drastic changes, such as flooding; and if scientific studies continue concerning their genetic makeup and habitat requirements, then possibly the species can be saved, despite disturbance from agriculture, road construction, and introduced plant species, among other hazards.*

It seems like a big order—saving the habitat to preserve a species, especially one that can't be propagated from seed, but there have been endangered species that were far worse off than this one and have been saved by just such a recovery plan. The Endangered Species Act of 1973, which mandates these plans, has had many success stories.

*However, habitat protection can only go so far. For many plants, such as the **valley oak** (Quercus lobata) of the Central Valley of California, which have lost most of their habitat, researchers have set up seed banks and grown seedlings in botanical gardens and arboreta, transplanting them into suitable habitats, usually purchased or donated land. (In the case of the valley oak, thousands of acorns were simply collected and planted in former oak habitat.)*

7-15 **The author** on the rim trail close to a tributary stream of the Whitewater River.

7-16 River Bend Park in Faribault: the **thirteen-lined ground squirrel—** does it eat lily bulbs?

But bulbs are a different story. Bulb-bearing plants like the trout-lilies multiply their bulbs very slowly. How long would it take for a seed bank to acquire, say, a hundred bulbs? And once planted in the wild, bulbs acquire enemies, such as molds, fungi, insects, and burrowing mammals. Because of predation by rodents (presumably pocket gophers, which eat nothing but underground stems and roots, and seldom come out of their tunnels), one species of trout lily in the Pacific Northwest has evolved poisonous bulbs. Facts like these cast the thirteen-lined ground squirrel in a new and sinister light.

Although I am genetics illiterate, I believe that some day geneticists will find a way to produce dwarf trout-lily seeds. I don't question the fact that Erythronium albidum is the parent of E. propullans, as conclusively proven by DNA analysis. But is it the only parent, and if so, why did such an evolution take place only in the Driftless Area and nowhere else in albidum's huge range—from the Missouri Valley to the Atlantic coast and from New York state to Florida? After much research, evolutionists may have the answer to these perplexing questions.

In the meantime, the Minnesota Department of Natural Resources is moving ahead to protect trout-lily sites in the Cannon, Zumbro, and Straight River watersheds and increase public awareness in urban areas, especially greater Faribault, where damage from erosion, pesticides, and all-terrain vehicles and motorcycles can be controlled at this stage.

And if present trends continue, we may never have to hear the dreaded voice from nature's kitchen, proclaimed in a tone that tolerates no substitutions: "We're outta dwarf trout-lilies!"

7-17 **The wildflower trail beside the Straight River at River Bend Nature Center.** Nearly all the clumps of plants on either side of the path are dwarf trout-lilies.

8-1 **Prairie Fens:** A typical prairie fen of west-central Ohio, **Gallagher Fen** consists of a wet bottomland, fed by alkaline springs from a nearby gravel hill.

The Knotted Dodder and Other Curiosities

Until the day I first encountered the **knotted dodder**, I had mainly good feelings about plants. After all, being at the bottom of the food chain, plants are responsible for making their own sugars and starches from water and carbon dioxide under the influence of sunlight and the green pigment **chlorophyll,** in a process called **photosynthesis.** And what's more, they feed the rest of the world as well in the form of grains, fruits, and vegetables. With all those green, chlorophyll-loaded leaves and stems working day after day to keep our refrigerators filled with groceries, who could criticize the quiet, efficient, unemotional behavior of the plant kingdom?

And yet when I saw the dodder choking the bejabbers out of an innocent sunflower—and in broad daylight, too! —I began to realize that even plants have their malcontents, have-nots, and criminal elements. They're as bad as we are!

Dodders (genus *Cuscuta*) belong to one of several families of plants with a long police record. These are the plants that have evolved, for obscure reasons, a different lifestyle, one that doesn't require a dependence on chlorophyll. Without green leaves or stems, some of them (the **parasites**, including dodders) adopt the characteristics of the fungi and steal the food that law-abiding plants carefully manufacture; while others (the **saprophytes**), like grave robbers, go underground in search of dead plant material. Still others, like assassins, take on animal characteristics—jaws that snap shut; stomachs that digest—and are called **carnivores**. Most carnivorous plants feed almost entirely on insects, although in the South, pitcher plants have been known to catch tree frogs.

Dodders must have turned to a life of crime a long time ago because they are found on every continent and even on oceanic island groups, such as the Hawaiian and Galapagos chains. Generally thought to have evolved from ancestral **morning-glories** (*Ipomoea* of the **bindweed family**), dodders retain the creeping and climbing habit of their ancestors but have lost their leaves and roots. Their yellow-orange stems grow in great profusion, covering large areas with such a web-like tangle that farmers in medieval Europe, whose crops suffered greatly from dodder infestation, were reminded of strands of egg yolk on the ground. In fact, the word *dodder* comes from a Germanic root meaning *egg yolk*, which is also the ancestor of another modern word, *doddering*, meaning trembling, referring originally to the quivering motion of egg yolk just removed from the shell.

Most of the twelve species of dodder native to northeastern US and eastern Canada look superficially alike. They bear abundant clusters of tiny white flowers,

8-2 Our leader at the Prairie Fen Open House, **Guy Denny, botanist from ODNR**, now retired, is shown here at the Urbana Raised Fen, making a path through a stand of cat-tails.

8-3 View of the **knotted dodder** (*Cuscuta glomerata–X, now T*) at Liberty Fen, showing the unique tight masses of yellowish flowers, wrapped around the host plant, a sunflower.

8-4 A closer view of the **knotted dodder**, with no stems visible.

scattered randomly on the stem or in loose **panicles**; these blossoms bear no outward resemblance to the big, colorful tube-shaped flowers of their morning-glory ancestors.

A few species of dodders—the generalists, such as **common dodder** (*Cuscuta gronovii*)—prey on a wide variety of **host plants** (euphemism for *victims*), largely in open areas, such as meadows, prairies, marshes, roadsides, and farm fields. Others are **host specific**, meaning they pick on certain plants and ignore the rest, and are seldom seen by amateur plant hunters, who after a while get into the habit of identifying every dodder as *C. gronovii*.

That's why I was so startled to see the knotted dodder for the first time; it actually had some individuality and was not part of the mob. For one thing, its tiny flowers were pale yellow, not the dead white that I would expect in *gronovii*. Secondly, its stems spiraled up particular host plants and were not cast over a wide area like a web. Oddest of all, the individual strands of the yellow stems were so closely parallel to each other as they climbed up the host and were so tightly packed with tiny flowers that no part of the parasite's stem was visible. The whole effect appeared as if someone had taken a thick yellow clothesline and tied it carefully around the stem of each host in the form of the knot commonly known as the hangman's noose. No wonder that I thought a crime was in progress!

All of this took place in a part of Ohio that I had never seen before, the **prairie-fen** country of west-central Ohio, roughly between Dayton and Columbus. The Ohio Department of Natural resources (ODNR) had invited the public to its annual open-house tour of five prairie fens, August 12, 1989, under the guidance of experts from its Division of Areas and Preserves. Alkaline wetlands formed after the glaciers receded 12,000 years ago, **fens** typically are found near limestone-gravel ridges and are watered by cold alkaline springs.

I had already seen **Canadian-type fens** in Portage, Geauga, and Summit Counties in northeastern Ohio, the kind of wetland that is often near a large pond or lake, surrounded by **tamaracks**, and filled with unusual Northern sedges, orchids, willows, carnivorous plants, and heaths. Now I was going to see a **Midwestern-type fen**, not near a large body of water; surrounded originally by grasslands and an occasional **bur oak** (*Quercus macrocarpa*) and now by acres of farm fields; and filled with a mix of Northern plants and prairie species from the Midwest and Great Plains.

After a three and a half-hour drive from Cleveland, I met our guides at a designated state park in the Dayton-Springfield area, where over a hundred people had converged from all over Ohio. We were given the itinerary—Buffenbarger, Urbana Fairgrounds, Liberty, Prairie Road, and Gallagher's Fens—and were asked to divide up into groups, each led by a knowledgeable guide. I chose the group led by Guy Denny, whom I had

8-5 A close-up of the **common dodder** (*Cuscuta gronovii*) with many visible stems, branching off from its host plant, and loose clusters of white flowers.

met several times before when he had lectured in northeast Ohio and who had written many informative articles on endangered plants in the ODNR *Newsletter*.

If anyone knew about rare species, it would be Guy, and I wasn't disappointed. At Buffenbarger Fen he pointed out **queen-of-the-prairie** (*Filipendula rubra*), a tall member of the rose family, sometimes over seven feet, with globular panicles of small pink, fuzzy flowers resembling those of spiraea. It has a large range from Pennsylvania to Iowa south to Georgia and is apparently an invader from the tall-grass prairies of the Midwest, still working its way east to New England and the Maritimes.

Also at Buffenbarger the **blue-leaf willow** (*Salix glaucophylloides*, now *myricoides*–P) grew in short, dense clumps. Guy told us that this species was once considered extinct in Ohio but is now rated as potentially threatened. Its leaves, bluish-gray as if dipped in ashes, certainly lived up to its common name.

Around noon we came to Liberty Fen, located in such typical flat prairie country, now turned into farms, that one could see for miles in all directions. The buildings of the small community of West Liberty seemed close at hand although they must have been several miles away.

As we passed through a weedy low spot in the prairie between the road and the fen proper, we noticed a stand of about ten goldenrods and sunflowers, not in bloom yet but infested with many pale-yellow, snakelike growths spiraling up the stalks. Someone wondered aloud of they were fungi because they did look fuzzy and unwholesome like certain mildews. I was sure they were dodders but of a kind I had never before seen in the wild. Somewhere, my memory screen informed me, in some wildflower book I had seen a picture of this one, but where?

"Say, Guy," I called out. "Is it all right with ODNR if I collect one of these?"

"Go ahead," he answered. "You can even eat it." This was said probably because we were scheduled to have lunch pretty soon, courtesy of the brown bags and thermos bottles in our backpacks. I stashed the specimen plus its sunflower host in a plastic bag, took several photos, and went on my way.

The rest of the afternoon went by quickly with many good sightings, and after thanking Guy for pointing out the highlights of a new and remarkable flora, we went back to our cars and drove home. I put the dodder specimen into a plant press and took it to the Cleveland Museum of Natural History herbarium, where I was a volunteer one day a week. A few days later I put it into the freeze-dry, to kill insect eggs, and later, on a shelf with the rest of my donated specimens.

Still later, while leafing through an out-of-print hardcover book that I had purchased from the Museum gift shop years before, entitled *Wild Flowers of Ohio and*

8-6 Close-up of **queen-of-the-prairie** (*Filipendula rubra*). Its many small, pink flowers show a relationship to the spiraeas, also in the rose family.

Adjacent States by former Ohioan Isabelle H. Klein, I finally found my hangman's noose. Isabelle Klein called it **knotted dodder** (*Cuscuta glomerata*), meaning having clustered as opposed to scattered flowers, and one of its favorite hosts was the sunflower.

It took several more days before I thought of looking up its rarity status in Ohio. With the latest ODNR listing of "Rare Ohio Native Plants" in front of me, I turned casually to the Cuscutaceae, and lo and behold, knotted dodder was X–rated—for extirpated, extinct. I had rediscovered a lost plant, not seen in Ohio since 1933, or fifty-six years before!

I lost no time in calling Guy in Columbus about my discovery, but he informed me that while I was lollygagging about, two of my botanist buddies from Cleveland, who had been at the same prairie-fen open-house but with a different group and leader, had reported the same discovery almost a week earlier.

"But you were the only one who collected a specimen," Guy went on. "If you want to, you can write it up and submit it to a botanical journal. Most of the botanical discoveries in Ohio, at least from this department, go into *The Michigan Botanist*." And thus my first and only scientific-journal article was born.

To write about a rare dodder with some understanding of the topic, I decided I had to learn about the life cycle of the whole dodder family as well as that of other non-green, leafless plants, which existed in Ohio and the Great Lakes region in more variety than I had imagined. For starters, as I quickly learned from my references, dodders have no roots. When their seeds germinate in the soil, they put down a structure that may have been a root in its past evolutionary history but now serves only as an anchor; it has no **rootlets** which can absorb water and minerals from the soil. At the same time, a non-green creeping stem develops that begins to search for a host plant to parasitize.

It lengthens to three inches at the most, moving imperceptibly in a circle, like the tentacle of a vegetable octopus, to find a green plant to attach itself to. Any plant not in the **grass family** will do. Once attached to a temporary host, its "root" in the soil withers and dies, and the young dodder will send out a branch, or perhaps a whole network of branches, to find its preferred host.

How it does this without a sense of smell or taste is unknown, but some chemical reaction is probably involved. In Ohio **hazel dodder** (*Cuscuta coryli–E*) and **buttonbush dodder** (*C. cephalanthi*) seek shrubs and small trees. **Smartweed dodder** (*C. polygonorum*) seeks plants of swamps and wetlands, such as the **water smartweeds** (*Polygonum*), **ditch stonecrop**, and **water horehound**. Knotted dodder seeks large members of the **composite**, or daisy, family, especially sunflowers, goldenrods, asters, and blazing stars. Common dodder will make do with any sort of host, except grasses.

8-7 Scattered **bur oaks** (*Quercus macrocarpa*) characterize tall-grass prairies in central Ohio. Their acorn cups, ringed with filaments, are the origin of their other common name— **mossy-cup oaks**.

8-8 The ashy blue color of the leaves of the **blue-leaved willow** (*Salix myricoides–P*) is caused by a type of bacteria called a **glaucous bloom**. Such blooms are found on stems, leaves and fruits of many plants, such as plums, and can be rubbed off easily.

Why dodders would rather die than victimize grasses is another mystery, but it's one of the luckiest breaks in the history of agriculture, since so many of the world's farmers have depended on cereal grains (wheat, rye, and barley) as well as oats, rice, and corn for their livelihood and their very survival. How would the great civilizations of the past have fared if their agricultural base, already besieged by fungi, such as **wheat rust**, and predatory insects, such as plagues of grasshoppers, had to fight off dodders with their superefficient absorption organs called **haustoria**?

The word *haustoria* comes from the Latin word *haustus*, meaning to drink, or draw in, water; or to drain or use up, as in our word *exhaust*. Only the first meaning applies to the dodder since the parasitic process never results in the death or critical injury of the host. Despite the appearance of being strangled, the host of knotted dodder actually is healthy and well nourished. If it were to weaken and die, the dodder, lacking its own roots, would also succumb.

Haustoria are generally considered to be modified rootlets and are perhaps similar to structures already present on morning-glory vines. I remember one year I trained a morning-glory to grow up a trellis leaning against the side of my house. Once it got started, it quickly twined itself around the vertical supports until it reached the top, where it would normally stop. But not this morning-glory. Sending out little green structures like suction pads on the sides of its stems, it continued to climb the clapboard siding of my house for about five more feet before calling it quits.

It's not clear how haustoria can enter the hard epidermal tissues of plants, let alone penetrate the bark and dissolve the dense woody cells of shrubs and trees. When plant anatomists discovered tiny, hair-thin rows of cells sent out by the haustoria, they named them *hyphae*, a term also used in describing the growth tissues of fungi. And perhaps there is a similarity in structure and chemical makeup in the absorption tissues of two totally different organisms.

8-9 A little-known composite, **fen Indian-plantain** (*Cacalia plantaginea–P*) is almost exclusively confined to wetlands.

119

Once the dodder establishes itself on its host plant, it turns into a seed factory, sending out prodigious quantities of tiny flowers, quickly pollinated by bees and wasps and followed by fruits containing four seeds each, packed with nutriments for next year's stems.

Like many fast-spreading weeds, dodders are **annuals** with well-developed methods of **seed dispersal**. Although their seeds are too heavy to float on water or be blown about by the wind, a heavy rain can wash them away after they fall to the ground and bring them to new areas with the right sort of hosts. Since they are waterproof, they will not rot. Also, because of their rough seedcoats, they may cling to the feet and fur of large grazing animals, such as deer, and be transported long distances. Furthermore, dodders have learned to use people, by clinging to their shoes, clothing, vehicles, farm machinery, and domestic animals.

Guy Denny to the contrary, dodder seeds are not appetizing to mammals or birds, or even digestible, but they can be swallowed accidentally, when mixed with grain or fodder, and pass through the intestinal tract unharmed. In the process, the tough seedcoat of the dodder is weakened sufficiently to allow germination. This seems to be the usual method, as proved by lab experiments that imitate the digestive conditions in grazing animals: dodder seeds are soaked in concentrated sulfuric acid, put in a blender filled with ground glass, and given the cold treatment (to duplicate overwintering) before they begin germination. Dodders have to be tough to survive these conditions.

8-10 **Parasites, Saprophytes,** and **Symbionts**: Even in full bloom, **beech drops** (*Epifagus virginiana*) a parasite of beech roots, looks like a dead stick. Note the gray bark of the massive **American beech** (*Fagus grandifolia*) behind it.

8-11 The tube-shaped blossoms of the **one-flowered cancer-root** (*Orobanche uniflora*) grow from an underground stem.

8-12 **Squaw-root**
(*Conopholis americana*)
in flower.

One wonders how many other non-green parasites have a similar life style. In Ohio there is a whole family of plants, the **broom-rapes**, distantly related to the snapdragons, which prefer to do their dirty work underground by parasitizing the roots of forest trees. Anyone exploring the mature forests of the Great Lakes region is sure to find **beechdrops** (*Epifagus virginiana*) growing beneath the canopy of the **American beech** (*Fagus grandifolia*). The erect, branching stems are brown with a few scales that probably once functioned as leaves for its non-parasitic ancestors. Its flowers, buffy brown with red-purple stripes, bloom and go to seed August to October, the same time as the beechnuts of its host. Perhaps its abundant seeds are dispersed by beechnut-loving animals, such as squirrels and wild turkeys.

An attractive pale-lavender wildflower with an ugly name, broom-rape or **cancer-root** (*Orobanche uniflora*) has no true stems above the ground, only one to four flower-stalks with a few small scales, vestiges of leaves, at the base. Because it prefers shaded wet woods with usually a thick understory of shrubs, broom-rape is not as conspicuous as its relatives. It has been known to parasitize trees, shrubs, and large composites, such as asters and goldenrods. Probably because its color is so subdued, it has evolved a delightful fragrance for attracting butterflies and other pollinators of its tube-shaped flowers.

Oak-hickory forests also have a member of this family: **squaw-root** (*Conopholis americana*), consisting of a spike of yellow-brown flowers alternating with scales of the same color (descendants of the original leaves), which harden as the fruit matures. The whole plant then resembles a pine cone stuck in the ground. One wonders if blue jays and squirrels are taken in by this mimicry and disperse the seeds. Like the famous European parasite, **mistletoe**, squaw-root victimizes mainly oak trees.

8-13 In fruit, it looks like an upright cone of a spruce or pine fallen to the ground.

8-14 A Western species of **dwarf mistletoe** (*Arceuthobium campylopodum*) photographed on a pine in Oregon's Siskiyou Mountains. The mistletoe resembles a dried-up cedar twig.

8-15 Related to our Indian pipe, this **snow plant** (*Sarcodes sanguinea*) was photographed on a mountain overlooking Yosemite Valley in California. As its name implies, it can appear even before the snow melts in late spring.

8-16 In the **snow plant**, the bright red flowers are tightly clustered in a spiral fashion, with each flower surrounded by a red *bract*, probably a vestige of the green leaves of non-parasitic ancestors.

Large woody knobs on the roots of its hosts are evidence that this species has been at work.

Most of our **American mistletoes** (from the family *Loranthaceae*) are from a more primitive group than the broom-rapes, but they retain their green leaves. They are widely distributed in tropical America and in the West; however, many parts of the Northeast and the Great Lakes drainage are subject to the infestations of the leafless, little-known **dwarf mistletoe** (*Arceuthobium pusillum*), which attacks spruce, tamarack, and white pine. To find a dwarf mistletoe is not easy, since the mature seed-bearing plant is no more than two inches high and usually sits in the middle of a growth deformity called **witches'- broom**, a tangle of short, skinny branches that grow out in all directions as the conifer host responds to the infection site. (Witches'-broom is also caused by certain fungi.)

Like dodders, mistletoes lack true roots, but they never disperse their seeds on the ground. When a sticky mistletoe fruit or seed lands on the branches of its host tree (usually through the agency of a bird), it sends out haustoria, which tap into the water and nourishment systems of the host tree by means of hyphae, the same as for dodders and fungi. But unlike the dodders, the dwarf mistletoe sends up a tiny stem with scale-like, deep-brown or purplish leaves that surprisingly resemble the scales of a **northern white-cedar**, or **arbor vitae**. This is a case of plant mimicry that is more effective in the Old World, where the parasite actually attacks cedars and related scale-bearing conifers. (*Arceuthobium* in Greek means "living off cedars.")

Some of the most remarkable non-green plants not only feed on dead plant material as many of the fungi do, but their waxy, spongy appearance reminds the plant hunter of mushrooms. The **pyrola** family, close relatives of the **heaths,** produce many normal green-leaved plants, such as the **shinleaves** (*Pyrola*) and **wintergreens** (*Chimaphila*), small plants

8-17 A small colony of **Indian pipe** (*Monotropa uniflora*), caught by a rare sunbeam illuminating the dark forest floor, its usual habitat. Indian pipe is now considered a **symbiont**, an organism that lives in a beneficial arrangement with others, in this case, mushrooms and trees.

often found on the floor of rich, moist woods. But it also contains the strange, ghost-white **Indian pipe** (*Monotropa uniflora*) and many of its weird-looking Western relatives, like the famous blood-red **snow plant** of the Sierras (*Sarcodes sanguinea*). Indian pipe even turns black when its flowering cycle is over, just as mushrooms do, and mushroom field guides warn novices not to pick it as a specimen.

Depending on what sources one uses, Indian pipes and their relatives are described as either strict parasites or parasitic-saprophytic, feeding on living and dead tree roots, as do their look-alikes, the mushrooms. Recent research finds the truth much more complicated. In the extensive coniferous forests of the West, snow plant has been discovered to tap into the nutrients produced by the **fungus associates** (**mycorrhizae**) of tree roots, especially of pines. Mycorrhizae are felt-like masses of mushroom tissue that invade and cover the rootlets of pines and provide them with minerals, nutriments, antibiotics, and moisture, which the fungi have recycled from decayed organic material in the soil. In this arrangement, the fungi also benefit by obtaining carbohydrates from the rootlets of the pine. Apparently mycorrhizae also invade the roots of the snow plants growing under pines, and all three organisms benefit in a benign form of partnership called **symbiosis**, living together for mutual advantage.

Mycorrhizae also play an important role in the orchid family. Some of the well-known leafless orchids are saprophytes, such as the **coral-roots** and the strange, but beautiful, **three-birds orchid**. Like the knotted dodder, the coral-roots never develop true roots; instead, they send out odd-

8-18 A **symbiotic orchid**, the **spotted coral-root** (*Corallorhiza maculata*–P) has flower stalks of various colors: yellow, brown, or red-purple, as in this example.

looking, many-branched underground stems called **rhizomes**, which become wrapped with mycorrhizal tissues. These supply the rhizomes with all the nutriments, minerals, and moisture that the coral-roots need for flowering and setting seed.

Since the **spotted coral-root** (*Corallorhiza maculata—P*) is the commonest of the group and most widely distributed in the East, it is the first orchid that plant-hunters usually find. Blooming in the dense shade of mature forests in rich organic soil, the spotted coral-root with its light purple flowers and spotted **lip** (the lowest petal of an orchid) is very often the only plant seen on the forest floor during the hot, humid days of July and August.

Very different are the big stands of the **crested coral-root** (*Hexalectris spicata—T*), a southern species just reaching into Adams County in Ohio along the Ohio River. Tall for an orchid, the crested coral-root can grow over two feet high and often in big, conspicuous clumps in light shade among oaks. With its elegant-looking flower, the buffy petals with conspicuous purple-red stripes being somewhat ribbon shaped, the orchid reminds the viewer of the kind of ornamental scrollwork found on awards certificates. Because its rhizomes store nutriments unevenly, it blooms very irregularly, a habit shared by all the saprophytic orchids, but carried to an extreme by the seldom-seen **three-birds** (*Triphora trianthophora—T*).

More often seen in wildflower manuals than in the wild itself, three-birds blooms in mature forests, such as beech-maple, on deep soil loaded with decayed material. Although a perennial, the plant puts no vegetative parts above ground until late July when the tuberous rhizomes trigger a growth hormone after certain conditions of soil moisture and air temperature have occurred. A stem arises, bearing the poorest excuses for leaves of any member of the orchid family: from six to eighteen millimeters long (at most, equaling the width of a dime), the roundish, clasping leaves probably contribute little in the way of photosynthesis and are perhaps evolving their way out of existence. Two to three weeks later, three flowers appear in succession, each in a separate leaf axil. The flowers are white, as benefits a plant blooming in deep shade, and of such a beautiful shape—like miniature corsage orchids, frilled lip and all—that orchid photographers will take endless pains to locate a colony, as a friend of mine and I experienced on August 21, 1983.

Jack and I had been all morning at the famous Oak Opening Park near Toledo, Ohio, a prairie and **sand-barrens** area with one of the richest and most diverse floras in Ohio. We were having great luck. We had found our first **Great Lakes goldenrod** (*Euthamia remota—T*), a native to only four areas on the southern shores of Lake Erie and Lake Michigan. At a small prairie adjoining a railroad right-of-way, we found the **tubercled rein-orchid** (*Platanthera flava var. herbiola—P*) just going out of flower.

8-19 The bare stems of the **crested coral-root** (*Hexalectris spicata—T*) are buffy in color and quite tall, for an orchid. This Southern species barely reaches Ohio in one county on the Ohio River.

Before noon we met a friend of Jack's, a park naturalist from a state-owned nature preserve in western Ohio, who gave us the great news that three-birds was in bloom at his park. He even gave us the name of the nature trail and the number of the station where it would be found. How could anyone miss this opportunity? And with all the location information, how could anyone fail to find the orchid?

Very easily. Although we got to the park in less than two hours, found the right nature trail, and found the small colony of three-birds, none of the plants was in bloom. Why? In Ohio, three-birds orchid blooms only in the morning! Naturally disappointed, we later found out that all bottom orchids in a single colony bloom at the same time; that is, the lowest orchid of every plant blooms on the same morning, then is pollinated, wilts, and begins to go to seed in the afternoon. Next day, the second orchid in each plant does the same, and on the following day, the third and last orchid repeats the procedure. Result: no more orchids until next year if conditions are right. And if not, try the year after that.

As it turned out, we didn't' have the time to return that week, and we didn't' hear there were any orchids in bloom in the park until August 15, 1985. This time we made sure to get there in the morning! We found at least fifty plants in bloom, scattered over a large area and, true to their saprophytic nature, most of them were growing by rotted stumps or dead tree trunks lying on the ground. In one group more than ten plants were growing close together, and some of the flowers were pink as well as white. For me this was a high point in my orchid-hunting career, and I learned a lot about saprophytes at the same time.

As for carnivorous plants, in Ohio there is only one species that can do without green leaves. It is neither the sundew with its sticky leaves nor the pitcher plant with its big, vessel-shaped leaves. (These two plants often have red leaves, but in many species red masks the green of chlorophyll.) Rather, it is the aquatic carnivorous group of the **bladderworts** (*Utricularia*), related to the **scrophs**, members of the snap dragon family, that seems to be moving toward a leafless condition.

Opinion is still divided on whether they have leaves to begin with. The famous **bladders**, which are traps to catch microscopic aquatic organisms, such as the well-known **water flea** *Daphnia*, seem to be part of a stem or root system, which may have been originally the veins of a set of large basal leaves. The bladders, which are unique in the plant kingdom, contain hairs that are a signaling device, acting somewhat as the sense of touch in animals. When *Daphnia* or a similar organism touches a hair, the bladder nearby suddenly opens, almost as if controlled by the equivalent of a jaw muscle, and the *Daphnia* is swept inside by the current. The bladder "door" closes behind it, and it is

8-20 A denizen of deep shade, the **three-birds orchid** (*Triphora trianthophora–T*) shows in its three outer petals (really sepals) the lifted tail and wings of a bird.

8-21 **Carnivorous Plants**: A dark red leaf of a **purple pitcher plant** (*Sarracenia purpurea–P*), seen in August in a bog in northeast Ohio, with its normal fall coloration masking the chlorophyll present in its cells. The thick layer of hairs inside the lid of the "pitcher" point downward and prevent small non-flying insects, such as ants, from climbing out.

trapped. After a victim is digested by *enzymes* similar to those in an animal's stomach, the bladder door opens again, and the hair-trigger is reset.

In all species of bladderwort, the highly dissected basal leaves (or whatever they are) may still manufacture food for the plant, but there is no doubt that the aquatic animals caught in the traps provide most of the calories. Most plant physiologists believe that nutrients containing important nitrogen compounds are in short supply in the bog or swamp habitat where carnivorous plants live; therefore, the process of catching and digesting animals has evolved to supply the needed nitrogen.

Although most bladderworts are aquatic, a few, such as the **horned bladderwort** (*U. cornuta*) of the Great Lakes region and Atlantic coast, are terrestrial, growing in wet sand or mud. Here it is fairly clear that the dissected leaves have no food-making function since sunlight doesn't reach them.

After studying all the different types of non-green plants that seem to function and even thrive without the benefit of chlorophyll and photosynthesis, I was better equipped to understand the knotted dodder.

First, I could see why it was so rare in Ohio, not only at present but ever since plant records have been kept. Since it is more or less host-specific on large composites, such as sunflowers, its usual habitat was the tall-grass prairies extending from the Great Plains into the Midwest in a sort of funnel shape, called, in Ohio, the **Prairie Peninsula**. Here the small end of the funnel seemed to have centered around Columbus, nearly in the middle of the state. There has been only one record of *C. glomerata–T* east of Columbus, in Licking County; this represents the easternmost point of its range, not just in Ohio but also in North America.

However, in the Great Plains, knotted dodder is one of the commonest species of its genus because large, colorful composites dominate the broad-leaf prairie flora, meaning all the plants other than grasses. The center of its abundance is the eastern half of Kansas, where it is found in nearly every county, and in the early days of settlement it was found from southwest Michigan west to South Dakota and south to Mississippi and Texas, a truly enormous mid-continental range. Why did such a successful plant become so uncommon in the eastern part of its range? Apparently agriculture did it in. In Ohio the natural prairie went down from 2,000 square miles to 2,000 acres. Corn and soybeans took the place of grasses and prairie composites, except in wetlands like prairie fens.

Another problem with knotted dodder is its distinctive appearance and color. Why is it the only dodder in the East to have yellowish flowers rather than white, and a ropelike inflorescence rather than a stringy or web-like appearance? From what I've seen of plant mimicry in the dwarf mistletoe, the squawroot, and the Indian pipe, my guess is that a furry, ropelike appearance is too reminiscent of mold or mildew to grazing animals, such as deer, and they will avoid it. On the other hand, bees will be drawn to the yellow color of the tiny, crowded flowers because they look like the disk flowers of its composite hosts, and they will be pollinated, just as the host's own flowers would be.

This brings up another problem: where *were* the flowers of the host plant? Shouldn't at least a few of them have been in bloom by August 12, the day of the prairie-fen open house? Is it possible that the knotted dodder is not only a thief, stealing its host's nutriments, but also a kidnapper, stealing its host's young? Could it be that the host plants never bloom? Although knotted dodder has not been studied in depth, botanists in California and Arizona have studied the **field dodder** (*C. campestris*), which is an important pest on alfalfa grown for seed, and which in some areas can destroy nearly all the crop. Somehow it does this by causing most of the flowers of its alfalfa host to fall off before being fertilized and preventing the remainder from setting viable seed. Perhaps knotted dodder does this to its sunflower and goldenrod hosts. In the underworld of criminal plants, it's either "us or them."

Will knotted dodder ever become a farm pest? So far, it hasn't been documented as such, principally because its favorite targets—the composites—have seldom been grown as commercial crops. In recent years, however, sunflowers have become the staple of the birdseed and margarine industries. In Ohio one sees fields of huge-headed **Kansas sunflowers** grown for seed.

Actually the biggest enemy of sunflowers right now is the rival rapeseed industry, mostly centered in Canada, where cultivation of an Old World mustard, called **oil-seed rape** (*Brassica napus*), has for the moment captured the low-fat, low-cholesterol cooking-oil industry. But even if knotted dodder should invade commercial sunflower fields by being transported by farmers and their machinery, there are several ways to control this species.

One is to plow up the sunflower fields and plant grass for two or more years before replanting sunflowers. This gets rid of most of the dodder, if not all, because newly germinated dodders must avoid grass. Secondly, to remove all hosts, get rid of all broad-leaf plants between the nearest road and the former sunflower field. (In the case of Liberty Fen, the area of infestation was between the fen and the road.) Finally, if there is a chance that dodder seeds have gotten mixed with sunflower seeds after the harvest, one can use a gizmo called a *dodder mill,* with moving, felt-covered rollers—something like a cotton gin, I imagine. The rough seed coats of dodder will stick to the felt, while the smooth sunflower seeds will go through.

Lastly, why did the knotted dodder return to Ohio after fifty-six years of absence? We may never know. The answer may have something to do with this era of fast,

8-22 The large nodding flower of the **purple pitcher plant** with its petals hanging down like curtains.

8-23 The **horned bladderwort** (*Utricularia cornuta*—E) lives in mud or wet sand. The few green leaves it has are buried in the soil and can't manufacture food in darkness. Photo taken in the Indiana Dunes National Lakeshore near Beverly Shores, Indiana.

8-24 **Green-Leaved Parasitic Plants:** In Ohio the **cow-wheat** (*Melampyrum lineare*—T) grows in very sandy soil or on rocky ledges. In Michigan it can be found in bogs.

8-25 **Bluehearts** (*Buchnera americana*—T) at one time was considered one of the rarest plants in the prairies of southern Ohio and was frequently mentioned by Lucy Braun. Since then, it has made a comeback. It is also found in boggy places behind the dunes on the shore of Lake Michigan in Indiana.

long-distance surface transportation. The tires of a truck, passing through Kansas, for instance, may pick up many dodder seeds; the next day, in Ohio, many of them may drop off. Or perhaps the viability of *C. glomerata* seeds in the ground is the answer.

Researchers can state that field dodder definitely loses its viability in five years, but other species may still retain it after ten to twenty years. It is entirely possibly that knotted dodder seeds remained dormant in the ground for fifty-six years or longer, waiting for…we don't know what: an increase in the deer population to transport seeds; a change of farm crops from corn to broad-leaf plants? No one is sure.

Anything is possible when one is dealing with a slippery crook that works boldly in the open, a master of many disguises, a rootless despoiler of green-leaved plants, a brazen thief that would deserve the hangman's noose if it hadn't stolen it first, *Cuscuta glomerata*—the mother of all dodders.

＊　　＊　　＊　　＊　　＊　　＊　　＊

2006 Author's Postscript

Thanks to a scientific journal article entitled "Fire and Cuscuta glomerata *in Ohio: a Connection?" by Jim McCormac and Jennifer Windus, (both of ODNR) appearing in* Rhodora *in 1993, the mystery of the strange appearance of the knotted dodder in Ohio, after more than half a century may have been solved. The authors believe that fires set by ODNR at various prairies in central Ohio (to burn sapling trees that would eventually take over the habitat) was the main cause of the reappearance of prairie plants in central Ohio. Seeds buried in the soil lost their hard coats and were stimulated to sprout. (See Chapter 3 on prairie fires.) There seems to be a close correlation between reappearance of the dodder and prairie fires set in the same area the year before.*

8-26 Feasting on the roots of other plants, principally oaks, the **yellow false foxglove** (*Aureolaria flava*), seen here in a prairie in northwestern Ohio, is a handsome member of its family.

9-1 **Birds: At White City Beach and the Easterly Sewage Plant** there is a strange mixture of the familiar and the exotic. When it comes to resident birds on the lakefront, the **herring gull**, which breeds on tiny islands in Lake Erie 80 miles west of Cleveland, is the most familiar. Its hawk-like bill and fierce yellow eyes go along with its reputation as chief scavenger on the lakefront.

9-3 Among waterfowl the green head of the **male mallard duck** is a common sight on or away from Lake Erie.

9-2 The slightly smaller **ring-billed gull** is familiar not only to lakefront visitors but to everyone who drives into a shopping-mall parking lot.

chapter 9

White City...What a Dump!

Author's Note: while most of the facts mentioned here may have been true of the middle '70s, when I wrote this article for the Cleveland newspaper The Plain Dealer, I haven't been to White City since the Sewer District closed it off to the public in the early '80s. However, even if only a tenth of the plants and animals mentioned in the article occur at White City, it would still be a remarkable haven for wildlife.

9-5 A **female common eider** on her nest. (Photo taken at the bird colony on Inner Farne Island off the east coast of Britain.) This species has turned out to be the rarest migrant on the Cleveland lakefront with three photographic records in all of the twentieth century to distinguish it from the slightly more common female king eider; and the locale was White City.

9-4 **Canada geese** are no longer spring and fall migrants. In the last 30 years they have become permanent residents in the Cleveland area.

9-6 The **male common eider**, also photographed at Inner Farne, with its resplendent black and white breeding plumage, has never been spotted on the Great Lakes in any plumage during migration. It apparently travels only along the Atlantic coast to and from its breeding grounds in Arctic Canada.

In all outward aspects, White City is a real dump. Walt Disney Enterprises would not make a movie about it. Time-Life's *American Wilderness* series would not publish a book about it. Nature Conservancy would not try to save it. Yet for all its pariah status as a "disturbed area," White City on the Cleveland, Ohio, lakefront has become a fascinating place to study wildlife.

For the uninitiated, a description of White City can sound very discouraging. Located off Lake Shore Boulevard near East 140th Street, White City was originally a popular bathing beach. Even in these days of notorious Lake Erie pollution, brave people still wade or take a dip along the stretch of sand protected by a breakwall, although the Cleveland authorities condemn the murky water as unfit for swimming. The real attraction lies next door. On the other side of a cindery parking lot, the Eastern Sewage Plant has established a "lagoon" for dumping sewage solids and effluent. At one time a single-track railway led out of the bowels of the sewage plant, and often a Toonerville string of tiny dump cars could be seen parked on the bank of the lagoon, filled with black muck of an indescribable smell. This material was dumped onto the banks of the lagoon, gradually raising them higher and higher like the layers of debris covering an ancient city. Weeds would take hold along this black, gooey shoreline, even bushes and small trees. Insects seemed to love it, especially a peculiar small fly that would buzz in swarms around any visiting bird-watchers and even accompany them back to their cars.

The little railway no longer operates, and the lagoon, protected by a breakwall, was fed by a constant stream of sewage effluent until two years ago. But the migratory birds keep coming back. Whether the super-charged nutrients in the muck have caused plants and insects to proliferate inside the lagoon or created a more complex food chain involving fish (and I've seen young catfish there), shorebirds and waterfowl from all corners of eastern North America have aimed toward White City like pilgrims toward Mecca.

In the winter, as long as the black lagoon waters are free of ice, gulls and ducks set up their headquarters. Among the hordes of herring and ring-billed gulls, the lucky visitor may spot a Bonaparte's gull, a Franklin's gull, a little gull, a great black-backed gull, or even a Sabine's gull from the far north.

The ducks are mostly mallards and blacks, but when the waters of the lake beyond the breakwall get stormy and tumultuous, the lagoon becomes a haven for diving ducks: canvasbacks, buffleheads, mergansers, scaup, and goldeneyes, with perhaps a rare eider or scoter making a sudden appearance. One winter's distinguished visitor from the North was a female harlequin duck, a species not seen in the Cleveland area since November 1966.

9-7 **Native Plants from Lake Erie Sand Dunes**: The familiar and the exotic of the plant kingdom also mix at White City. Next to a beat-up fence are a few scrubby grass plants, which turn out to be **American beach grass** (*Ammophila breviligulata—T*), the species responsible for stabilizing the Lake Erie dunes and seldom found away from the lake: a true **strand plant**.

9-10 **Eurasian Plants Adapted to Wastelands:** Although its name suggests that it is related to the well-known thistles of the daisy, or composite, family, the **Russian thistle** (*Salsola kali var. tenuifolia*) from Eurasia, is a prickly-leaved species from the large, weedy **goosefoot**, or **chenopod**, family, found commonly in deserts and grasslands.

9-8 A Great Lakes variety of a familiar Atlantic coast plant, the **inland sea-rocket** (*Cakile edentula*–P), despite its exciting name, belongs to the edible but rather drab-flowered mustard or cabbage family. (*Rocket* is an old word, derived from the Italian, for a kind of cabbage.) As with many salt-tolerant plants, its leaves are fleshy. (Photo courtesy of Jack Selby.)

9-9 **Seaside spurge** (*Euphorbia polygonifolia*–P), also from the Atlantic coast, belongs to a family that is famous for producing a poisonous milky juice, called **latex**. (The rubber tree is a useful member of this family.) Perhaps the red stems of this ground-hugging plant are a warning to animals not to eat it.

133

9-11 The **cocklebur** (*Xanthium spinosum*) shown here below with its spiny fruit, is a European species from the real thistle family. Since it seeks waste places exclusively, White City is an ideal second home.

9-12 The spiny capsule of the **jimsonweed** (*Datura stramonium*) of the **nightshade family**, famous for many plants used for food (potato, tomato, bell pepper, eggplant) as well as for drugs and poisons (tobacco, henbane). This species perhaps originated in India or the Middle East. All parts of the plant have poisonous alkaloids, which also are used for their medicinal value.

9-13 **Escapees from the Garden**: Cucumber (*Cucumis sativus*) often escapes to disturbed areas from cultivated plots, as do other members of its family: musk-melon, squash, pumpkin, and watermelon.

Shorebirds come in the winter too. Next winter there may be northern or red phalaropes bobbing in the lagoon, or purple sandpipers clambering over the breakwall, as they have done in the past.

Spring migrations of waterfowl occasionally hit White City. The dabbling ducks do not seem to appreciate it, but small groups of Canada geese and even tundra swans seem at home in the lagoon. Incongruously the swans dip their necks down into the filthy water, acting as secure as in the bogs of their homes in the Canadian tundra, and perhaps there is a similarity.

It is in late summer and early fall that White City comes into its own. The shorebird migrations from Canada make White City a busy place: not only the common species such as sanderlings, yellowlegs, peep, semipalmated plover, turnstones, dowitchers, and killdeer; but the rarities such as golden plover, stilt sandpiper, Baird's sandpiper, piping plover, and red knot. A September afternoon may reveal a whimbrel quietly feeding among turnstones, peep, and willets while a Caspian tern meows overhead like an angry Siamese cat. Or the lucky birdwatcher may spot an avocet from the western plains, standing on pale blue legs in the shallows, while buff-breasted sandpipers skulk among the sedges on the shore. It's not wise to get too close. White City muck has a deceptively firm appearance as the shorebirds blithely run over it. A human visitor, however, will find himself sinking in up to his ankles.

Fall brings warblers, kinglets, and sparrows to the few trees and bushes around the lagoon, and hordes of swallows to sit on the wires. The gulls and terns from their breeding islands in western Lake Erie join the shore birds in great numbers and spill over onto the bathing beach. Herons stalk through the clumps of arrowhead that have sprung up over the summer—probably hungry for a catfish dinner. The big flocks of "undesirable aliens"—pigeons, starlings, and house sparrows—are occasionally joined by escaped cage birds, such as parakeets and strawberry finches. All find their way to White City.

9-14 The most stately and attractive member of the buckwheat family–**prince's-feather** (*Polygonum orientale*), cultivated in Eurasia–is right at home with its relatives, the more humble smartweeds, most of which are natives.

9-15 Close-up of one nodding spike of **prince's-feather**.

9-16 **Native American Plants Adapted to Sandy Environments:** The **common sunflower** (*Helianthus annuus*) is such an easy plant to recognize with its great height (nine feet or over) and huge single flower that it almost comes as a shock to find that no recent plant authority will pinpoint its place of origin. Fernald (1950) claims it as a native of the Great Plains from Minnesota to Texas and westward.

The wildlife enthusiast will find not only the unusual among birds but also among plants. The sedge-willow association beside the lagoon is typical of a wet environment, but it is on the dry, cinder-strewn disturbed areas away from the banks of the lagoon that the plant hunter can have a field day. This is truly a dump in the sense that individuals and commercial firms clandestinely mock the "No Dumping" signs to heave household goods, piles of stone, old mattresses, building materials, old tires, bottles, and cans. City-owned cement mixers wash out their excess cement at White City. Besides attracting rats, all this debris makes a challenging environment for a large variety of plants.

The strand plants of the Lake Erie shoreline, some of which are on the Heritage List, frequently put in an appearance at White City as if it were just another dune at Mentor Headlands State Park, thirty miles away. One will find **beach grass** (*Ammophila breviligulata*–T); **inland sea rocket** (*Cakile edentula var. lacustris*–P), a member of the cabbage family with four-petaled lavender flowers; and **seaside spurge** (*Euphorbia polygonifolia*–P)—all descended from common plants on the Atlantic coast, perhaps reaching Lake Erie through the St. Lawrence in post-glacial times.

These often accompany **Russian thistle** (*Salsola kali var. tenuifolia*) of the spinach family, and not a thistle; and **cocklebur** (*Xanthium strumarium*) of the aster family—coarse, homely species, lacking petals and originally from Europe or Asia. A tall, graceful native plant called **switch grass** (*Panicum virgatum*) keeps them company. Hosts of alien species, mostly from gardens and empty lots in the cities and including **spider-flower** (*Cleome spinosa*) and **garden portulaca** (*P. grandiflora*), are often very attractive, and then there are the vegetables: tomatoes, in such profusion as to make the home gardener wince, thrive on apparently barren soil, along with squash and cucumbers.

9-17 Another Westerner, the **buffalo-bur** (*Solanum rostratum*), as one of the **nightshades**, protects itself by poisonous **alkaloids** as well as numerous spines on its seed capsule. Its common name perhaps refers to the dispersal of its burs by attaching themselves to the shaggy fur of buffalo in its Great Plains habitat.

9-18 Although **sand-vine** (*Cynanchum laeve*, once listed as *Ampelamus albidus*), of the milkweed family, is common only in southern Ohio and further south and west, it is slowly making its way north to Lake Erie, by way of many disturbed habitats.

Mixed in with homely **lamb's quarters** and **pokeweed** may be found gorgeous clumps of carmine plumes marking the **prince's-feather** (*Polygonum orientale*), a showy relative of the common knotweeds and smartweeds that thrive at White City. That bluish-white umbel with the large outer petals turns out to be **coriander** (*Coriandrum sativum*) from the herb garden while the pink-flowered mint, **henbit** (*Lamium amplexicaule*) an invader from Europe nestles among the rocks as if it always belonged there. Nearby may be discovered such useful aliens as the tall grass, known as **sorghum** (*Sorghum bicolor*); **flax** (*Linum usatissimum*); and **broomcorn millet** (*Panicum miliaceum*), a grass once grown for brooms and now for feeding wild birds on game refuges.

9-20 **Mystery plant**: strong smelling, with apparently simple, unlobed leaves, and a flower similar to the bur-marigolds or beggar-ticks (*Bidens*). **What is it?**

9-19 The large green seed-pods of **sand-vine** clinch its relationship to the milkweeds.

137

9-21 **Bur-marigolds** (*Bidens*) are found almost worldwide, including oceanic islands, such as the Hawaiian chain. Most of the species of the Great Lakes region are found in wetlands or on sandy or rocky soil, including beaches. They produce the well-known barbed seeds, known as stick-tights or beggar-ticks, which catch on to fur, feathers, and clothing. This adaptation helps them to disperse seeds to every available wet habitat. Pictured here is the **nodding bur-marigold** (*B. cernua*), found throughout northern Ohio and noted for its wide flowers.

9-22 **Garden Ornamentals**: The **common morning-glory** (*Ipomoea purpurea*), one of many tropical vines or creepers in its genus, comes originally from Latin America. Besides the purple form shown here, it can also be bluish, red, or white.

Many White City plants seem to prefer the most sterile ground. Exotic, poisonous **jimsonweed** (*Datura stramonium*, of the **nightshade family**), protects its seeds inside large burs. Its huge, petunia-like flowers, which bloom only at night, seem ready to open up or to close, typical of the ephemeral quality of much of White City's flora. A White City specialty is the **buffalo-bur** (*Solanum rostratum*), also of the nightshade family, a spiny native American plant usually found further west. It creeps along the ground like a squash vine, a type of mimicry further carried out by its large lobed leaves and yellow, squash-like blossom. However, there is no mistaking its fruit, a spiny bur, no longer transported by buffalo yet somehow spreading to favorable sites like White City.

The nature photographer visiting White City should take his pictures when he finds a suitable subject, for with the transient nature of the environment, the wildlife may not be there the following day. The birds may be off again on their migratory journeys, and somebody from the sewage plant or the city may bulldoze a section of the lagoon bank or dump a truckload of rocks, obliterating a thriving stand of plants.

9-23 Another immigrant to White City is the **moss-rose**, of the **purslane family**, mostly a very weedy, inconspicuous group, but including the **spring beauty** (*Claytonia virginica*). The flowers of the moss-rose come in a variety of glowing colors. Gardeners commonly call this plant **portulaca** after its scientific name *Portulaca grandiflora*.

9-24 A longtime garden favorite, originally from the tropics, is the **spider-flower** (*Cleome spinosa*, now called *C. hassleriana*). Although it belongs to the **caper family**, well known in the spice trade, it could easily pass as a legume: bicolored and asymmetric flowers, palmately compound leaves, and fruit in the form of long pods.

Nevertheless, new birds and plants will return. Like a naturally disturbed area—a sandy Lake Erie shore, for example—White City makes up in diversity of species what it lacks in stability as a habitat. While we would not want every natural area to be so constantly in flux, White City remains a source of unexpected wildlife visitors, tucked away in the urban landscape.

*Author's postscript (2006): Shortly after submitting this essay for publication back in the '70s, I saw two unusual plants that had never been documented for the Cleveland area before. The first, **sand-vine** of the milkweed family (Cynanchum laeve, formerly Ampelamus albidus), a native of southern Ohio, was a puzzler until I noticed its long, dark green, milkweed-like pods. Its flowers, like small, dusty-white tassels, gave no hint of the milkweed clan.*

*The other was clearly a type of **composite**, or member of the daisy family, like a **bur-marigold** (Bidens), the plants with golden flowers that supply the annoying beggar's-ticks in the fall. But the strong odor from the leaves was not mentioned in the description of any bur-marigold that I had read about in the standard references.*

9-25 **A Miscellany of Lake Erie Strand Plants: Clammyweed** (*Polanisia graveolens*, now called *dodecandra*), a native plant of the caper family, with a strong, spicy odor typical of that group. Note the bicolored purple and white petals and large green pods.

9-26 The most cosmopolitan of Lake Erie's sand-dune flora, the **inland beach pea** (*Lathyrus japonicus–T*) is part of a large species complex occurring on the ocean coasts of northern North America, Eurasia, Greenland, Japan, and Chile, and on the shores of many inland lakes, including the Great Lakes. Currently, Ohio specimens are rare and need protection against nibbling herbivores, such as rabbits.

9-27 **Lyre-leaved rock cress** (*Arabis lyrata–T*) of the **crucifers**, or **cabbage family,** has a large population behind the dunes at Mentor Headlands, 30 miles east of Cleveland, where this photo was taken.

Years later, when I was working on Chapter 5, on halophytes, or salt-tolerant plants, Jim Bissell, the curator of botany at the Cleveland Museum of Natural History, mentioned that he had found a new halophyte growing on I-71 near Columbus. It was a creeping species called **fetid marigold** *(Dyssodia papposa) that had migrated from the western states, following the salt-treated roads of the interstate system. Closely related to the garden marigolds, which also have a strong odor, the fetid marigold was apparently the same plant I had seen at White City years before.*

9-28 The **cinquefoils** (*Potentilla*) on the Lake Erie shore are well represented by **silverweed** (*P. anserina*, of the rose family) with its large compound leaves and cosmopolitan distribution.

9-29 Close-up of the flower of **silverweed**.

9-30 A legume genus of warm regions, *Strophostyles* also occurs on Lake Erie in the form of the **wild bean** (*S. helvula*), now called the **annual woolly-bean**. Rather inconspicuous because of the sandy color of its flowers.

9-31 **Lake Erie Dune Rarities Seen in 2003:** Many recent Ohio sightings of **Canada hawk-weed** (*Hieracium canadensis var. fasciculatum*–T), a member of the composite, or daisy, family, have confused it with an introduced plant, the **Savoy hawkweed** (*H. sabaudum*) of Italy. The latter has hairy leaves and favors grasslands and poor soil. The specimen in the photo was found at Walnut Beach, near Ashtabula, Ohio, on a sand dune, and has smooth, shiny leaves, characteristics of *H. canadensis*.

9-32 A recently named rare plant on the Lake Erie shore, **northern poison ivy** (*Toxicodendron rydbergii*—E) was once considered a geographical variety of the notorious common species (*T. radicans*). Found among the sand dunes in Ashtabula County, the bushy plant in the photo has shiny leaves that do not lie flat, quite unlike the dull stiff leaves of *T. radicans*. Due to a lifelong allergy to poison ivy, I did not take a herbarium specimen.

However, there was one problem: fetid marigold has deeply lobed leaves, while the "mystery plant" seemed to have regular leaves without lobes. The picture of the newcomer to White City, appearing as photo 9-20 in the illustrations within this chapter, was taken indoors the evening after I collected the specimen, so I'll let any of my botanist readers offer a guess as to its identity. Unfortunately I didn't know about the Cleveland Museum's herbarium at the time, so I didn't save the specimen.

Orchidophilia

10-2 A close-up of the **showy lady's-slipper**.

10-1 **Lady's-slippers:** A clump of **showy lady's-slippers** (*Cypripedium reginae*—T) from a fen in Portage County.

10-3 On the **Bruce Peninsula of Ontario**, jutting into Lake Huron, the pink coloration of many orchids is replaced by a deep red, such as illustrated by this **showy lady's-slipper**.

10-4 Also, on the Bruce Peninsula one may see an **albino**, or all-white, **showy lady's-slipper** (*forma albolabium*).

10-5 The **ram's-head lady's-slipper** (*C. arietinum*) never reaches Ohio. However, it does occur in the Upper Great Lakes region in Ontario, Michigan, Wisconsin, and Minnesota.

Who doesn't like orchids? They're the Hollywood glamour queens of the plant kingdom. They wear bizarre outfits, crazy hairdos, colors that don't match. They're demure and exciting at the same time, full of little fun tricks like popping up in unexpected places ("I swear they weren't here last week!") or displaying odd variations ("Hey, here's one that's all white with purple stripes!").

Who can resist **calypsos**, three inches high and shaped like a miniature lavender slipper with a gold tongue? And the **fringed orchids** with their thick clusters of red-purple or white or tangerine flowers resembling ballerinas with fringed skirts? And the **lady's-slippers**, with their huge pouches of yellow or pink or white? It's exhilarating, almost intoxicating, to find huge stands of these floral wonders in Ohio, Michigan, the Carolinas, Ontario, and all the far-flung provinces of the Orchid Kingdom.

But orchids exert weird effects on people. Perhaps they emit plant hormones that affect our psyche. Just looking at an acre of orchids at the peak of bloom is enough to turn an ordinary plant hunter into an orchidophile for life. In fact, we can't just look at them. It isn't enough. Who'd ever believe us? Orchids make us take photos, many photos, photos that can be shown to appreciative members of garden clubs and senior-citizen groups and native-plant societies and all the other stay-at-homes who will envy us for The Best Arethusa Slide Ever. We may modestly mention that it took five hours of slogging through knee-deep bogs, loaded with poison sumac, swarming with mosquitoes and black flies, just to bring back this slide, and much of this is true.

10-6 The **albino ram's-head** (forma albiflorum).

Besides, who would ever actually pick an orchid, even to be pressed on a museum **herbarium sheet**, even for the cause of science? They're too rare. Most of them are endangered. And so we join the ranks of the Orchid Photographers, or OP's, with our reflex cameras, multiple lenses, flash attachments, and tripods.

Orchids made OP's act in predictable ways. It's easy to spot a group of them in the woods. They're the people standing patiently in line, as if waiting their turn at a nonexistent restroom. Around them hover the members of a higher orchidophile echelon, the Orchid Discoverers, or OD's. These are usually long-time natives of the area who have an encyclopedic knowledge of each species, its habitat requirements, and its time of bloom. OD's are like press agents: they know that some orchids are publicity-shy, act coy, put on camouflage. If an ordinary OP combs a hemlock grove for orchids and finds nothing, the OD will lead him back and point out a round-leaved orchid growing

10-7 In Ohio the **pink lady's slipper** (*C. acaule*) shown here in close-up, is no longer considered rare, perhaps because it favors a variety of habitats besides wetlands, especially dry or wet woodlands.

10-8 The **albino pink lady's-slipper** (*forma albiflorum*) is still very scarce. (Photo courtesy of the late Lindley Vickers)

10-9 Close-up of the **large yellow lady's-slipper** (*C. parviflorum var. pubescens*).

10-10 The only hybrid orchid I've ever seen in the wild. Found in Mill Prairie, it is a hybrid between the **small yellow lady's-slipper** (*C. parviflorum var. p.–E*), which I've never seen in Ohio, and the **small white lady's-slipper** (*C. candidum–E*). It has the yellow "slipper," referring to the lower petal, or **labium**, of the former species, and the small size of the latter and is officially named *C. x andrewsii*, or **Andrews' lady's-slipper**.

here, a spotted coral-root growing there, and a **downy rattlesnake-plantain** that *might* survive if the OP will only move his foot off it.

Orchids make us talk funny. When referring to the Bruce Peninsula of Ontario, which probably has more orchid species growing in greater profusion than any comparable area in Eastern North America, we say "the Bruce." Knowledgeable OP's will often be overheard, when choosing a head-quarters for a Bruce foray, arguing over the advantages of Red Bay over Tobermory (always "Tub-m'ry"). Many OP's sound as if they speak in tongues: "Yes, Flowerpot Island was the place where I mistook *Corallorhiza maculata var. flavida* for *Corallorhiza trifida var. verna.*" Only among orchidophiles and lawyers is Latin a living language.

Orchids make many OP's argumentative. Occasionally one can hear long, loud discussions that may come to blows. These are caused by disagreements over orchid nomenclature and taxonomy, precipitated by a hint from Case, a footnote in Luer, a sentence in Voss, or any of the various books by Orchid Authorities (OA's). Aside from causing hard feelings, the biggest disadvantage of discussing taxonomy is that it keeps an OP away from the next promising orchid site. A beginner should realize that orchidophilia is a dawn-to-dusk affair with hardly any time off for meals. That is why McDonald's is the restaurant of choice for the average group of OP's. They are already conditioned to getting up at the crack of dawn and waiting in lines.

All members of the orchid family exert the same fascination. If we admire the Hollywood glamour goddesses, we also have to like their poor relatives, those that take character roles, bit parts, walk-ons. It's as if we have forgotten an obvious truth, one that OA's never mention: **most orchids are little and homely**. A great many of them are a few inches high and are colored green, brown, or dirty white. If they were reclassified as members of the chickweed or smartweed families, no one would look at them twice. Although the life histories of these obscure species are probably fascinating (for instance, many of the **twayblades** look like little green moths on a stem), the average OP doesn't bother with such details. The fact that they're orchids is enough.

By the same token, orchids make us ignore attractive or rare plants that grow in the same habitat but don't happen to belong to the orchid family. (An exception might be made for **carnivorous plants** and **moonwort ferns**.) In the South, so I've heard, **trilliums** take on this role. The trillium photographers, in their search for all twenty-three species of **sessile trilliums**, most of which will never win beauty prizes, ignore many rare and intriguing plants growing in the same habitats.

10-11 **Fringed Orchids:** The **yellow fringed orchid** (*Platanthera ciliaris*–T) is really a light orange in color. In Ohio it is found in wet sandy prairies west of Toledo as well as in the southeast portion of the state. (More about this elegant species in Chapter15.)

10-12 One of the few orchids I've seen that has petals of a genuine orchid color, the specimen of the **small purple fringed orchid** (*Platanthera psycodes–E*) shown here was photographed at the Ridges Sanctuary on the Door Peninsula of Wisconsin, an orchid hotspot.

Certainly the most unhappy orchidophiles are the OA's. They are the popularizers, the ones who write books and give lectures. They ought to be happy, for they actually make a living at what the rest of us peasants do at great expense. But should a group of OP's meet an OA in the field, he has a pained look as if he's thinking, "My God, what have I done?" You tell one you were among the audience who admired his lecture in Pittsburgh, and he'll say, "Lord, what a mob!" You tell another that this group came all the way from Tennessee to visit a particular orchid site, and he'll say, "The visitors are ruining this place. We're going to have to close it off for the next three years."

In a sense he's partly right: orchids make OP's forget about the environment. They also begin to ignore the scenery, the human history, the ecology, and the animal inhabitants of a choice orchid habitat. A gorgeous Blackburnian warbler can be singing a few feet above the heads of a group of OP's waiting in line, and no one will even bother to look up.

10-13 The **prairie fringed orchid** (*Platanthera leucophaea–T*), which appears to be covered with large wet snowflakes, is one of the rarest orchids nationwide.

10-14 A close-up of the crystalline petals of the **prairie fringed orchid.**

10-15 **Northern Bog Orchids**: In June 1984 I returned to Titus Bog south of Erie, Pennsylvania, where I had first seen the **dragon's-mouth orchid** (*Arethusa bulbosa*–E), as described in the Introduction. This time I took a camera and was able to take this photo of the orchid facing forward.

10-16 At Oliphant Fen in the southern part of the Bruce Peninsula, in Ontario, pink bog orchids are abundant, such as the **rose pogonia** (*Pogonia ophioglossoides*–T). In Ohio this species is found in Willow Bog, along with the dragon's-mouth and the grass-pink. Unfortunately, all three do not bloom at the same time.

10-17 The **grass-pink** (*Calopogon tuberosus*–T), seen from a distance at Oliphant Fen, is equally rare in Ohio. This photo shows petals of a deeper pink than are seen in Ohio.

10-18 This close-up of the **grass-pink** gives some idea of the bizarre way this species is pollinated. The uppermost petal with a sort of pollen brush attached is really the **lip petal**, which in most orchids is the lowermost petal. (While in the bud the whole flower is turned 180 degrees.) When a bee comes looking for nectar, the weight of the insect causes the brush to fall down on its back and covers it with pollen. Now the bee is able to pollinate another grass-pink, and the procedure is repeated.

10-19 **Forest Orchids: Fairy-slipper** (*Calypso bulbosa*), prefers coniferous forests both on Flowerpot Island, next to the Bruce Peninsula, where I took this photo, and in the northern Rockies and coast ranges of the west.

10-20 The **albino form** of the **fairy-slipper** is called *forma candida*. Photo taken at Misery Bay alvar. (See Chapter 4.)

Orchidophilia can sometimes reach the dangerous stage of orchidomania. At this point, the OP starts concentrating on strange color variations, hybrids, and albinos and forgets everything else. If he starts publishing, watch out! He's about ready to join the OA's. Right now the **splitters** are in the ascendancy. They are upgrading color forms into new subspecies, subspecies into new species, groups of species into new genera. If they are thorough enough, they will get their own name appended to the new scientific name and become immortal—that is, until a new generation of OA's, this time the **lumpers**, get their chance and restore the orchid family to its former status.

10-22 **A Miscellany of Homely and Inconspicuous Orchids:** A large-flowered orchid, often overlooked because of its green petals, the **whorled pogonia** (*Isotria verticillata*) can be found on shady, rocky, forested slopes, as are commonly seen in the Cuyahoga Valley National Park south of Cleveland, Ohio. Its cousin with short, dirty-white petals, the **small whorled pogonia** (*I. medeoloides*–E) is the rarest orchid east of the Mississippi and was not found in Ohio until the 1990's.

10-21 The **showy orchis** (*Galearis spectabilis*), despite its striking color pattern, is actually very inconspicuous in its habitat—shady forests on limestone soil. Although blooming at the same time as the well-known spring wildflowers, it is seldom seen in northern Ohio.

153

10-23 The **ragged fringed orchid** (*Platanthera lacera*) is extremely common in Ohio. I have seen it only around ponds, but it is found in a variety of grassy and forested habitats, wet or dry.

10-24 The **ladies'-tresses** are a large group of inconspicuous orchids with white flowers spiraling up a stem. At the southernmost edge of its range, the **hooded ladies'-tresses** (*Spiranthes romanzoffiana–T*) is the rarest of this group in Ohio. I have seen it only in sphagnum bogs.

10-26 The leaves of the previous plant, showing the arrangement of white veins, resembling a reptile's skin.

10-25 The abundant flowers of **Goodyera**, the **rattlesnake-plantains**, resemble those of the ladies'-tresses in small size and white coloration, but they also have another method of attracting pollinators—white-veined leaves. Pictured here is the **downy rattlesnake-plantain** (*G. pubescens*) growing in a woodland at the Holden Arboretum near Cleveland.

The reverse side of orchidomania is orchidophobia. At times one hears about severe withdrawal symptoms. In an extreme case, an OP was heard to say, by at least two witnesses, "**Ram's-head lady's-slippers** are a nothing plant, and **albino ram's-heads** are nothing squared!" When they finally got him to a doctor, he was taken off orchids and put on sedges, which can't be photographed satisfactorily and produce no known side effects. With no more waiting in line, his work day went from fourteen hours down to eight, and he could wake up at a civilized time and eat in sit-down restaurants. While his comrades were stalking orchids elsewhere in Michigan, he began to savor what he termed "the wholeness of life." He visited Mio to see the Kirtland's warblers and Mackinaw City for the restored fort of Michilimackinac. He explored the Porcupine Mountains, Sleeping Bear Dunes, and the Pictured Rocks. He spent three days at Isle Royale looking for moose. With the pressure to produce taken off, he learned to relax and enjoy the world without peering through a camera lens. Orchid taxonomy became so much Greek to him, and he reverted to speaking English.

10-27 The green flowers of the **early coralroot** (*Corallorhiza trifida*–E) are tiny and inconspicuous but still have the orchid shape. Photo taken June 1992 at Pictured Rocks National Lakeshore in the Upper Peninsula of Michigan. It is very rare in Ohio. (See Chapter 8.)

10-28 Bright green and lacking the typical orchid shape, the flowers of the **long-bracted orchid** (*Coeloglossum viride*–E) rank among the homeliest in its large family. Specimen found the same day and location as the previous orchid.

Nowadays, according to rumor, he occasionally sneaks out to take a quicky orchid photo and has definitely been known to give slide shows to garden clubs. He has even been heard to say that ram's-heads are "curious" and "not all that bad." When asked whether he will ever become an orchidophile again, he smiles enigmatically and says: "I see the orchid family socially, but we are just good friends."

10-29 **Insect Mimics:** The only all-brown species I have photographed in Ohio is the **crane-fly orchid** (*Tipularia discolor*), an insect look-alike with long petals split in half to resemble the outstretched wings of a cranefly at rest. Since so many orchids, especially in Europe, resemble female moths, flies, bees, and spiders, this type of mimicry is thought to attract males of the same species and achieve pollination by trickery.

10-30 The **common twayblade** (*Listera ovata*) of Europe was never known from North America until 1968, when it was found on the Bruce Peninsula of Ontario. As is the case in the six native American twayblades of the genus *Listera*, the common twayblade's prominent lip petal is clearly divided into two segments, resembling the wings of a green perching insect. (Photo taken near Red Bay, Bruce Peninsula, Ontario.)

11-1 and 11-2: **Pennsylvanian Plants: Diorama of a coal forest, in the Cleveland Museum of Natural History**, with a huge **seal tree** (*Sigillaria*) at far left; a massive **scale tree** (*Lepidodendron*) at far right; and **tree ferns** (*Psaronius*) in the middle. A decaying trunk of a scale tree lies at the bottom of the diorama. Small trees with jointed trunks (like our modern bamboos) are *Calamites*, **giant horsetails**. Flying insect is a giant dragonfly.

chapter 11

Pennsylvanian Nature Trail

Care to join me for a short walk through an **equatorial rain forest** and **mangrove swamp**? Wear light, loose clothing, for the cool breeze off the ocean unfortunately does not penetrate very far inland, especially through this thick tangle of tree trunks, vines, and shrubs. Also, wear a hat because the lacy foliage of the canopy trees lets through a lot of sun. In fact, you can see the blue tropical sky most of the time—when it isn't raining, that is.

Good sturdy boots are a must. The path is muddy in places, and also you don't want to stub your toes on all the roots sticking out. Forget about insect repellent. There are no mosquitoes or black flies here. That yellow dust in the air? Only **spores** or pollen drifting down from the trees, and they have never been proven to cause allergies.

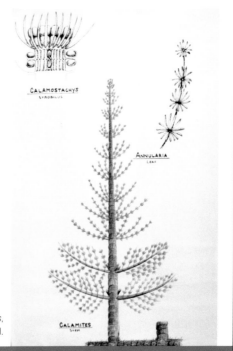

11-3 Drawing of **Calamites**, the **giant horsetail**.

Actually, except for the damp odor of decaying vegetation, it's quite pleasant here. The gurgle of the tidal rivers, hidden behind the mangroves, combines with the sleepy drone of crickets and the occasional booming of frog-like croaks from creatures hidden deep in the undergrowth. No screams of parrots or raucous calls of monkeys disturb the quiet atmosphere. The eye is soothed by the countless shades of green. Since there are no flowers on the forest floor, the only colors are in the yellows of the fallen leaves, and the metallic reds and blues glinting off the bodies of dragonflies.

The undergrowth seems to consist largely of young trees. Here, around a giant **tree-fern**, *Psaronius*, is growing a colony of young ferns, each with a buttress of rootlike structures to shore up the weak, spongy stem. The many half-buried roots which make such rough walking on the path all seem to come from the **scale trees**, *Lepidodendron*, with their hard, diamond-patterned bark and crown of needlelike leaves 100 feet above our heads. Golden clouds of spores descend from their many cones hanging down from short branches among the leaves. The lack of lower branches gives the scale trees a palm-like appearance. Despite the great reproductive potential of the **spore cones**,

11-4 **Fossil showing the jointed stems of Calamites.** Similar structures in the modern horsetail, or scouring rush (*Equisetum*), proves its relationship.

most of the young scale trees sprout from the roots, which are really underground stems or **runners**.

Many of the other trees in the forest have adopted this habit. Bizarre-looking **seal trees** (*Sigillaria*), with a bark pattern in vertical parallel lines and a ridiculously undersized tuft of leaves at the very top, alternate with the graceful **giant horsetails**, or *Calamites*, with their jointed, bamboo-like stems. From every joint arises a **whorl**, or ring, of leaves, from which arises a **whorl** of branches. The branches then put out whorls of leaves and branchlets in the same manner, giving the whole tree a bushy effect, almost like that of a willow.

Our walk is interrupted by a sudden gust of wind followed by the crash of small, heavy objects from the top of a nearby tree-fern. Luckily they miss our heads and land in the path. We pick them up—hard, round, heavy-bodied seeds resembling hickory nuts. Since a true tree-fern does not produce seeds, the nuts must have been produced by the *Medullosa*, or **seed-fern**, growing close by. As we look up at its graceful fronds rustling in the wind, we can see how closely it resembles a fern with the main difference being the presence of large seeds dangling here and there from the main trunk.

The large **conifer** *Cordaites* also produces seeds which are hidden in the tufts of narrow sword-like leaves. When we find a fungus-riddled stump of a *Cordaites* that was blown down in a hurricane, we stop to calculate its age from the **growth rings**, but we are disappointed: due to the uniformly warm climate year round, tropical trees do not put out annual growth rings.

Our footing becomes very precarious now as the path enters a mud flat and skirts a mangrove swamp. (A **mangrove** is any tree that tolerates salt water and sends down **aerial roots**.) **Stilt roots** from the *Cordaites* arch into the mud flats and the water of the estuary beyond. As in all tropical lowlands, the mangrove roots collect soil and eventually make new land. In the estuary the shallow water around the mangrove roots serves as a nursery for aquatic animals. Climbing cautiously over the maze of roots, we can see that the tidal rivers swarm with young fish—mostly sharks, lampreys, and **coelacanths**—and many forms of invertebrates, such as snails, **brachiopods**, and jellyfish. Immature **horseshoe crabs** like to crawl out of the water and perch on the stilt roots of the mangroves, as if to sun themselves, but most likely to protect themselves from predators . . .

. . . If you are wondering why the pages of this essay should be devoted to a habitat so different from those found in northern Ohio, rest assured that the locale of the rain forest just described *is* Ohio—of 300 million years ago, in the latter part of the **Carboniferous Period**, or **Coal Age**, known as the **Pennsylvanian**. And, yes, this rain forest was equatorial in the literal sense because the equator ran right through the Midwest back in those days. North America was then connected with all the other continents in a giant land mass called **Pangaea**. Thirty million years later, during an **Ice Age** known as the **Permian Period**, the giant continent began to break up, and North America drifted to its present position in the Northern Hemisphere. The drastic change in climate caused large-scale extinctions among the plants and animals just described. Thanks to the science of **paleobotany**, this particular kind of forest and swamp can be reconstructed in fine detail from the many fossils left behind when the decayed plants in the swamps turned into coal. From all the fossilized marine animals left behind, we know that there was a shallow inland sea covering a great part of what is now the Mississippi drainage basin. However, at that time there was no Mississippi River, nor Great Lakes, nor any of the familiar Midwest landmarks.

11-7 **Fossil showing the diamond-patterned bark of the scale tree.** These forest giants grew to an estimated height of 100 to 150 feet.

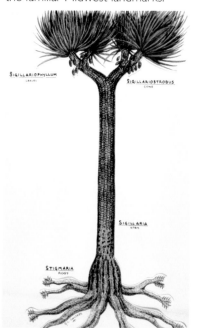

11-6 **Drawing of the scale tree** (*Lepidodendron*). Its bark has a diamond-shaped pattern of leaf scars, reminiscent of a fish's scales. Both scale trees and seal trees bear leaves only at the top (like our modern palms) and **spore cones** dangling below the leaves.

11-5 **Drawing of the seal tree** (*Sigillaria*), so called because its bark has parallel rows of circular leaf scars, resembling old-fashioned seals stamped on documents or envelopes.

11-8 **Close-up of diorama,** caption 11-1 and 11-2. Note the seal tree (gray bark) at the left and the fallen scale tree (tan bark). In front of both appears an ordinary fern, but notice the odd lumps, which look like fruit hanging form the central stem. These are giant-sized seeds, and the fern is really *Medullosa*, a seed-fern.

11-9 **Fossil leaflets** (*Neuropteris*) of the seed-fern *Medullosa*. Although they look like part of a typical fern frond, *Neuropteris* leaflets differ in two aspects: they have short **petioles** (leaf stalks) connecting the midvein of each leaflet at one point to the central axis of the frond; and they bear **netted veins** (that meet each other), instead of **forked veins** (that spread out over the leaf), as in ordinary ferns. These are two features of most modern flowering plants.

11-10 The fruit of *Medullosa* is a giant seed called *Pachytesta* in this photo of a **coal-ball peel** (See text). In structure it appears close to that of the modern relative of conifers, the **gingko** (*Gingko biloba*).

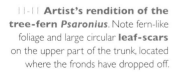

11-11 **Artist's rendition of the tree-fern *Psaronius*.** Note fern-like foliage and large circular **leaf-scars** on the upper part of the trunk, located where the fronds have dropped off.

11-12 **Coal-ball peel of an ancient tree fern *Psaronius*** with central part of trunk surrounded by many **aerial roots** (cross section) These structures descend from the top of the tree and serve to keep the weak trunk from falling.

In the last 200 years one of the unexpected byproducts of the coal industry has been thousands of fossils, many of which preserve parts of the ancient plants described above. These fossils come in two major forms. In the **compressions**, a plant part (seldom a whole plant) is caught between two layers of mud or sand and under pressure turns to coal. The external parts of the plant retain their structure down to the very cell walls, but the interior structure disappears. However, in **petrifactions**, the interior structure of the plant is replaced by minerals from water, usually molecule for molecule, often preserving the contents of the cells themselves. The exterior of the plant usually disappears.

Except in the case of huge tree trunks, such as in the Petrified Forest of Arizona, most petrifactions are a hodgepodge of stems, leaves, cones, seeds, and roots, from different individual plants of the same species and plants of different species, all rolled together in a roughly globular shape called a **coal ball**. Coal balls, dug out of strata above the coal seams, usually contained very little coal and so were dumped on slag heaps, to be later retrieved by paleobotanists, once their scientific value was realized.

At one time, coal balls were ground down mechanically by abrasives to produce thin sections suitable for study under a microscope. Nowadays these thin sections, called **peels**, can be produced much more easily by planing a surface of a coal ball by sawing it level. To remove the mineral content of the planed surface but retain the organic structure, such as cell walls, one must etch the surface with acids in this order: hydrochloric, hydrofluoric, and nitric, for two minutes each. Neutralize the surface; dry it; then flood it with acetone. Apply an acetate sheet, which looks like cellophane, and let it dry. This is the peel, which by its chemical nature can adhere to organic material only.

Carefully remove the peel from the coal ball, and it will prove to be an exact duplicate of the surface, down to the microscopic level. It may be stored for reference or cut up for microscope slides. The whole process takes only about twenty minutes. By preparing a series of peels, the paleobotanist can analyze the complete internal structure of a seed, a cone, or a woody stem, almost as easily as one can look at a living plant.

The big difficulty in studying peels is in assigning plant parts to species. It's a little like imagining a tossed salad turned to stone and cutting through carrot slices, celery stalks, olives,

11-13 **Modern Descendants of the Pennsylvanian Flora: A colony of club-mosses** (*Lycopodium sp.*), showing the prominent greenish cones filled with yellow spores and raised high above the leaves. (Pennsylvanian ancestors such as *Lepidodendron* also had yellow spores.)

11-14 **The woodland horsetail** (*Equisetum sylvaticum-T*) has a bushy appearance and jointed stems, similar to that of its ancestor *Calamites*.

tomatoes, and lettuce leaves all at different angles. Does leaf A go with stem B and fruit C, or are they all from different plants? Does stem A differ from stem B, or are they both forms of the same plant at different stages of maturity? For this reason, each part is assigned a different scientific name, called a **form genus**. This can be confusing. The seed of the seed-fern *Medullosa* is called *Pachytesta*, and the leaf is called *Neuropteris*. Only by applying statistical studies of plant remains found together in the same stratum, or by getting a lucky break (like finding a seed attached to a leafy branch) can the paleobotanist figure out what structure goes with what.

"Assembling" a tree from its separate parts is only the first step in reconstructing the Carboniferous landscape. Next comes the hard part: determining which plants grew together and in what sort of habitat. One technique is to dissolve fossil-bearing rock with acid to recover microscopic spores and pollen grains, which are distinctly different for each plant species, much as fingerprints are different for each individual person. Luckily spores and pollen grains are virtually indestructible, and studying them carefully through the science of **palynology** will indicate which plants were living nearby even if the rest of the plant parts are not preserved in the fossil record.

Now that we have the plant community, with different species living together, we must call upon another science, still in its infancy—**paleoecology**—to supply the animals (called **herbivores**) that ate the plants, and other animals (called **carnivores**) that preyed upon the plant eaters. It has not yet been demonstrated whether living plant tissue during the Carboniferous was eaten by the primary herbivores (mainly insects and giant millipedes). For one thing, very few fossil leaves or stems seem to have suffered obvious damage, such as having pieces bitten out of them. However, we do find great numbers of fungus spores, which may indicate that only after the death of the plant and the start of the decay process did the insects get their jaws around plant material. Then the **giant cockroaches** performed their function as scavengers (much as their descendants do today) and crickets and grasshoppers found their niche,

11-15 **A modern tree fern**, photographed in the Australian rain forest of northern Queensland, shows fern-like leaves and a massive trunk, draped with **aerial roots** and similar to that of a modern conifer, such as a redwood.

11-16 **Bark of a young tree fern**, photographed at the Denver Botanical Garden, shows circular leaf scars similar to that of the ancient *Psaronius*. These scars are later covered up by aerial roots coming down from the top of the tree and serving to support the weak central trunk.

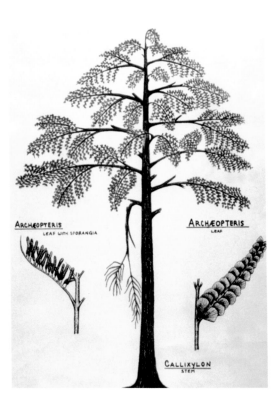

ARCHÆOPTERIS
LEAF WITH SPORANGIA

ARCHÆOPTERIS
LEAF

CALLIXYLON
STEM

11-17 **Late Devonian Plants: Artist's rendering of Archeopteris**, the first known tree; it was first thought to be a fern because of its leaves. Later, reproductive structures were discovered that seemed closer to those of the seed plants. Now it is considered a **pro-gymnosperm**, i.e., an ancestor of the present non-flowering seed plants, as conifers and gingkos.

to be preyed on in turn by spiders, mantises, and the **giant dragonflies** with their two-foot wingspan. Apparently huge amphibians, looking like bulky, muscular salamanders, stood at the top of the food chain.

Only recently have paleooecologists found a fossil of a cockroach with a body pattern similar to the shape and veining of a *Neuropteris* leaflet—evidently one of the first cases of plant mimicry. Did this pattern camouflage the cockroach as it went about scavenging the remains of a seed fern? And what were its specific enemies? And what animal preyed upon these enemies? All of these questions may some day be answered by paleoecologists, as they painstakingly reconstruct the total communities within the estuaries, the mangrove swamps, and the forests further inland.

Paleobotany also answers the question "What happened next?" by charting evolutionary patterns over a long period of time. By comparing the fossils of the Carboniferous with those of the **Cretaceous** (of a mere 65 to 140 million years ago), we find that the giant scale-trees and seal-trees have disappeared, leaving only the tiny **club-mosses** (*Lycopodium*), which we still find in northern Ohio, to carry on their line. The **giant horsetails** were similarly succeeded only by our diminutive **scouring-rushes** (*Equisetum*). Tree ferns still survive in tropical forests, but not the genus *Psaronius*. Our Ohio ferns descend from different ancestors. Seed ferns like *Medullosa* completely disappeared. Perhaps the **gingko tree** from the Orient is one of their remote descendants, with its fernlike foliage and heavy seeds. *Cordaites* faded out of the picture when conifers with needles and scale-like leaves took over. These were the ancestors of our present-day pines, cedars, and tamaracks. By the Cretaceous Period all of these relatively primitive plants were dominated by the **flowering plants**: the oaks, sycamores, magnolias, birches, legumes, cat-tails, and the thousands of other plants that brighten up our world.

Where did they come from? What plants were their ancestors? Why were they so successful? Did it have something to do with their insect pollinators—the beetles, butterflies, and bees that originated around the same time? These questions are also being attacked by paleobotanists the world over. In the cavernous sub-basement of the Cleveland Museum of Natural History and in similar institutions, truckloads of plant fossils, coal balls, peels, and microscope slides from all periods of geological history may provide future scholars with an answer.

Author's postscript–2006: Some day a chapter like this one, but entitled "Devonian Nature Trail," will be written, utilizing all the discoveries made from compression fossils and petrifactions from the Cleveland Shale of 400 million years ago, in the **Devonian Period***, or* **Age of Fishes***. One notable fossil on display at the Cleveland Museum of Natural History will be an important part of the "Devonian forest." The fossil shows a three-foot woody plant with a large cylindrical spore-bearing cone on top of a slender trunk, from which narrow, grass-like leaves hang. At the bottom is a round, compact root-like structure that is most likely an underground stem.*

Miraculously recovered in one piece when the road crew was building Interstate 71 on Cleveland's West Side in the 1960s, the fossil, now named Clevelandodendron ohioense (or the "Cleveland tree from Ohio"), depicts a sapling of a large ancestral club-moss that probably grew up to at least twenty-five feet in height at maturity. When my curator of paleobotany, Dr. Shya Chitaley, arrived at the Museum from India in 1980, she found this fossil on the shelves of the department, along with hundreds of other Devonian fossils, and named and described it in a scientific journal in 1996, the year of the 200th anniversary of the founding of the city of Cleveland.

Although most of the ancient cone-bearing trees have proven to be ancestors of our modern club-mosses Lycopodium and Selaginella, Clevelandodendron has an anatomical structure closer to that of the modern **quillwort** *(Isoetes), with the cone, growing on top of the underground stem, practically invisible. The only obvious structures are hollow, quill-like outgrowths that emerge from the scales of the cone and are not true leaves at all, except in function.*

At present the only member of this family known to occur in Ohio is the **Appalachian quillwort** *(I. engelmannii–E), found in only one county. In June of 1986, I was lucky enough to be taken to a shallow pond next to a railroad track near Warren, Ohio, where a small colony of quillworts were growing. If it hadn't been for my guide, who gently pulled up one of the "quills" to show the spore-bearing cone scale attached to the bottom, I would have thought that I had been looking at an aquatic grass or sedge. With a 400-million-year pedigree, the Appalachian quillwort probably qualifies as Ohio's most ancient surviving vascular plant.*

11-18 **The only fossil of *Clevelandodendron*** known so far is this three-foot specimen at the museum miraculously recovered in one piece, from root to cone. Initially placed with the **club-mosses** (*Lycopodium*) because of the prominent terminal cone, the specimen, under anatomical study, revealed a relationship closer to the present-day aquatic **quillworts**: club-mosses that have lost their erect stems and have developed a cone-like, spore-bearing structure above their underground root.

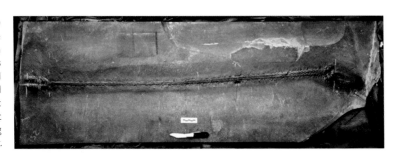

11-19 A typical modern **club-moss** that resembles *Clevelandodendron* in miniature, the **bog club-moss** (*Lycopodiella inundata*) bears a cone that is located at the top of its stem and produces spores.

11-21 A living **quillwort plant**, (at above, left), emerging from a temporary pool beside a railroad track, looks like nothing more than some sort of aquatic grass or sedge. Actually it's a living fossil, related to a long-extinct Devonian tree, which was perhaps 25 feet in height or more, and flourished 360 million years ago.

11-20 The **Appalachian quillwort** (*Isoetes engelmannii*–T) is a rare aquatic that lacks an external stem and bears spore-producing structures on top of a thick underground stem called a **corm**. In this dried specimen, courtesy of the Cleveland Museum's herbarium, one can see the very flattened corm with a root protruding from the bottom and many bulbous structures, which produce spores, crowded on the top. A false leaf, green with chlorophyll, emerges from each reproductive segment, and outwardly resembles a blade of grass.

All photos of fossil plants courtesy of the Paleobotany Department of the Cleveland Museum of Natural History.

Drawings are by artist Gayle Sanders.

The Elusive Gentians

Looking for members of the **gentian family** in northern Ohio?

It can be frustrating.

I remember the first gentian I ever found, as a result of a "hot tip" that the plants were blooming on the **shale bank** adjoining Chagrin River Road south of US 422 in eastern Cuyahoga County. On a clear October day, after locating the shale bank and doggedly climbing up the slope, slipping down two feet for every three feet ascended, I found on the few level places, growing under the first autumn leaf-fall, a delicate-stemmed plant with narrow, opposite leaves; one or two vase-shaped flowers at the top; and lightly-fringed petals of a peculiar smoky blue. As anyone might be, I was justly proud of having discovered the celebrated wildflower—*Gentianopsis crinita*–P, the **fringed gentian**.

chapter 12

Actually I hadn't. The diminutive gentian growing on shale banks was, as in most cases, *G. procera*, the **small fringed gentian** (or in Ohio a hybrid between the two species). To become acquainted with the real thing, I found out years later that one has to travel to mucky **bottomlands**, such as in Stumpy Basin of Summit County, or to sterile **borrow pits**, waste areas depleted of topsoil by construction projects, such as the well-known location on Boston Mills Road, north of Peninsula, also in Summit County, which is next to, and created by, the Ohio Turnpike. Here in all its glory grows the true fringed gentian, with stout stems ranging up to three feet in height, broad leaves surmounted by dozens

12-1 **Ohio Members of the Gentian Family: Smaller fringed gentian** (*Gentianopsis procera*–P) found on a shale bank near the Chagrin River. (See Introduction.)

12-2 **The fringed gentian** (*Gentianopsis crinita—P*), a three to four-foot species with many flowers, prefers open, grassy, or bushy areas, such as the borrow pit (an area denuded of soil to build up a neighboring road bed), where I photographed this specimen.

12-3 The giant of the gentian family in Ohio, the **American columbo** (*Swertia caroliniensis*) grows up to 6 feet in height and can be recognized by its huge basal leaves.

12-4 The greenish, butterfly-shaped flower with a huge **gland**, a swollen group of cells, on each petals marks the **American columbo.**

12-5 The midget of the gentian family in Ohio, the **yellow bartonia** (*B. virginica*), has greenish-yellow flowers and tiny leaves. Mostly found in wetlands.

12-7 In the **stiff gentian** (*Gentianella quinquifolia var. occidentalis*) the flowers are arranged in upright clusters.

12-6 The pink gentians (*Sabatia*) have one representative in Ohio, the **rose-pink** (*S. angularis*), which has the typical yellow central spot that acts as a guide to pollinating insects. This specimen was found in a wet spot among the rocks of an abandoned stone quarry in the Cuyahoga Valley south of Cleveland.

12-8 There are several gentians whose flowers never seem to open. Of the two closed gentians in northeastern Ohio, the **bottle gentian** (*Gentiana andrewsii*) usually has a blunt-looking apex where the petals come together, with a little bit of white membrane showing at the opening.

12-9 Conversely, the rarer of the two closed gentians, the **blind gentian** (*Gentiana clausa–P*) has a more pointed apex with no white membrane showing at all. It is found only in northeastern Ohio at the western edge of its range.

12-10 The **yellowish gentian** (*Gentiana alba–T*), with cream-white petals tightly closed until just before maturity, likes forest openings in southern Ohio, where I saw it in leaf, and sand barrens at the western end of Lake Erie. (Photo courtesy of Marilyn Ortt.)

of flowers, and petals all deeply fringed at the ends and along the sides—a beautiful but hardly delicate wildflower, and an unlikely companion to the coarse, hardy **mulleins,** asters, and grasses that it competes with in a marginal type of habitat.

For the gentian family, competition is the name of the game. Like the North American heaths and orchids, attractive but rare plants, the gentians seem to prosper in habitats shunned by most plants as too dry, rocky, sandy, or boggy. They seldom are found in large stands or among familiar **climax vegetation,** such as a **beech-maple forest,** but in poor, treeless habitats, since they do not run the risk of being shaded out, most gentians bloom from midsummer to late fall, as do their relatives in the milkweed and dogbane families.

The giant of the family in Ohio, the **American columbo** (*Swertia caroliniensis*) blooms in June on sunny slopes, such as the toboggan-run in Virginia Kendall Park, north of Akron in Summit County. Its small, greenish-white, butterfly-like flowers do not resemble those of the other gentians. Even when not in bloom, it can be recognized by its great size and the rosette of huge, strap-like leaves growing from the base. By contrast, the midget of the family, the **yellow bartonia** (*Bartonia virginica*) pokes its wiry leafless stems only a few inches above the moss in dark swamp forests, such as Towner's Woods near Kent or Grand River Terraces in Ashtabula County. In a striking case of plant mimicry, the tiny,

12-11 Formerly classified as a gentian, the **buckbean** (*Menyanthes trifoliata*–T) has been segregated (along with the **floating-heart**) into its own family. The spectacular clusters of white-bearded flowers are seldom seen in bloom in the bogs and fens that it inhabits in Ohio. (One explanation: the buds are killed off by late frosts.) Therefore, I had to include one of my slides from Alberta, Canada, to illustrate this remarkable Northern species.

12-12 **Gentians from outside Ohio:** Like a miniature water-lily, the **floating-heart** (*Nymphoides cordata*) of fresh-water ponds has white flowers and floating, heart-shaped leaves. I have seen this uncommon Eastern coastal species in New Jersey and Rhode Island, where I took this photo.

12-13 The **pink gentians** (*Sabatia*) are also well represented on the East Coast, often in a saltwater habitat. Some are halophytes. (See Chapter 5) The photo of the **slender marsh-pink** (*Sabatia campanulata*) was taken in a marsh at Tobay Sanctuary on Long Island.

12-14 A close-up of the **slender marsh-pink** reveals the tell-tale yellow patch in the center. The species features a five-lobed central spot.

12-15 The **Plymouth gentian** (*S. kennedyana*) is one of the rarest East Coast species, named on the Federal Heritage List as "endangered." It is a true aquatic, as shown here, rooted in the mud of a pond in Rhode Island.

12-16 The large flower of the **Plymouth gentian** shown here in close-up has 10 large petals with a complex yellow center, consisting of 10 lobes, each edged with red and subdivided into a group of three. This species has been found only in limited coastal regions of Nova Scotia, Massachusetts, and Rhode Island.

yellow-green flowers of bartonia look for all the world like the inedible spore capsules of the **haircap moss** (*Polytrichum*) that it lives among, and thus perhaps it escapes predation from herbivores.

A large group of attractive, pink-flowered gentians (genus *Sabatia*) live in the Cuyahoga Valley's Deep Lock Quarry Park, growing quite comfortably in the quarry itself, where water seeps out of the rocks. Most of the *Sabatias* have a yellow, star-shaped pattern in the center of the flower to attract pollinating insects.

In contrast, many of the blue gentians found in Ohio have flowers partly closed at the top, as if to discourage insects. **Stiff gentian** (*Gentianella quinquefolia*), found on dry hillsides, such as the shale bank on River Road, has many small tube-like flowers clustered near the top. The petals point inward and partially block the flower tube. The **bottle gentian** (*Gentiana andrewsii*) and the rare **blind gentian** (*G. clausa*), both found on slopes, roadsides, or stream banks, go further. They have "elastic" strips along the petals to make sure that even if the flower is forced open, it will snap shut again. One would expect that the chief pollinators would be tiny flies that can creep into the narrow opening at the top. A little observation soon dispels the notion. The major pollinating insects are large, clumsy bumblebees that force an entry past the elastic-lined opening and disappear inside the flower, which closes on top of them. After a few seconds, in which they somehow turn around, they emerge head first, pushing their way out of the "bottle," having gathered nectar and pollinated the plant at the same time. Undaunted by the effort, they usually aim for another closed gentian and repeat the process.

Perhaps the rarest gentian in Ohio, a white-flowered aquatic called **bog-bean** (or **buck-bean**), now known from only five locations, resembles the fringed gentian most closely with its cup shape, abundant flowers, and deeply fringed petals. Now placed

in a separate family of its own, *Menyanthes trifoliata*–*T* seems to be a Northern plant displaced by the last glacier and surviving only in cold bogs, a companion of pitcher plants and rose pogonia orchids. Although it blooms in July in Canada, bog-bean blooms in mid-May in Ohio, if at all, for late frosts often kill the flower buds.

Because of their habitat preferences, many of Ohio's gentians are listed as endangered, threatened, or potentially threatened, by Ohio's Natural Heritage Program, which has been mapping and inventorying the 600 rarest of the native plants since 1978. Since the fringed gentian chooses a wide variety of marginal habitats, it is rated as potentially threatened; however, due to its great fame and attractiveness, it tempts too many people to pick or transplant it from the wild. They might be disappointed when they find it is a **biennial** or annual. A better garden subject, the bottle gentian, which is a perennial and not on the endangered list, can be bought as cuttings from wild-flower dealers, transplanted easily into ordinary garden soil, and expected to bloom every year, attracting the bumblebees to perform their eccentric acrobatics before winter closes in. Frustrated plant hunters can thus enjoy one of the elusive gentians close to home.

12-17 A representative of the many dark-blue gentians of the Far West, this **pleated gentian** (*Gentiana calycosa*) was seen at Paradise Meadows in Mt. Ranier National Park, Washington.

12-18 My favorite Eastern gentian, the handsome **pine-barren gentian** (*Gentiana autumnalis*) of central New Jersey and from south-east Virginia to South Carolina. I saw it only in leaf, but my friend, Dr. John Glasser of Wyckoff, New Jersey, kindly supplied me with this photo.

177

13-1 **Forest Grasses:** One of the first grasses I ever identified on my own, using Lucy Braun's book on the monocots of Ohio, was **bottle-brush grass** (*Elymus hystrix*). It is closely related to barley, which also has long **awns**, or bristles.

chapter 13

Let's Look
at the Grasses

13-3 The very common **squirrel-tail barley** (*Hordeum jubatum*) is not a native Ohioan. However, it is native all through Arctic North America and the Eastern Seaboard. In Alaska the long awns are pink instead of pale yellow.

13-2 **Beach Grasses: At Mentor Headlands, American beach grass** (*Ammophila breviligulata*—T) holds down the dunes, as it does elsewhere along the Great Lakes and the Atlantic Coast.

Looking at grasses for most people means standing on a high hill overlooking a field of wheat and admiring the view as the wind makes waves and ripples in the golden sea of grass. To come down to earth and actually examine the flowers and fruits of this family of plants is supposed to be forbiddingly difficult, presumably the province of specialists, such as the experts working for the Department of Agriculture. Even the popular plant guides warn the reader away from grasses. Like sedges, umbels, crucifers, and aquatics, details on this family (they say) can be found only in "the technical manuals." One gets a mental picture of heavy, dusty volumes resting on a high shelf in some agricultural-school library.

The reason for ostracizing this large and important family is simple. Grass flowers are small and **imperfect**, lacking colorful petals and sepals to attract pollinating insects. Being mostly **wind pollinated**, grasses produce large numbers of minute stamens and pistils, arranged in an almost infinite variety of complex **heads, spikes, racemes,** and **panicles** (called **inflorescences**), colored green or brown for the most part, and apparently designed to frustrate the best intentions of amateur naturalists in classifying them. In the popular view there are too many kinds of grasses, and they all look superficially alike. Yet even a sobersided botanist like Lucy Braun was moved to uncharacteristic admiration: "...The grasses and sedges ... should not be neglected by the layman," she once wrote, "for among these plants are some of the most graceful and beautiful forms of inflorescence."

Once we drop our prejudices against minute and colorless flowers, we will find that grasses, besides literally furnishing our daily bread, really serve as an unobtrusive background to many of our life's activities. At home the ground covers we carefully cultivate and many of the weeds we roundly curse are grasses. (In fact, the American

13-4 Close-up of a single head of **squirrel-tail barley**.

obsession with grassy lawns has been the subject of serious study among social historians.) Green-carpeted suburbs, public squares, athletic stadiums, and industrial parks, not to mention cemeteries, testify to our need for a living background restful to the eye.

Grasses help fill in bare spots where more colorful flowering plants could not survive; they cover sterile tracts of soil disturbed by man's activities: roadsides, railroad tracks, dumps, vacant lots, and construction sites. Wherever nature limits trees, grasses simply take over: in Arctic tundra, wetlands, prairies, deserts, sand dunes, and mountains above timberline. One of the two flowering plants found in Antarctica is a grass.

One of the advantages of studying grasses is that they are as readily available as the nearest vacant lot. In fact, in disturbed areas one finds a greater number of species than in a natural habitat because many of the foreign grasses (mostly agricultural escapes) prefer

13-5 **Prairie Grasses:** The golden-yellow heads of **Indian grass** (*Sorghastrum nutans*), a hallmark of tall-grass prairies.

13-6 The dominant prairie grass, **big bluestem** (*Andropogon gerardii*) grows up to ten feet and is often photographed against the sky. It's often called turkey-foot grass because the long flower-spikes, in groups of two to six, spread out like toes on a bird's foot.

a dry, sandy, or rocky environment. It is closest to their ancestral habitat, the treeless plains of Eurasia or the savannas of the Mediterranean. These Eurasian grasses are often joined by immigrants from our own Western plains and deserts.

To learn the names of the grasses, two methods are feasible. The first, called the "leaf method," is to leaf through a book of grasses until you find a picture of the unknown plant. In some cases you will find the correct genus and sometimes the species without even having to read the description. A good book for this purpose is E. Lucy Braun's *The Vascular Flora of Ohio*, Vol. 1, *Cat-tails to Orchids* (Ohio State University Press, 1967) or the paperback *How to Know the Grasses* by Richard W. Pohl (Dubuque, Iowa, William C. Brown, 1954), part of the H. E. Jacques *Pictured-Key Nature Series*. The first covers only Ohio; the second, the whole country.

I remember how easy it was to name a peculiar bushy-headed grass which I first found in North Chagrin Reservation near Cleveland. Without much leafing, I found it in Lucy Braun's book, which I had borrowed from the library. (Probably every Ohio library has a copy.) There, big as life, on page 96 was a picture of *Elymus hystrix*, the **bottlebrush**

13-7 **Close-up of big bluestem**, showing the **racemes** (long flowering heads) spreading out.

13-8 **Little bluestem** (*Schizachyrium scoparium*), found in prairie habitats throughout most of the US, tends to dominate more of the dry, short-grass prairies than its tall cousin.

13-9 A very colorful grass in the fall when its leaves turn dark red, the **common broom-sedge** (*Andropogon virginicus*) favors old fields, pastures, and disturbed ground rather than prairies.

grass. Anyway I was hooked. Soon I began looking at weedy gardens, vacant lots, and cracked sidewalks and came up with **foxtail grass**, **orchard grass**, **velvet grass**, **timothy**, and **wild rye**. Grasses were easy! What's more, they could be gathered quickly and brought home intact in a plastic bag without much fuss. Occasionally people would look at me suspiciously as I wandered around vacant lots, eyes glued to the ground, but they probably thought I was looking for a lost wallet or a contact lens.

The second method for identifying grasses is the scientifically correct method of learning the twelve tribes of the grass family (as found in Ohio and around the Upper Great Lakes) and their distinguishing characteristics. This requires learning something about anatomical structure and the special terminology that goes with it. For the record, the twelve tribes are commonly called **bamboos**, **fescues**, **cereals** (wheat, rye, and barley), **oats**, **bent grass**, **cord grass**, **canary grass**, **rice**, **wild rice**, **panic grass**, **beard grass**, and **corn**. These account for 74 genera and about 300 species in the Ohio flora, native, and introduced. Their differences have to be determined by studying minute structures of the flowers under a ten-power magnifying glass.

The following diagram is of a typical grass flower (from the fescues, which are the most unspecialized of the tribes). This information was gained from the introduction to Pohl's book, referred to above.

Anatomy of a flower from the grass family

Fig. 1

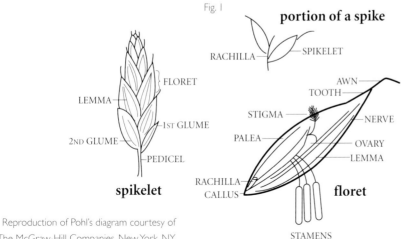

portion of a spike

RACHILLA — SPIKELET

AWN

TOOTH

STIGMA — NERVE

PALEA — OVARY

LEMMA

FLORET

LEMMA

1ST GLUME

2ND GLUME

PEDICEL

RACHILLA
CALLUS

spikelet

floret

STAMENS

Reproduction of Pohl's diagram courtesy of The McGraw-Hill Companies, New York, NY

The fruit of grasses, called the **grain,** usually very minute and ignored by the textbooks, develops inside each **floret,** which consists of two **bracts** (the **lemma** and **palea**) wrapped around the **stamens** and the **pistils** (the male and female reproductive parts). All the florets plus the two bottom bracts (called the **glumes**) compose one **spikelet.** The sum of all the spikelets on a flowering stem (or **culm**) makes up the **inflorescence.** Sometimes there are hundreds of spikelets on one inflorescence. In wheat, the **glumes, lemmas,** and **paleas** are called **chaff** and have to be separated from the grain. In corn, they are called **husks.**

In some of the more specialized tribes the glumes are large envelopes covering the florets, as in oats, or they are reduced to tiny vestiges, as in rice. In still others, the spikelets contain only one fertile floret and the rest are empty or staminate. In the last two tribes the florets (either fertile or sterile, or female and male) take on a different appearance and sometimes assume a different location on the plant. Again, corn, which is the least typical grass, is a good example with the male **tassels** on top and the female **ears** along the side of the stem.

No matter which way you learn the grasses, you will find that knowing ten or twenty major types will add greatly to your knowledge and appreciation of the green world around you.

There are a wide variety of grasses growing in the Cleveland region, some of which are handsome enough to be transplanted into a garden or gathered as a supplement to dried-flower arrangements (but don't touch them if they are Heritage Plants: E, T, or P).

Starting at the Lake Erie shore, one can find the tall, stately **switch grass** (*Panicum virgatum*), with big panicles of dark purple spikelets, and the **beach grass** (*Ammophila breviligulata*—T) with stiff, yellow-brown spikes. Both of these grow in sand dunes and are seldom found far from the water's edge.

In disturbed areas throughout the city, one can find grasses that prefer to grow in rocky, gritty soil. Many of these are aliens from Europe or the Western states. One of the most beautiful is **purple love grass** (*Eragrostis spectabilis*) with an inflorescence consisting of bright, red-purple spikelets, shining with a metallic gleam in the sun. Unfortunately its color fades somewhat when the plant is gathered and brought inside the house. Another plant frequently found around industrial areas and heavily salted roadways is **squirrel-tail barley** (*Hordeum jubatum*), a short relative of the familiar cereal. A large stand of this plant presents a solid, shimmering mass of golden awns. (I have seen a variety of this plant in the Arctic with pinkish awns.) It may make a good rock-garden plant.

The tall prairie grasses native to the counties west of Cleveland require plenty of space for their cultivation. **Indian grass** is a favorite (*Sorghastrum nutans*) is a favorite with

13-10 **Wetland Grasses:** a grass of wet prairies, with flowers along only one side of the stalk, the **prairie cord grass** (*Spartina pectinata*) belongs to a genus well represented along the Atlantic as **halophytes** (salt-tolerant species—see Chapter 5). Found commonly in tidal marshes and salt meadows, these grasses help build up solid land behind the coastal dunes.

graceful panicles of a beautiful golden-brown when ripe. It is often associated with **big bluestem** (*Andropogon gerardii*), which has bluish-green stems often tinted with a purple or pinkish cast. A shorter relative of big bluestem, **common broom-sedge** (*A. virginicus var. v.*) grows in weedy fields and along railroad tracks. Its stems and leaves turn dark red in the fall.

Certain Ohio grasses are well adapted to a woodland garden. The bottle-brush grass referred to above grows in small, isolated clumps in fairly dense shade. Wet woodlands would be suitable for the **wild-rye** species known as **downy wild rye** (*Elymus villosus*) with fuzzy, nodding spikes. (Its tall relative **Canada wild-rye** (*E. canadensis*) can be found among the sand dunes of Lake Erie.) Another grass fond of wet woodlands that most likely will introduce itself into a woodland garden is the close relative of rice called **white grass** or **Virginia cutgrass** (*Leersia virginica*). Like domestic rice, it is semi-aquatic and probably grows beside every woodland stream or wet spot in northern Ohio. The yellow-green color of its leaves is distinctive, as well as their saw-toothed edges. One should not walk barelegged through clumps of white grass.

Among the grasses of meadows and wetlands, the introduced **reed canary grass** (*Phalaris arundinacea*) sometimes has red-purple panicles instead of the usual green. However, it has the reputation of crowding out the other plants in its habitat. Another grass which grows in dense stands along mud flats, **Walter's barnyard grass** (*Echinochloa walteri*) is a fairly recent immigrant to the Lake Erie estuaries. Its large, long-awned, wine-red panicles set it off as one of the most striking members of the grass family in Ohio.

Whether one tries to cultivate native grasses or simply encounters them in their own habitat, a knowledge of this important family of plants adds immeasurably to the enjoyment of the natural world.

13-11 One of the few food crops originating in northern North American, **wild rice** (*Zizania aquatica*–T) is usually associated with the Upper Great Lakes, where the **Ojibways** and related peoples originally gathered it in the wild. Nowadays it is cultivated commercially. Very rare in Ohio, it prefers wetlands, much like its distant relatives in the Orient. Photo taken in New Jersey where it may have escaped from cultivation, although it is native there. In Ohio I have seen it at a marsh at Winous Point near Sandusky Bay.

13-12 **A Southern Ohio Specialty:** In the counties near the Ohio River, **giant cane** (*Arundinaria gigantea*) grows in swamps and wet places along roadsides, where this specimen was found—near the Davis Memorial Preserve in Adams County. The leaf shape should look familiar because giant cane (growing up to 30 feet in Texas) is a **bamboo**, the only native woody grass in the eastern US. Large stands of cane are called **canebrakes**.

14-1 **Sedges in Genera Other than** *Carex:* The **low umbrella-sedge** (*Cyperus diandrus*–P), photographed on a Lake Erie beach leading to the amusement park at Cedar Point, near Sandusky, Ohio, always has its fruiting bodies arranged in two rows, typical of most species of *Cyperus*.

chapter 14

14-2 The **bulrush** now known as **chairmaker's-rush** (*Schoenoplectus pungens*) was once classified as the **three-square** (*Scirpus americanus*). The former common name refers to the three-angled stem, triangular in cross section. A colorful caterpillar is seen climbing down from the cluster of spikelets, apparently having eaten the long terminal bract.

Why I Won't Write About the Sedges

14-3 **Spike-rushes** (*Eleocharis*) are aquatic sedges, usually having a single spike of fruiting bodies atop the single stem. Most of them are delicate species except the coarse **four-angled spike-rush** (*E. quadrangulata*), pictured here, which grows in large colonies in or beside ponds.

14-4 One of the most colorful species in a generally colorless family, the **white beak-rush** (*Rhynchospora alba–P*) has brilliant white scales surrounding its fruiting bodies.

Dear Editor,

Thanks for asking, but no thanks: I won't be writing about the **sedges** of the genus *Carex*. First of all, sedges are dull. Like their relatives, the grasses, they have lost their colorful sepals and petals, but even so, did Walt Whitman ever write a book called *Leaves of Sedge*? Did the Bible ever say, "All flesh is sedge"?

Sedges may feed grouse and mountain goats, but what have they ever done for people? Not even the pioneers ate sedges when they were starving. Nowadays not even the most adventurous chefs use them. Do we ever hear of turkey with sedge dressing?

It's hard to get excited over a plant family that has only one celebrated member—**papyrus**, the huge, fan-shaped **umbrella-sedge** of the genus *Cyperus* that flourishes mainly in Cleopatra movies. But who writes on papyrus scrolls nowadays? Even the Egyptians consider it a nuisance for clogging up their waterways. Moses in the **bulrushes** was probably actually nestling in a bed of papyrus, unless it was really the sedge *Scirpus*, now known as the bulrush. See what I mean about sedges? Even the common names are

14-5 **Green cotton-grass** (*Eriophorum viridicarinatum*–P), once known as **bog cotton,** when going to seed, somewhat resembles a tiny milkweed with its silky white bristles.

ambiguous. Sedges are also confused with just plain **rushes,** which are of a different family altogether. Thus we have **spike rushes, beak rushes, nut rushes,** and **twig-rushes**—all of them sedges, not to mention **cotton-grass** of the Arctic tundra and **saw grass** which covers the Everglades—also sedges.

Only *Carex* is definitely known as a sedge, and it has a bad press. There are just too many species: 1,500 worldwide, 267 in Eastern North America, and 161 in Ohio alone. The wit who said one of the attributes of the Creator must be "an inordinate fondness for beetles" would have been pleased to substitute *Carex*, if he had thought anyone had ever heard of the plant.

Not only are there hundreds of **carices,** but they all tend to resemble the basic plan: long, grass-like leaves that come off the stem in three ranks; a tall stem, or **culm,** that bears the **male and female flowers** in a variety of clusters, mostly spikes; and the inflated **sacs** that contain the fruit—minute vase-shaped, green or brown things called **perigynia**. It's the perigynia that drive botanists either blind or crazy, because each species of *Carex* has sacs of a slightly different shape. Some look relatively huge and bloated, as if pumped full of air, like those of *C. tuckermanii*, while others are paper thin, as if crushed by a steam roller, like those of *C. scoparius*. (Sorry about these Latin names, but until recently nobody has come up with English equivalents for every species, or even wants to.)

Then there are the **beaks.** They are short, long, straight, crooked, toothed, untoothed. Some perigynia don't have any at all, and others have long-necked beaks with little sawteeth on them, or they have beaks on the other end (called **stipes**). As if that's

14-6 **Twig-rush** (*Cladium mariscoides*) is the sedge growing in huge expanses in wet prairies of northwest Ohio, such as Irwin Prairie. (See Chapter 3.) Pictured here is the sedge going to seed, bearing a dark brown fruit, called an **achene** (a dry fruit bearing a single seed almost as large as the fruit itself.) (Photo by Jack Selby)

How the one-seeded fruits of *Carex* may have developed into *stick-tights* and dispersed more easily

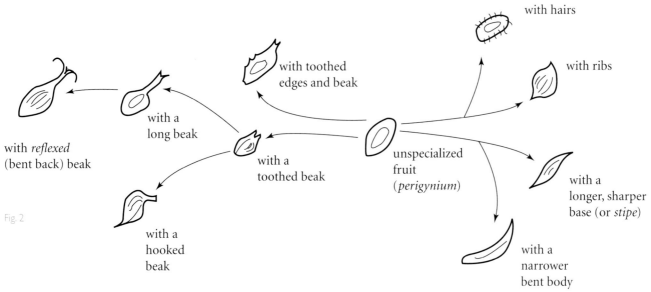

Fig. 2

with *reflexed* (bent back) beak

with a long beak

with toothed edges and beak

with hairs

with ribs

with a toothed beak

unspecialized fruit (*perigynium*)

with a longer, sharper base (or *stipe*)

with a hooked beak

with a narrower bent body

not enough, some **perigynia** are fuzzy while others are smooth; some have ribs (called **nerves**) while others are plain; and some are round and can roll while others have sharp angles. If anyone studies the latter, he should be warned. One slight careless touch causes them to pop up like tiddlywinks and fly over to the other side of the room. I won't even mention what a job it is to break open a perigynium and see what the actual fruit, called the **achene**, looks like. Nobody likes to work with *Carex*.

It's because of its peculiar structure that *Carex* has spread everywhere. All the little beaks or rough edges or hairs of the perigynia are well adapted for hitchhiking a ride on clothing or animal fur or the feathers of birds. Walk through the woods, and chances are that some of the **stick-tights** on clothing and skin are these tiny, vase-shaped fruits. Perhaps that is how they are dispersed. No one has bothered to investigate, but it stands to reason that any animal, even a small one, walking through swamps and meadows, where carices abound, is likely to carry off at least a few of the easily detachable fruits, if not a whole head or spike. The spikes are well armed with long awns and toothed bracts that catch onto things easily. To top it off, many species of *Carex* also have rough stems and leaves, enabling an animal to carry off unwittingly a whole plant.

14-7 **Various Species of Carex: Tasseled sedge** (*Carex crinita*), a tall, easily recognized plant in a genus with 151 species in Ohio alone (year 2001 figure), not counting varieties, hybrids, and foreign species. Even the serious Lucy Braun called this sedge "striking and beautiful," as it arches over the water.

14-8 A single spike of **tasseled sedge**, hanging by a narrow stalk, resembles a caterpillar hanging by a silk thread. Just a coincidence?

14-9 In mature beech-maple forests the **plantain sedge** (*C. plantaginea*) appears in Ohio usually in April, when most wildflowers are still in bud. It can be instantly recognized by its red-purple stems and terminal **male spikes** (pollen-bearing bodies). All this colorful display, uncommon in most sedges, perhaps serves as a lure to pollinating insects early in the season. Also, the leaves are broad and lily-like, perhaps mimicking those of many common spring wildflowers.

This brings up another vexing feature of *Carex*. Along with its other sedge relatives, it does well in swamps and bogs and other mucky places and is not so common in dry, open areas, where the grasses take over and where most people like to walk. Who besides a handful of fanatics wants to risk wet feet for the sake of finding a rare sedge or two? About 63 of Ohio's 161 carices are extirpated, endangered, threatened, or potentially threatened, using the Ohio Natural Heritage Program's terminology. Their presence is a rough index of the health of our wetlands in Ohio and the wildlife that depend on them. If anyone is interested in charting environmental stresses, carices may well be the best indices.

Despite the problem of the rare carices, the genus is much too common. Just about any trip to a river bank, lake shore, wet woods, meadow, or even a puddle of rainwater in a vacant lot will net many different species, each associated with a particular habitat.

Some of these commoner species, one must grudgingly admit, are striking in their form. *Carex crinita* grows very tall and bends over with its long fruiting spikes hanging down on wiry stems. They look so much like hairy caterpillars dangling on silk threads that one wonders if birds are deceived and try to eat them, or if animals like deer pick them up on their backs as they make their way through the marshlands.

One peculiar northern *Carex*, which is common on Isle Royale in the middle of Lake Superior, is *C. michauxiana*. Growing out of the water, this bears large, skinny perigynia with long needle-like beaks. It would take a large, furry, aquatic animal to carry off and disperse these oversize fruits. By an odd coincidence, there just happens to be a thriving herd of moose on Isle Royale. No one has investigated the **symbiotic relationship** between moose and sedges, if there is one, because no one beyond a few eccentric plant hunters finds *Carex* interesting.

As I've said before, the genus *Carex* is a dull, colorless, confusing, complicated, irritating, little known group of plants. Next time ask me to write about orchids.

Author's postscript–2006: Hardly any other aspect of botany is in a greater state of flux than the assignment of scientific names to Carex. *Former geographical races have become full-fledged species in recent years, and vice versa. Discarded names (called* **synonyms***) have been resuscitated as acceptable names, and vice versa.* Carex complanata, *once a synonym for* C. hirsutella, *is now a species in its own right. And new species are constantly being discovered. In 1993* **juniper sedge***, or* C. juniperorum, *was first named and described by Catling, Reznicek, and Crins in* Systematic Botany, *as living in Ontario, Kentucky, Ohio, and Virginia in* **red-cedar** (Juniperus virginiana) **openings***, one of the commonest habitats in southern Ohio, consisting of prairie grasses and other plants surrounded by a forest dominated*

14-10 The fruiting bodies of carices come in many shapes. **Gray's sedge** (*C. grayi*) has spikes that are roughly spherical with a bur-like appearance. Note the very slender, pale-green male spike above the bur.

14-11 **Bladder sedge** (*C. intumescens*) looks like an immature Gray's sedge crushed into a hemisphere.

14-12 The cylindrical shape of the **long-fruited sedge** (*C. folliculata*) is typical of many carices.

14-13 **Two Recently Described Ohio Sedges:** it's easy to understand why **juniper sedge** (*C. juniperorum*–P) was not discovered in Ohio, or anywhere else, until the '90s. As this picture shows, the distinctive fruiting bodies are found close to ground level at the base of wide grass-like leaves. If no fruit is visible, the species looks much like a grass.

14-14 **Purple wood sedge** (*C. purpurifera–T*) has purple stains at the base of the leaves. Without the fruit, it could be taken for a large number of other sedges with purplish stains.

14-15 **Isle Royale, Michigan:** A distinctive plant from the northern coniferous forest of Newfoundland to Ontario and south to interior New England, New York, and northern Michigan, **Michaux's sedge** (*C. michauxiana*), shown here in a marsh, has straw-colored, almost needle-like fruiting bodies.

14-16 **A cow moose** and her calf, crossing a river in Ontario's Algonquin Provincial Park. It would be interesting to plot out the ranges of the moose and Michaux's sedge to find out if they matched.

by red-cedar. As in the case of all native species newly discovered in Ohio, juniper sedge was given a Heritage rating of E, until Allison Cusick, then chief botanist of ODNR, discovered it in many other locations in southern Ohio. It is now rated P.

To eliminate some confusion about common names, a relatively new publication has come to my attention: Seventh Catalog of the Vascular Plants of Ohio; by Tom S. Cooperrider, Allison W. Cusick and John T. Kartesz, editors, (2001, Columbus: The Ohio State University Press), with special chapters contributed by Barbara K. Andreas, John V. Freudenstein, and John J. Furlow. Each species and subspecies of Carex now have a common English name, including a few that have two common names, numbering 166 names in all at last count. Perhaps this will eliminate some confusion, in Ohio at least. Now if all the Departments of Natural Resources of every state could get together, this situation involving the giant genus Carex may some day be alleviated.

chapter 15

Ohio's Rarest and Fairest Plants—and How to Find Them

15-1 **Cardinal-flower** (*Lobelia cardinalis*):
fair but not rare, Ohio's most attractive lobelia
is found in wetlands throughout the state.

15-2 **The Botsocs Annual Field Meeting, Southern Ohio, May 2002: Chaparral Prairie, Adams County,** a view of a typical scene in southernmost Ohio, showing three habitats: **forest**, **prairie** (including **prairie openings** and **savannas**, with scattered red-cedars); and **wetlands**, illustrated by a stream. A fourth habitat, **dolomite ledges** and slopes, are present in the hill I'm standing on to take the picture.

Author's note: As is my custom when writing about rare and endangered Ohio plants, I use pseudonyms for many locations to avoid the triple threat of tramplers, collectors, and transplanters—the bane of all plant hunters in nature preserves that lack governmental protection. For this essay I will also use pseudonyms for certain people who gave me important directions.

Since this article follows up in a general way my first chapter—on the famous Ohio botanist Dr. E. Lucy Braun—written a quarter- century ago, I occasionally refer to her well-known book The Vascular Flora of Ohio, Vol. I, Cat-tails to Orchids *(Ohio State University Press, 1967) simply as "Lucy Braun's book."*

People occasionally ask me, "You've been photographing and writing about so many **rare** plants in Ohio; how do you go about finding them?" I usually tell them that it depends on how a person defines rare. When I first started hunting for plants in the beech-maple forests of northeastern Ohio near my home, any plant that I hadn't seen before was a rarity.

15-3 One of our guides, **Jim McCormac**, botanist of ODNR, showing our group the leaves of **silver plume grass** (*Saccharum alopecuroideum–E*) a roadside plant in Scioto County. (See Chapter13.)

The first time I ever laid eyes on the **cardinal-flower** (*Lobelia cardinalis*) in a grassy opening near a small creek in the woods, I thought it was the rarest and most beautiful species I had ever seen in the wild. I wondered why I had never seen it before until, much later, I realized that it was a wetland plant, growing abundantly in mucky, buggy places that I usually avoided, and that it flowered abundantly in late summer, a hot, humid season to be out in, especially in northern Ohio. That was when I found out that rarity depends on **habitat**, **population density** within a large area, and **growth habits**, especially flowering time, when even an amateur botanist can identify a species.

Later, when I started sending reports to ODNR for its annual Heritage List and contributing to TNC, I started receiving their newsletters, which list the schedule of field trips held in nature preserves all over the state. After going on many of these excursions, led by experienced field botanists and often to nature preserves containing habitats I had never heard of before, I learned the first two unwritten axioms of plant hunting: **Rule I: rare habitats yield rare plants, and if you find one rare plant, there are probably others nearby, and Rule II: seek professional help whenever possible.**

These axioms have proven true every year, and especially in May 2002, when I attended a three-day "field meeting," in what turned out to be the mother of all field trips. The sponsors of this marathon were three national botanical associations, known informally as the **BotSocs**: the Botanical Society of America, the Torrey Botanical Club, and the Philadelphia Botanical Club. Each of these three societies produces its own very prestigious scientific journal, but members never meet during the year except for one week in the field, and the field meeting is always held in a different place in the Northeast or Great Lakes area every year. Amateurs are welcome to these get-togethers, so when I found out that the field meeting of 2002 was in extreme southern Ohio, specifically Adams, Scioto, and Highland Counties close to the Ohio River, I jumped at the chance to attend.

Ever since I studied the career of Lucy Braun, who discovered and wrote about many of southern Ohio's rarities and their habitats, I have tried to visit the area at least every other year. This is the home of **limestone, short-grass prairies; red-cedar woodlands surrounding prairie openings; limestone and dolomite cliffs and river banks; and shady, mixed-hardwood forests** with many Southern trees—all sheltering a uniquely Ohio River type of flora not completely duplicated in any other part of the country.

I have been turning in rare-plant sightings to ODNR every year since 1977, but 2002 was a banner year for me: 22 new sightings from southern Ohio alone with 20 of these species new to me and most of them fairly recent newcomers to the Heritage List. I could have never found them by myself. A short rundown of the most interesting of these with their Heritage List ratings is as follows:

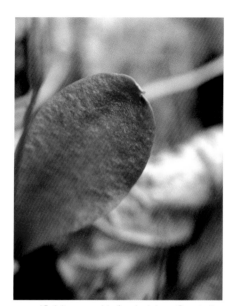

15-4 A rare prairie fern in Adams County, the **limestone adder's-tongue** (*Ophioglossum engelmannii–E*) has a plantain-like leaf with a barely discernable sharp tip.

15-5 Another prairie rarity, the smallest club-moss in Ohio, is the **limestone** or **Midwest spike-moss** (*Selaginella eclipes–T*).

Limestone adder's-tongue fern (*Ophioglossum engelmannii–E*), a tiny relative of the grape ferns with one or two unfernlike fronds growing from the base. These are shaped like the leaves of the **common plantain** that grows in everyone's front lawn and so are easily overlooked. Also, the fern's **spore cases** grow on a central stalk similar to the straw colored stalk of flowers of the plantain.

Southern black-haw (*Viburnum rufidulum–P*), a tree-sized member of the **honeysuckle family**, is perhaps the largest member of the *Viburnum* genus.

Silver plume grass (*Saccharum alopecuroideum–E*, formerly X) was in leaf only, but some day I hope to see it in bloom, since I've seen its red-plumed relative, the **giant plume grass** (*Saccharum*, formerly *Erianthus, giganteum*) on the Atlantic coast in Maryland, and it's a beauty. (When the plume of flowers goes to seed, the huge pink seed-head resembles a stick of old-fashioned cotton candy.) Since the plume grasses have been reclassified in the **sugar-cane** genus *Saccharum,* it would be interesting to see if any farmers in southern Ohio will start growing them as a money crop.

Perhaps the most unexpected plant seen on the BotSocs field meeting—the **Kentucky lady's-slipper orchid** (*Cypripedium kentuckiense*—is not a native as yet, but since it grows across the river from Scioto County in Kentucky, it may some day soon be found in Ohio. A close relative of the glamorous **large yellow lady's-slipper** (*C. calceolus var. pubescens*) of Ohio, the Kentucky orchid has a pouch that is white rather than the bright yellow of the former, and curly brown side petals, rather than greenish-yellow. Found from Texas and Oklahoma east to Virginia and taking in every Southeastern state except the Carolinas, Georgia, and Florida, the Kentucky orchid was never listed in any major US flora until Gleason and Cronquist's 1991 edition. Mr. D., on whose farm we saw a huge clump with 35 flowers growing on multiple stems, admits to obtaining the specimen outside of Ohio and transplanting it—but for educational purposes only. He hopes that plant-hunters will some day see this species growing naturally in a southern Ohio woodland, recognize it for what it is, and add it to the Ohio flora officially so that it can obtain state protection.

If a plant hunter wants to find a particular species that is not known to be protected in an ODNR or TNC nature preserve open to the public, **Rule III** may apply: **ask a friend; get into a network; and don't forget to return a favor.** This applies also to organizations of friends, such as the Native Plant Society of Northeastern Ohio or the Cleveland Museum of Natural History's **NEON** (Northeast Ohio Naturalists), run by the curator of botany, Jim Bissell. These and similar organizations also have newsletters and schedule field trips.

15-6 Not a full-fledged Ohio citizen yet, the **Kentucky lady's-slipper** (*Cypripedium kentuckiense*) is found in several neighboring states and is closely related to the **yellow lady's-slipper** (*C. calceolus var. pubescens*) (See Chapter 10.).

In late July of 1986, I had a great experience looking for **featherbells** (*Stenanthium gramineum—T*, of the lily family), one of the most striking plants in Ohio, although I didn't know that at the time. I was in southern Ohio, talking to a longtime friend from the TNC, Marilyn Ortt, about rare mallows, information that would be useful for my chapter on this colorful family of plants, when somehow the conversation got switched to featherbells, also a plant confined to the southern counties. Marilyn did not know of any location for this species but had a friend Brian who could give me more definite information. When I spoke to Brian, he was very helpful: "You want to find featherbells in bloom? Well, go down Chinaberry Road, and after it crosses Potluck Creek, park and look over the mudflat on the other side of the bridge."

Chinaberry Road? Potluck Creek? Driving down the narrow county road, I kept wondering whether I was still in Ohio, and not Kentucky. I had no problems finding the little bridge or the mudflat, but at first all I could see were the spikes of **scaly blazing-star** (*Liatris spicata*), a handsome, pink-flowered species in the daisy family, often found in wet prairies or meadows, and the pink-purple heads of **spotted phlox** (*Phlox maculata*) in great abundance. It wasn't until I passed a grove of **river birch** (*Betula nigra*), which provided a dark background, that I saw six plants almost eight feet tall, each covered from top to bottom with tiny white flowers, like a small tree spangled with ice crystals. I had been expecting a plant no more than three feet tall with a few flower stalks, but not this giant with hundreds of narrow-petaled flowers all blooming at once. But it was really featherbells—of the tall variety named *robustum*—and all its bell-shaped blossoms constituted a single, many-branched inflorescence, called a **panicle**, that was breathtaking.

According to some authorities, featherbells is the only species of its genus and occurs from Texas to Virginia, mainly in the Appalachians. The Ohio populations represent the northernmost extension of the species, and this distribution pattern was noted long ago by Lucy Braun for dozens of plants native to southern Ohio, some of them of ancient origin. She too was interested in variety *robustum* and observed that it and the normal-sized variety never bloomed at the same time, always separated by two to four weeks, and never occupied the same patch of wetland together. However, middle-sized hybrids were known. In her day, the species was reported from nine counties, with variety *robustum* found only in three; at present (2006) the range is down to six counties, and it is unknown in how many of these *robustum* may occur. In the coming decades ODNR may have a double problem: saving this unique, seldom-seen species from human encroachment of its wetland habitat as well as preserving the tall variety from the genes of its commoner cousins.

15-7 **Fern Wall, a Rocky Ledge in Northern Adams County:** The **umbrella magnolia** (*M. tripetala*–P) has a large pale-yellow flower and is often found on rocky hillsides.

15-8 The flower of **bigleaf magnolia** (*M. macrophylla*–E), found only in Jackson County and south to the Gulf states. Photo of the flower with its indefinite number of petals and reproductive parts shows a similarity to water lilies (See Introduction.), and both families go back to the Age of Reptiles, over 60 million years ago.

15-9 **Jennifer Windus**, botanist of ODNR, illustrates the remarkable size of the leaf of **bigleaf magnolia**, which reaches up to 35 inches in length.

15-11 The dolomite ledges of Fern Wall play host to the attractive, low-growing member of the carnation family, **Wherry's catchfly** (*Silene caroliniana var. wherry–E*), a disjunct found in only four states and in only two counties in Ohio. In Ohio it comes in white and pink color forms.

15-10 Also at Fern Wall we noted the many hand-shaped leaves unique to the **American climbing fern** (*Lygodium palmatum*), which we saw twining around the trunks of young umbrella magnolias. Remarkably enough, fossils from the Green River Shale, a Western rock formation dating back to the Eocene Period of nearly 55 million years ago, contain species of *Lygodium* and *Magnolia* together in what must be one of the most ancient of plant associations.

If ever a plant-hunter needs a friend, as in rule III, finding the **fringed orchids** of the genus *Platanthera* (formerly *Habenaria*) will provide a real test case. With their large **lip** petal divided up into many fringelike segments, the showy members of this group of orchids have often been compared to ballerinas wearing fringed skirts; but to find them in the wild is a different story. Lucy Braun's book lists 13 native fringed orchids in Ohio: three are rated X, two are E, two are T, one is P, and only five are common. But *common* is a relative term, because fringed orchids have the disconcerting habit of moving around, being abundant in one year at a given place, the next year gone. A fringed orchid may become common only in very specialized habitats—open areas, usually wet, with poor soil over a substrate of sand, clay, gravel, or peat, but these habitats themselves are rare in Ohio, occurring mostly in the sand prairies of the northwest (Lucas and Ottawa Counties especially) or in bog or fen country of northeast Ohio (Summit, Geauga, Portage, or Wayne Counties especially). If a fringed orchid is found at the east end of a bog in, say, Portage County in a certain year, it may have disappeared from that spot the following year, only to turn up at the west end of the bog, or perhaps in another bog in the same or neighboring county. This is where "hot tips" from a network of friends really help.

One of the most notorious movable orchids I know of is the **prairie fringed orchid** (*Platanthera leucophaea*–T), with its beautiful, creamy-white fringed lip petal as elegant as a magnified snowflake. It is so rare nationwide that it is also placed on the federal Heritage List, issued by the Department of the Interior, as T. I first saw it in 1987, thanks to a hot tip from friends in Wayne County who saw a colony growing in a marshy area near a cemetery. Naturally I was delighted to hear the news, so I informed long-time orchid-hunting friends Jack and Florence Selby, and we drove down together. When we arrived, we spotted 60 specimens scattered through a wet prairie, which is the ideal habitat. (For a picture of the Prarie Fringed Orchid, see 10-13 and 10-14.)

Ten years later, I heard that the orchids were no longer in or around Wayne County, and that the center of abundance had moved to the northwest counties and the area around Sandusky Bay, into poorly drained areas that now occupy former lake bottoms, dating back to a larger incarnation of Lake Erie in preglacial times called Lake Warren. The last time I saw this species, a numerous colony of perhaps 100 plants, I had to wear boots and wade into ankle-deep water. It's anyone's guess where this wandering orchid will turn up next.

While the prairie-fringed orchid usually occurs in wet **marl**, a crumbly soil composed of limestone, clay, and sand, its glamorous relative with yellow-orange petals and a white-fringed lip—the **yellow fringed orchid** (*Platanthera ciliaris*–T)—prefers a wet, acid, sandy soil, only common in treeless isolated spots in northwest Ohio.

15-13 The other forest plant, **nodding mandarin** (*Disporum maculatum–T*) of the lily family, should also be called spotted mandarin. Of the flowers shown in this photo, both are nodding, but careful observation shows that the *inside* of the petals is covered with tiny purplish-black spots, similar to the freckles of the true lilies (genus *Lilium*). Species is found in only two counties in Ohio in steep wooded ravines.

15-14 **Finding Feather-bells: Marilyn Ortt** of Marietta, Ohio, long associated with TNC and ODNR, has helped me a great deal with southern Ohio Mallows (Chapter 6) and with the lily known as **feather-bells** (*Stenanthium gramineum–T*). Photo taken when she was clearing away brush in a TNC preserve in Athens County, southern Ohio.

In late July of 1982, I heard of a large colony of the yellow fringed growing in an extensive TNC preserve that I was fairly familiar with, having visited parts of it on field trips. However, the part I wanted to visit was surrounded by private land, and I had heard that near the only entrance a local rifle club had set up a firing range. I had hoped that there would be no target practice scheduled for that day, and I was lucky. As I walked past the entrance, not a sound could be heard.

Proceeding down the path, I encountered several circles marked by a ring of stones, painted white, and littered with spent shell casings. These were the firing positions where the riflemen would stand and aim at the targets. From constant use, the sandy soil within the circles had become compressed into wet, shallow pits. I had been told to look into these pits for bog plants, and sure enough, I found some Heritage species: the **cross-leaved milkwort** (*Polygala cruciata–E*) and two kinds of carnivorous plants—the **spatulate-leaved sundew** (*Drosera intermedia–E*) and its abundant relative, the **round-leaved sundew** (*D. rotundifolia*). The milkwort was new for me and, as it turned out, is found in only three counties in the state. It looks like the common **purple milkwort** (*P. sanguinea*), but its pink flowers are larger and in larger heads, and its leaves are in whorls of four.

I could see that this was going to be a good day for me. As I walked slowly down the path, I noted that the vegetation resembled that of southern New Jersey, except for one big difference: sand replaced sphagnum moss. Thirteen bog plants on the Heritage List were here, notably the beautiful **grass pink orchid** (*Calopogon tuberosus–T*), with its **lip petal** arranged like a brush to spread pollen on a bee's body. Also present were the **colic-root** (*Aletris farinosa*), a lily with tiny white flowers on a single stalk, and a strange

15-15 The very tall form of **feather-bells**, now included in the present species, was once called *robustum*, and this photo brings out its great height, over 8 feet, equal to the **Turk's-cap lily**. All the flowers are part of a single, branched inflorescence called a **panicle**, but the flowers at the very top are the only **fertile**, that is, seed-bearing, blossoms on the whole plant.

little plant with a single yellow, three-petaled flower shaped like a ship's propeller, the **twisted yellow-eyed grass** (*Xyris torta–E*) in its own family. It's not a grass but has grass-like leaves.

The big show of the day was provided by the yellow-fringed orchid itself, with 12 specimens in full bloom and others in bud, extending in large yellow heads above the grasses and ferns of the sandy wetland. Looking at this ethereal vision of yellow-orange in perfect symmetry, I knew that the next thing I had to do when I returned home was to contact some nature photographers in my "network" and share the vision with them.

The return trip, occurring three weeks later, went off as planned—the orchids were still in bloom, and my three buddies got some good pictures. But there was one hitch: the gun club. There was no sign or sound from them when we entered the sand wetland, but as we approached the exit, it was "POW!" every ten seconds. Target practice had resumed in earnest.

We debated whether we should just wait, but that might take hours. Then I had an idea. Years before, when I was in the Army and taking basic training at Fort Knox, I remembered that during target practice, all shooting stopped when the sergeants yelled, "Hold your fire!" It might work here. As loudly as I could, I shouted the three words, and after several moments, strangely enough, the shooting stopped. Some Army veterans among the gunners, perhaps? When we passed the firing pits, no one was in sight. We never did find out how many gunners were there, and why they left so suddenly.

Next to the yellow-fringed orchid, the most beautiful and striking *Platanthera* (*P. peramoena*) in Ohio is the deep rose-colored **purple fringeless orchid**. It is the fate of this species to bear a self-contradictory common name … How can a fringed orchid be fringeless? . . . but it actually has a lip petal with the tiniest fringe imaginable, to be seen only under magnification. Another oddity is its life style: it has adapted to disturbed areas more than most other Ohio fringed orchids, and thus it is found in man-made habitats, especially in wet spots along roads. So common that it is not on the Heritage List, the orchid has a range much more southern than the other Ohio fringed orchids. Very tall for its genus (over three feet in some specimens), it should be a candidate for the title "the orchid that everyone knows" – but it isn't.

The reason is simple: like the famous "purloined letter" of Poe's mystery story, it can't be found even though it is in the open where everyone can see it, namely, along well-traveled roads. Why not? Because it resembles something else very common, namely, **spotted phlox** (*Phlox maculata*) in color, shape, and size.

In late July of 1989, when I asked Jack and Florence Selby to join me in searching for this elusive species, I had heard from the grapevine that it favored roadsides, especially in a certain county of southern Ohio. However, I had forgotten to check out Lucy Braun's book on the close resemblance between the orchid and the phlox, and this is what we were learning the hard way as we drove down mile after mile of a narrow state road. Whenever we saw a rose-purple panicle of flowers, we stopped, got out, and examined the specimen. It was always spotted phlox. This was getting monotonous. Discouraged, we decided to stop at a lodge of a state park nearby, one of several occupying former strip mines, have a bite of lunch, and drive home.

As we got out of the car and were walking toward the lodge, Jack lagged behind us, and I heard him say, "Hey, wait a minute. Look at this!" He was pointing to another spotted phlox growing in a weedy strip next to the parking lot. But this time it was the real thing, the purple fringeless orchid, and so was the next one, and the next . . . the whole parking lot was loaded with them!

After many photographs, we were starved, so with mission accomplished, we entered the lodge's coffee shop to splurge on the best lunch special they had—only to be told by the manager that it was so late that they were not serving from the lunch menu any more ". . . but we have sandwiches." The reader can well believe that those sandwiches were some of the most delicious we had ever eaten.

There is one final group of plants that occupy such little-known habitats as shale banks and cliff tops, or have such very small populations that no general rule can apply, except **Rule IV: keep alert; great discoveries are made when you are looking for something else; and don't rule out plain dumb luck.** Even if one tries to be scientific and systematic, field botany has so many variable factors that accidental discoveries are bound to happen. In Ohio they seem to happen more frequently in the southern counties involving Appalachian-type plants.

As a boy growing up in an Appalachian small town in western Maryland, I loved to climb around the foothills of Haystack Mountain, looming up right behind the houses of my neighborhood. In summer my friends and I would go on Boy Scout hikes and gather crawfish (in the North pronounced "crayfish") from the mountain streams, chase gray fence lizards but never could catch them, and stop to admire the "moccasins," big purplish flowers, which we were told not to pick. I later found out they were **pink lady's-slipper orchids** (*Cypripedium acaule*), rare in Ohio at one time.

But the early-spring wildflowers that everyone knew were "Johnny jump-ups," which grew especially on loose-shale slopes and riverbanks, as long as there was a bit of soil for their roots. No one connected them with violets. Violets were small with all five petals colored yellow, white, or pale purple and didn't lie flat. These had five large petals, two of which were a most unusual deep-purple color, and the other three were a more

15-16 Close-up of a single section of the panicle of **featherbells**.

15-17 Close-up of individual flowers of **featherbells**, revealing their narrow petals, which are somewhat bell-shaped, thus the common name.

commonplace lavender. All five petals lay in the same plane, not twisted, and revealed an orange spot of color in the center, which I now know was the tip of the stamens, perhaps useful in attracting bees as pollinators. Lastly, violets had a round or heart-shaped leaf; these had a divided leaf, somewhat shaped like a bird's foot.

One peculiarity of Johnny jump-ups was that they had two types of plants—one bearing the beautiful bicolored flowers, and the other with conventional flowers, with all petals of the same color. Modern botanists now regard these two types of flowers as color forms of the same species and call the whole complex the **birdfoot violet** (*Viola pedata*–T).

In Ohio the distribution of the birdfoot violet—along the Ohio River, in the extreme northeast, and at the west end of Lake Erie—is perhaps determined by the species' preference for open sandy or rocky grasslands, or shale and sandstone banks and road cuts—and these habitats are localized in Ohio, as they were back home in Maryland. Many rare plants in Ohio follow the same pattern.

In mid-May of 1987, I joined an ODNR field trip through a part of Scioto County that was managed by Shawnee State Forest. Our guide was mainly interested in pointing out showy, pink-flowered azaleas, known as **pinxter-flowers** (*Rhododendron nudiflorum var. nudiflorum*–T), which were at the height of their blooming season. The roads were lined with them. One of the most beautiful shrubs of the heath family in the eastern US, the pinxter-flower likes the same acid-soil conditions, in bogs and edges of woods, as does its close relative, the **roseshell azalea** (*R. nudiflorum var. roseum*–P). The main difference is that the blossoms of the pinxter-flower lack the wonderful fragrance of its cousin, which I have seen lining the sphagnum bogs of northeast Ohio.

15-18 **Finding the Yellow Fringed Orchid:** in the wet **sand prairies** of northwest Ohio, a **yellow fringed orchid** (*Platanthera ciliaris*–T) is seen at the height of its bloom.

While everyone in the group was exclaiming over this great display, sort of a southern Ohio version of the famous cherry-blossom festival in Washington, D.C., I noticed clumps of smooth-edged, bright green, sword-like leaves beside the road. They looked like those of irises, but what kind? Our guide confirmed my guess by identifying them as the leaves of **dwarf iris** (*Iris verna*–T), a species I had never seen before, and one of three dwarf irises in the eastern US. It is mainly an Appalachian plant at the very edge of its range in Ohio in only two Ohio River counties, and it grows in woodlands, rather than in wetlands, as in the case of the typical irises.

Naturally I was disappointed that I didn't find *Iris verna* in bloom, but years later I saw its violet flowers, very large in comparison to the size of the plant, in an open woodland in northern Alabama.

Of the two other dwarf irises, only the **dwarf crested iris** (*I. cristata*) is common, occurring in many counties of northeast and south-central Ohio. I first saw it in one of the Cleveland metropolitan parks in a well-shaded creek bottom. The **lake iris** (*I. lacustris*) grows on sandy, peaty shorelines of the Upper Great Lakes and doesn't extend into Ohio. I was

15-19 In the same wet area, the **cross-leaved milkwort** (*Polygala cruciata*–E) thrives, an Atlantic and Gulf Coast species that has found suitable wet, sandy habitat in only one county in Ohio.

lucky to find it growing with **calypso orchids** (*Calypso bulbosa*) on the tip of the Lower Peninsula of Michigan in wet, sandy soil.

On the roadside in Shawnee State Forest, in the same vicinity as the leaves of *Iris verna* were clumps of another plant, one closer to the ground and with dissected leaves. Only when I got nearer and saw the bicolored purple flowers did I realize that I had stumbled on the Johnny-jump-up of my boyhood. This was the first time I had seen it in bloom in Ohio, and it was in the same type of habitat as in western Maryland—a clay or shale slope, in an unshaded area. What a great habitat this roadside turned out to be, with three rarities for the price of one!

In the case of finding two of the most famous **disjuncts** in Ohio extensively studied by Lucy Braun—**golden-star** and **mountain lover**—dumb luck needs to be followed up by a hunch or an educated guess. There won't be any guided tours or hot tips from friends to help find the places where these two species are lurking. The first disjunct, which is defined as a plant located far from the center of abundance for the species as a whole, is a type of **adder's-tongue lily** known as **golden-star** (*Erythronium rostratum*–E). Golden-star resembles the common spring wildflower, the **yellow adder's-tongue** (*E. americanum*) of every woodland in eastern US north of Florida. The similarity is so great that the two species were never differentiated until 1963, when *rostratum* was first

15-20 Like a tiny ship's propeller, the three-petaled flower of **twisted yellow-eyed-grass** (*Xyris torta*–E) looks more at home in the sandy pine barrens of New Jersey and the Southeast than in the Midwest or Appalachians. In its huge range, which goes from the Atlantic and Gulf to Minnesota and Iowa, it skips all but three counties in Ohio.

15-21 **Finding the Purple Fringeless Orchid:** a flowering stem of **purple fringeless orchid** (*Platanthera peramoena*) from south-central Ohio.

15-22 Close-up of the above, showing the hardly visible fringe on the lip petal.

named and described as a Southern plant ranging from northern Louisiana and central Alabama, north to southeast Kansas, Missouri, and Tennessee. That same year Lucy Braun reported that she had discovered it in forests within the drainage of one creek in one county of southernmost Ohio and nowhere else in the state.

Although the two species are superficially look-alikes, with solitary yellow flowers and spotted leaves, the beaked seed capsule of *americanum*, when ripe, points downward, while the capsule of *rostratum* twists around and points upward. Likewise, the petals of *americanum* are *reflexed*, that is, they curve backward until they almost touch, while those of *rostratum* simply spread but do not recurve.

In the late 1980s an article in an ODNR *Newsletter* caught my eye. It stated that golden-star is still found in **mixed-hardwood forests** sloping down to Hickory Creek but occurs in no other part of Ohio. Oddly enough, the yellow adder's-tongue lily has never been found in this creek's drainage, although common everywhere else in the state except the western prairie counties. This may be due to a genetic antipathy between related pairs of species, or it may be purely accidental. To confuse the issue, neither of the two closely related species are found in the county to the east, although the **white adder's-tongue** (*E. albidum*) is common there. (For a parallel, see Chapter 7 on the Minnesota **dwarf trout-lily**.)

After reading the *Newsletter* article, I made plans to stop in southern Ohio on my way back from Tennessee the following spring and photograph golden-star. That spring I found myself following the state highway that parallels the Ohio River, and when the sign proclaiming Hickory Creek came into view, I turned north. A few miles from the intersection the small farmhouses dropped out of sight, and a fine forest appeared. After noting the absence of "No Trespassing" signs, I judged this a good place to stop and explore.

I could tell the place was loaded with *Erythroniums* because of the spotted leaves everywhere, but when I knelt down to examine the flowers, ——oh, no! not one of the tapering buds was open! I then realized that it had been raining earlier that morning; the sky was still overcast; and adder's-tongue lilies and golden-stars open only under sunny skies. What a bummer!

On one of the buds I pushed away the petals and noted that the fruit, a capsule, was twisted so that its beak was pointed upward—a tell-tale sign that the species was really golden-star after all. I had found another Heritage species to report to ODNR, but I really had wanted to photograph it.

15-23 **Finding the Birdfoot Violet:** The bicolored flower of the **birdfoot violet** (*Viola pedata–T*) and the **palmately compound** leaves (looking like a bird's foot) are features startlingly different from those of other violets.

15-24 The **pinxter-flower** (*Rhododendron nudiflorum var. n–T*), one of many attractive native azaleas, is a close relative of **roseshell azalea** (*R. nudiflorum var. roseum–P*) of bog edges in northern Ohio. (Chapter 2)

I got my second chance in late April of the following year. Same time of year, same place, but it was "*deja vu* all over again." The woodland was loaded with clumps of golden-star, but all the buds were tightly closed. Thinking that this situation could go on for years, unless I stuck around all day waiting for the sun to penetrate the thick canopy of trees, I decided to put into action a back-up plan, which I had recently heard about. I had a good hunch it would work.

I knelt down, bent over to a nearby plant, and started exhaling hot air on one of the buds that looked ready to open. This was going to be a slow process, I thought, but the petals actually started to roll back slightly. I kept at it, thinking if any people walking by saw me, they might think I was a crazy emergency medic giving CPR to a nonexistent patient. Fortunately no one came by, and soon the petals were fully open and ready to be photographed. In their final stage, the petals were spread but not reflexed, proving again that the species was golden-star.

Acting on hunches was the method I used when all else failed in hunting down the rarest woody plant in Ohio, a creeper called **mountain-lover** (*Paxistima canbyi–E*) or **cliff-green**, and named for William Canby, botanical explorer from the mid-nineteenth century. Mountain-lover is an obscure member of a large family of trees, shrubs, and vines, called the **bittersweets**, sandwiched in between the hollies and maples and known for their ornamental red fruits. As its name implies, mountain-lover is adapted to only one habitat: thin soil on top of cliffs in areas of very steep elevation, as commonly found in the Appalachian Mountains and Plateaus of the South. In Ohio the closest approach to these conditions occurs in Highland and Adams Counties, where the rugged Appalachian

15-25 **Three dwarf irises:** the **dwarf iris** (*Iris verna–T*), common in the South, barely finds its way into extreme southern Ohio. The yellow-marked petals are very distinctive.

Plateau meets the gently rolling Bluegrass Region, extending into Ohio from Kentucky, in a series of dramatic escarpments that dominate the landscape. This line of cliffs in Adams County marks the **Edge of Appalachia** preserves, managed by TNC and has its counterpart in Highland County in a huge rock formation called Fort Hill. In places the visitor on these peaks can imagine himself standing on the Skyline Drive in Virginia and looking down into the Shenandoah Valley, although the difference in elevation is measured in hundreds of feet rather than thousands. To the mountain lover plant, however, there is no difference, as its total US distribution consists of sites scattered over only 6 states: eastern Kentucky, West Virginia, western Virginia, Tennessee, Pennsylvania, and southern Ohio (Adams and Highland Counties), where its ground-hugging habits adapt the plant to any altitude, as long as the substrate is a neutral soil associated with **dolomite** (a type of alkaline rock containing calcium and magnesium, and similar to limestone).

15-26 The **dwarf crested iris** (*I. cristata*), found throughout Ohio, also has yellow marks on the lavender petals, but they are covered by a white curly material (the crest) which, as someone once observed, at first glance looks like cake frosting.

The mountain lover cannot be called a disjunct, because there is no center of abundance with a few outlying areas. All the known sites are small populations of plants, isolated from each other by many miles of rocky terrain, and separated by thousands of miles from their nearest relative, the **Oregon boxwood** (*P. myrsinites*) of the Montana Rockies. (I saw Oregon boxwood on a trip out West in 1966. It was a bushier and larger plant than mountain lover, perched on a cliff overlooking a waterfall in Glacier National Park, Montana.) When a whole species suffers this type of isolation, plant evolutionists call it a **relict,** a species left over from more favorable times in the past, such as before the glacial period. Relict species are usually considered candidates for extinction in the near future, unless they develop adaptations to a variety of habitats.

Ever since I knew that Fort Hill was a site studied by Lucy Braun, I was anxious to see what Heritage plants may live there. In this, I was disappointed, but my first visit gave me at least some idea of the lay of the land. Basically the highlands of the Edge of Appalachia resemble what geologists in the Great Basin Desert of the West call **block mountains.** One side is a fairly gentle slope with easy walking, usually through a forest. The other side is a sheer drop down to the valley. The dolomite cliffs on the other side are bare of vegetation except for short, ground-hugging plants reminiscent of **alpine tundra** in the Rockies or Sierras. In southern Ohio these cliffs are called **hanging prairies.**

15-27 The **dwarf lake iris** (*I. lacustris*) never reaches Ohio. (Photo taken in Michigan.) Notice the yellow stripe on the petals surrounded by a zone of white, which is further encircled by a zone of deep purple. All three irises are on very short stalks, much shorter than the leaves.

My first visit was in spring of 1985, and many distinctive spring wildflowers were in bloom in the rich forest around the base of the rock, including quite a few that don't reach northeast Ohio. The beautiful dark-purple **dwarf larkspur** (*Delphinium tricorne*); the **wood poppy** (*Stylophorum diphyllum*) with its large yellow petals; and the **large-flowered valerian** (*Valeriana pauciflora*), its pink flowers in tight clusters called umbels—all these were new to me. The biggest surprise was the huge field comprising many acres

15-28 **Finding the golden-star:** Lucy Braun was the first Ohio botanist to find the rare trout lily called **golden-star** (*Erythronium rostratum—E*) in Ohio. Note that the anthers are yellow instead of brick red, as in the common **yellow fawn-lily** (*E. americanum*), and that the petals spread but do not **recurve** (reach back and touch each other). (See Introduction.)

of **moss phlox** (*Phlox subulata*) in full bloom. I never even suspected that this springtime rock-garden flower planted so commonly around Cleveland was a native! Thinking back to the few times that I've tried to plant it in my own garden without success, perhaps I should have tried dolomite soil.

All the colorful plants disappeared as I took the path through a dense forest to what I thought was the top. The path started winding around large stone boulders, which some authorities claim are foundations of an Indian fortification. In the dim light, it was difficult to see if there was any pattern in the way they were arranged except that they all seemed about the same size. Eventually I thought I would reach the cliff side of Fort Hill, but the path seemed to be winding in circles, so I came down the way I started, before I got completely lost. Although Lucy Braun in her late 70s managed to find the cliffs of Fort Hill, I didn't have her luck and so decided to try Tanglewood instead.

In mid-May 1989 I was again at the Edge of Appalachia in a forested preserve full of hills and gullies, all by myself, and equipped with camera, compass, and a rather poor map that did not show any trails to the cliff-tops. However, I had been here many years before, and at that time I remember there definitely was a trail up to the top.

Since I had started late, it was already close to six o'clock, with the shadows lengthening, when I reached a point where many years before I had seen a signpost pointing to the cliffs. But the present signpost said nothing about cliffs, just the name of a trail. I followed it to where the path divided. The left fork was a narrow, rocky trail that looked abandoned, so I took the right fork, which was wide and well kept. This path slowly curved around through the woods and returned to the signpost again. It was just a loop and went nowhere, but I had lost valuable time. At this point I realized I hadn't taken a flashlight, but somehow I would have to go up to the top, come back down and find my way to the parking lot. Could I do all that in the dark?

15-29 **Exploring Fort Hill, Highland County: dwarf larkspur** (*Delphinium tricorne*), with its deep-purple flower, is not rare in Ohio but favors limestone soils, more common in the western or southern portion of the state.

15-30 The **wood-poppy** (*Stylophorum diphyllum*), with its large deep-yellow petals, resembling those of the yellow opium poppies of the Arctic (genus *Papaver*), has a mostly Appalachian range that doesn't reach to the Great Lakes.

Suspecting that TNC was protecting the cliff-top from being trampled by too many visitors, I started off again down the trail to where it divided and took the left fork this time ("The road less traveled by," I kept repeating.) It was 6:30 already and not relishing the idea of staying here overnight, I started to hurry when I noticed the woods had become strangely silent: no birds, no crickets, not even any deerflies buzzing around my head. Suddenly, as I started to climb the left-hand trail on hands and knees, trying to balance myself on the dolomite rocks jutting out into the path, a loud, raucous, two-note call filled the air. It seemed to say, "It's here! It's here! It's here!"

What in the blazes was this? Then I realized it could be the evening call of only one bird—the great crested flycatcher. No other squawk that I had ever heard in the woods sounds so comical and frantic at the same time, but now, instead of seeming merely hysterical, it had assumed a depth that I had never noticed before. Was it verifying my hunch that I was finally taking the right path? I would see in a few minutes.

Reaching the top of the rise, I emerged into full, blazing sunlight, as intense as a hammerblow for anyone walking in semi-darkness all afternoon. The sun seemed at eye level, barely above the trees on the opposite ridge across the creek. Looking down, I saw that I had reached a hanging prairie, a cliff-top opening carpeted with odd, low-growing plants. I had better take some photos while the light was still good.

As it turned out, the flycatcher was right—my guardian spirit in bird form. In the patch of vegetation about nine square feet in extent, I recognized a ground-hugging plant with narrow, glossy leaves, irregularly toothed and crowding the stems, as the long-sought mountain-lover. I was a month too late to see the tiny, green-petaled flowers in bloom, but where were the seed capsules? I later found out that no Ohio specimens of *Paxistima* have been known to set fruit, and it is suspected that the two colonies are

15-31 One of the few Ohio natives that is widely used in rock gardens, the **moss phlox** (*P. subulata*) is found mainly in open sandy or rocky habitats in the eastern half of the state. Photo shows a huge stand of moss phlox at the entrance of Fort Hill State Monument.

15-32 A close-up of **moss phlox**, showing creeping stems with flowers much larger than the very narrow leaves, a growth habit common in Arctic plants.

15-34 The graceful clusters of purplish-pink, appearing white at a distance, mark the **large-flowered valerian** (*Valeriana pauciflora*), of its own family. Hardly known in northern Ohio, it becomes more common as one approaches the Ohio River. Photo taken along shady, forested streams at the base of Fort Hill.

15-33 One of the most curious of Ohio's flora, the **sullivantia** (no other common name) was first found in southern Ohio by William Sullivant, an Ohio botanist, and named after him in both genus and species (*Sullivantia sullivantii*). A member of the saxifrage family with rounded leaves and tiny (2 mm) white florets, barley visible as a cluster in the upper right of the photo, sullivantia is found growing exclusively from dolomite rocks along shady forest streams in southern Ohio, northern Kentucky, and southeast Indiana—truly an Ohio River **endemic** (found nowhere else).

simply large clones, getting larger by sending out runners or underground stems—a dangerous genetic trait that may lead to extinction.

Since rare habitats yield rare plants, next to the mountain-lover and scattered in crevices between the boulders was a tiny, low, tundra-type plant with five-petaled white flowers, which proved to be **rock sandwort** (*Arenaria stricta–P*) of the pink family, once mistakenly thought to belong to a subspecies found mainly in Texas and the Southwest, a seldom-seen, limestone-tolerant plant with very narrow mosslike leaves.

A third plant was not in bloom, but I photographed the very distinctive twisted seed capsules. Later I found out that this was another Northern-type plant called **wedge-leaf whitlow-grass** (*Draba cuneifolia–T*), a small-flowered member of the crucifer or cabbage family with 14 related species in eastern North America, especially in remote Arctic or mountainous habitats.

15-36 Irregularly toothed leaves of **mountain-lover** (*Paxistima canbyi*–E), or **cliff green**. No flowers of fruits ever appear on the two Ohio populations.

15-35 **Cliff-top species:** View from Tanglewood, Adams County, at sunset, with the valley of Ohio Brush Creek down below.

It was seven o'clock now, but I had just enough light to see my way back to the parking lot. Returning to my motel in West Union, the "metropolis" of Adams County, and taking out my trusty ledger book to enter all the important sightings of the day, I felt that my time had been well spent. I had found the least common plant in the most inaccessible habitat in Ohio—truly the land of the fair and the home of the rare.

15-37 **Rock sandwort** (*Arenaria stricta*–P) of the pink family is often associated with dolomite rock and the few stands of mountain-lover in Ohio. Recently this sandwort has been renamed *Minuartia michauxii*.

213

Putting Back the Pieces

Ep-1 **Rediscovering Lost Lake Erie Beach Plants:** The **inter-dune pond,** rebuilt in 1991 at Mentor Headlands, on Lake Erie. The zone of grass surrounding the pond is almost entirely **American beach grass** (*Ammophila breviligulata*–T).

epilogue

Ep-2 One of the Ohio plants that were rated X and reappeared after this pond was dug was **bushy cinquefoil** (*Potentilla paradoxa*–E). (Photo courtesy of Jack Selby.)

Ep-3 Another success story on Lake Erie revolves around a woody member of the heath family—**bearberry** (*Arctostaphylos uva-ursi*–E), rediscovered in 2000 on private beach property in Ashtabula County. (Photo taken on Manitoulin Island.)

214

Ep-4 **Herrick Fen in Portage County**: TNC in the '90s put in a boardwalk to prevent trampling in the fen. Photo taken where the marsh in foreground (grasses and cat-tails) meets the fen (tamaracks, *Larix laricina*–P) in the distance.

Sometimes I feel very discouraged when considering all the native American plants that have been teetering on the brink of extinction since the days of exploration and settlement. In Ohio alone, plant experts estimate the number of native species of higher plants (excluding mosses, fungi, algae, and lichens) at around 1,850, while the number of endangered and threatened (**E** and **T**) species at the latest count (January 2002) totals 393. Add to that the 85 presumed extirpated (**X**) and the 101 potentially threatened (**P**), and the total of rare plants in Ohio (and this is only one of fifty states!) rises to 579, or almost one-third of the total native plants. Is it possible to save them all?

Numbers, however, don't tell the whole story. Although we can never hope to restore all of Ohio's rare plants to their former abundance and in their former habitats, ever since the enactment of the Endangered Species law in 1973, professional biologists have registered many successes in locating and putting back some of the pieces of the ecological jigsaw puzzle. They have done this, as I have shown in many of the chapters, by discovering, acquiring, and restoring habitat through consulting maps and historical records of lost species; fencing off promising areas to discourage herbivorous animals (such as the surging deer population); and by "land management," using such methods as removing intrusive non-native plants by hand, mowing, or controlled burning.

Just as the federal government has been enlisted in the fight against air, water, and soil pollution, so has the Act of 1973 enabled national agencies to acquire and upgrade habitats for wildlife. For instance, south of Cleveland the federal government now protects the remaining wild areas near the Cuyahoga River between Cleveland and Akron, Ohio, in a district called the Cuyahoga Valley National Park, on land first purchased over twenty-five years ago. As a result, woodland areas near the river sheltering clumps of the large yellow lady's slippers (*Cypripedium calceolus var. pubescens*–T) have been freed from the threat of development, trampling, and water pollution. The species is now rated P due to protective measures such as this.

State agencies are also heavily involved. The Ohio Department of Natural Resources (ODNR), through its Division of Natural Areas and Preserves, has acquired to date (1999) 24,000 acres of rare plant and animal habitat all over the state gathered into 122 preserves. Northern Ohioans who swim at the popular Lake Erie beach at Mentor Headlands State Park in Lake County are probably unaware that just east of the beach lies a state nature preserve, one of the few on Ohio's "north coast" that protects rare sand-dune plants occurring within 300 feet from the water's edge and nowhere else in the state.

Not many years ago state biologists supervised the construction of a small body of water that would simulate a kind of natural reservoir behind the dunes—called by ecologists an **inter-dune** pond. In less than a year, seeds of dune plants long buried in the sand sprouted beside the pond, including a low, yellow-flowered member of the rose family, the **bushy cinquefoil** (*Potentilla paradoxa*–T), which had disappeared from Lake County after 1960. Thus, another piece was added to the Ohio jigsaw puzzle.

Ep-5 **Bayberry** (*Myrica pensylvanica*–E) is found at only one other site in Ohio (also a fen) but is extremely common as an Atlantic coastal plant. The Ohio sites are the furthest inland for the species. The "berry" is really a hard nut covered with grayish wax, at one time used in candle making.

The latest plant on the Lake Erie shore to be brought back from presumed extinction in Ohio is a low shrub common around the Upper Great Lakes—**bearberry** (*Arctostaphylos uva-ursi*–X) of the heath family. In 2000 a Lake County park naturalist, who was looking for short-eared owls on private property, just west of a municipal beach, found three individual specimens of bearberry by accident and recognized them in leaf even though they hadn't bloomed yet. Jim Bissell of the Cleveland Museum of Natural History later confirmed their identity. Although the Heritage List status of bearberry has been upgraded to E, recent exploration of the same area has turned up no new specimens; in fact, the original three shrubs have disappeared (temporarily, it is hoped), perhaps due to the voracious rabbit population on the lake shore. However, other privately owned tracts on Lake Erie may contain this rare plant as well as other surprises.

Private agencies also save many rare habitats in Ohio. A sort of "duplicate ODNR" is the Ohio chapter of The Nature Conservancy (TNC), a mammoth land-acquiring organization of over a million members in the U.S. and Canada alone and owner and protector of eleven million acres of preserves. In Ohio alone it boasts of 32,000 members and manages 29,000 acres. Some of its holdings are so large, such as the many so-called Edge-of-Appalachia preserves it has taken over in Adams County, that it provides its own permanent preserve managers.

Ep-6 A close-up of a cluster of grayish **"berries" of the bayberry**, growing directly from the main branches.

Not only does TNC include among its members large land-holding corporations, such as in the timber, agricultural, and mining industries, but it has many contacts with international corporations that own large holdings in the rain forests of tropical third-world countries. Like the World Wildlife Fund, TNC's International Program is helping the people of these countries to set up their own system of national parks and nature preserves and earn valuable tourist dollars, rather than cut down the trees for short-sighted agricultural and mining projects.

Furthermore, TNC hasn't forgotten our northern neighbor Canada. Following reports of overdevelopment of beaches on both U.S. and Canadian sides of the Great Lakes, TNC in 1997 set up its first Great Lakes Initiative, a comprehensive aid program to lakefront communities in both countries. Readers may remember that in Chapter 4 I described the magnificent dunes at Carter Bay on Manitoulin Island as a habitat that could easily become unraveled if the dune grasses anchoring the sand were obliterated by beach and harbor development. By an almost eerie coincidence, these dunes have actually been purchased by a developer in the last few years and have been featured in widespread advertisements as the newest complex of projected marinas, golf courses, and condominiums on Manitoulin's south coast. Moreover, some of the large **alvars** (natural limestone pavements) on the island and elsewhere in the region are also being threatened, by mining development. With a dose of good luck and a lot of help from TNC's Great Lakes Initiative, these threats may diminish. In the meantime, it is white-knuckle crises like these that make me realize the importance of stressing habitat in my articles.

TNC has needed many volunteers to serve as "watchdogs" (the old term) over the various preserves it owns, so ever since 1977, I have been a "surveillance committee of one" (the new term) to oversee developments in Herrick Fen, in Portage County, the bog capital of Ohio. This job usually involves making one annual visit to the preserve and writing up a short report. One of only two places in Ohio where one can find the E-rated **bayberry** (*Myrica pensylvanica*)—a shrub with waxy berries once prized for candle making—Herrick Fen has always been one of my favorite wetlands, partly because it contains so many different habitats: a **beaver pond** now dammed up to form a small lake, a **cat-tail marsh**, a **swamp forest**, a **beech-maple forest** on higher ground, and two **fens**, one on either side of the lake.

Ep-7 The rarest plant of Herrick Fen, the **bunchflower** (*Melanthium virginicum*–T) of the lily family can't be missed in its flowering season, when it sends up tall, conspicuous panicles of white flowers, of which mainly the terminal ones bear seeds. (See featherbells, Chapter 15.)

For me, observing how TNC has managed the property year after year has been like taking a course in applied ecology. To prevent damage from trampling, TNC put in a boardwalk. To control the growth of invasive plants—**giant reed** or **phragmites** (*Phragmites australis*), and **narrow-leafed cat-tail** (*Typha angustifolia*) in the marsh, as well as **European buckthorn** (*Rhamnus frangula*) in the fen—TNC sends in a volunteer work crew, called **land stewards**, each year to cut down by hand the tall weedy plants when they get too close to the boardwalk and the endangered fen species.

Walking the boardwalk at Herrick Fen has also been a good introduction to many wetland plants that I've seldom found elsewhere, especially two attractive state-listed lilies—**white camass** or **wand-lily** (*Zigadenus elegans var. glaucus*–P) and **bunchflower** (*Melanthium virginicum*–T). These two have similar large, white flowers, with a conspicuous yellow gland on each petal. At the right time of year, the wand-lily was easy to spot from the boardwalk, but I could never find the bunchflower, even though it was on the ODNR list of plants attributed to Herrick Fen. Finally I sent away for a topo map and discovered that the bunchflower grew only in the fen on the other side of the lake, a place I had never visited before. Luckily my friend Cal from the Education Department of the Museum of Natural History, where I volunteer, lived near Herrick Fen, and together we made an expedition via some obscure paths and dirt roads to the other side of the lake and actually found a thriving stand of the bunchflower. Fortunately for us, we had the correct blooming date, and the bunchflower was loaded with tall panicles of white flowers that towered conspicuously above all the other plants in the fen. I now know, from this map-reading exercise, what some of the ODNR researchers go through in rediscovering sites of plants that haven't been reported for many years—with probably more failures than successes.

There are other private organizations, such as the National Audubon Society and the Ohio Historical Society, that acquire and protect sites of rare plants in Ohio, but the one I'm most familiar with is the Cleveland Museum of Natural History, where I have been a volunteer in the Botany and Paleobotany Departments, and have submitted articles to its magazine, the *Explorer*, over the last twenty-five years. More than anyone else, Jim Bissell, curator of the Botany Department, including the herbarium, with its 60,000 specimens of pressed plants, has a talent for scouting out areas that may harbor rare species. He does this by careful reading and reinterpretation of herbarium labels, with the location information supplied by the original collectors of the specimens, some of whom were active over 100 years ago. Ownership of farms has changed; tiny, four-corners communities have disappeared; railroads have been abandoned; and county roads have been assigned new numbers—but Jim is still able to nail down a specific locality most of the time.

Many of his greatest successes are with wetland plants. Once in 1982 I was standing beside Jim on a bridge overlooking a creek in northeastern Ohio when I spotted a rather large pondweed (*Potamogeton*) floating in the water. After I casually pointed it out to Jim, the next thing I knew he was wading in the creek and pulling out a sample leafy stem. A few weeks later, the specimen was determined to be **Hill's pondweed** (*P. hilli*–X), not definitely collected in Ohio after 1913—a lost plant for sixty-nine years!

The whole flood plain of this creek, with its adjacent swamp forest and a rare hilltop fen, has proved extremely productive in rare plants. In the course of time, the Museum has acquired this site as one of twenty-two that it manages in northern Ohio, amounting to 2,700 acres. In the flood plain are located several clumps of the **small purple fringed**

Ep-8 Close-up of the terminal cluster of the **bunchflower**.

Ep-9 Close-up of the individual flowers of the **bunchflower**, showing the conspicuous yellow glands on the petals.

Ep-10 The **white wand-lily** (*Zigadenus elegans var. glaucus*–P) also has yellow glands on its petals, possibly as a visual aid to pollinators. (Bees especially like combinations of yellow and white.) Species of *Zigadenus* out West, where they are called **death camass**, are notorious for lethal alkaloids in their bulbs.

orchid (*Platanthera psycodes–E*), blooming in mid-summer, with its handsome flowers a true orchid color. In the hilltop fen can be found a thriving colony of **hooded ladies'-tresses** (*Spiranthes romanzoffiana–T*); like others of its genus, this northern orchid is distinguished by small white flowers spiraling up the stem.

The biggest surprise was the discovery of a second Ohio colony of the rare **globeflower** (*Trollius laxus–E*) down in the swamp forest. This was originally labeled E on both federal and Ohio lists, but with the discovery of new populations it has been taken off the federal list completely (see Chapter 2) although it still retains the E rating in Ohio. Just recently Jim's discovery team has found a new colony of globeflower in the hillside forest adjacent to the fen, and there are probably other surprises in this creek system waiting to be uncovered.

The search for rare and endangered plants continues. In June of 1999, I spent four days in Tennessee looking for a rare member of the camellia family that I hope some day to write about—*Stewartia ovata*, or **mountain camellia**, a small tree with a beautiful white magnolia-like flower—when I unexpectedly ran into two plants that are part of the Lucy Braun story of Chapter 1 but that I had not seen before.

Along a mountain stream in a grassy meadow above Lula Lake Falls, atop Lookout Mountain, where a famous battle was fought in the Civil War near Chattanooga, Tennessee, I found an odd creeping plant with three-lobed leaves and an inch-wide greenish-yellow flower with many narrow sepals and petals, almost like a small cactus flower. It took a while before I recognized this as the **yellow passion-flower** (*Passiflora lutea*), the same species that Lucy Braun had documented in Lynx Prairie, but which I had never before seen in bloom in several trips to that unique Ohio Preserve.

Shortly afterwards, my Tennessee friends began to explore the thick woods upslope from the meadow and found a small grove of mountain camellias in full bloom. On our way back to the meadow we passed a few large azalea bushes, or small trees, bearing flowers of a brilliant orange-red, a much deeper color than that of the **flame azalea** (*Rhododendron calendulaceum*), common in the Southern Appalachians. Our leaders casually mentioned that this bush was actually the **Cumberland azalea** (*R. cumberlandense*), but as they went on their way, the wheels started to go around in my memory. Wasn't this the famous red azalea that Lucy Braun discovered and named when she was exploring for new plants in the Cumberland Plateau of eastern Kentucky? Of course, it was. I dashed back to the woods, camera bag on my shoulder, and took some photos that I hoped would be worthy additions to a book inspired by Lucy Braun's career.

The latest experience I have had with a plant associated with Braun's career occurred in early October of 2003, at the same time I was putting this book together.

Ep-11 **Following Jim Bissell:** In a newly explored creek in Ohio's most northeastern county, Ashtabula, Jim Bissell, curator of botany at the Cleveland Museum of Natural History, points to the rare aquatic, **Hill's pondweed** (*Potamogeton hilli–E*), which he discovered the year before. This species, last noted in Ohio in 1913, is one of 15 pondweeds on Ohio's Heritage List, including five still rated X.

Ep-12 **Exploring for Plants in Tennessee:** The **mountain camellia** (*Stewartia ovata var. grandiflorum*) is a forest-loving American cousin of the gorgeous camellias of the Far East in the tea family. Resembling a magnolia in size and showiness, it is actually closer to the **St. John's-worts** (*Hypericum*) in structure.

Ep-13 In the same forest a few steps from the mountain camellia was a large azalea bush with small, intensely red flowers. This small tree was the **Cumberland azalea** (*Rhododendron cumberlandensis*), first discovered in eastern Kentucky by Lucy Braun. (See Chapter 1.)

Ep-14 In contrast, the **flame azalea** (*R. calendulaceum—E*) of the South, with a few stands in south-central Ohio, has larger flowers of an orange cast, although some bushes have yellow, orange, and red flowers mixed together. (Photo taken in Great Smoky Mountains National Park.)

This was when I joined a four-day tour hosted by the Cleveland Metropolitan Park System. We were to visit Kentucky's Natural Bridge State Park, southwest of Lexington, in a limestone region featuring unusual plants, animals, and rock formations. One such formation, called a **rockhouse**, is an overhang resembling a cave opening or a natural bridge that hasn't completely eroded away and supports a flora that receives little direct sunlight or moisture. It was here, in this part of Kentucky, that Lucy Braun first discovered the **white-haired goldenrod** (*Solidago albopilosa*).

Using Gray's *Botany*, I jotted down the features of this plant before we left: sprawling rather than upright; a few tufts of large flowers at the end of the creeping stem; a noticeable covering of white hairs, especially on the main stems; October blooming time; and location in only two counties.

Sure enough, on the third day near a huge rock formation called Gray's Arch we noticed a few scattered, creeping goldenrods that fit the above description exactly. I took a few pictures. Then right under the arch itself was a large penned-off enclosure containing hundreds of these plants. Attached to the fence was a notice proclaiming that this species was endangered in Kentucky and in the United States as a whole and was therefore both state and federally protected. In my career as a plant hunter, I have seen very few plants in the wild with such qualifications, so this was a real prize.

In 1999, while I was still in the Appalachians and very close to southwest Virginia, the only known home of the **round-leaf birch** (*Betula uber*) that is mentioned in the Introduction, I thought I would take one more day and hunt down this rare tree. I had phoned people at the National Forest Service headquarters closest to the site where the birch was rediscovered after being lost for some sixty years, and they gave me directions to a county road, where a Forest Service work camp was located. The trees would be somewhere nearby.

Leaving my hotel the following morning, within two hours I was standing by a county road in front of the Forest Service camp and reading a sign that simply said "BETULA UBER" with an arrow underneath it pointing to a trail on the other side of the road. I thought: "This is almost too easy." And I was right.

The trail dead-ended at a creek, which I recognized as the famous Cressy Creek of the *New Yorker* article, the only landmark which the 1975 search team could use to find the last population of the tree. I crossed the shallow, fast-running creek. No trail. No birch trees. What then? Would I need to get a map from the Forest Service work-camp officials? I recrossed the creek and then noticed a wooden platform built next to a large enclosure protected by a wire fence. Of course. This was a viewing platform, and the rare trees were inside the fence. But when I stepped onto the viewing platform, the

Ep-15 **Searching for the Round-Leaf Birch:** The only known site for the **round-leaf birch** (*Betula uber*) in the world: the drainage area of Cressy Creek, a small, shallow stream with a rocky bed, in a cutover woods in the mountains of western Virginia. (See Introduction.)

light was terrible for taking pictures. Only when I looked at some of the branches of the birches against the sky could I see that the leaves were round. I had found the right place, but it just wasn't made for photographers.

Very disappointed, I drove back to the main highway, passing by the district headquarters of the Forest Service, the same place from which I had received such promising information a few weeks before. Perhaps they would know of some other locations of *Betula uber*. I found a place to turn around and drove back to the headquarters building.

It looked like a lost cause: the naturalists and district rangers were out of the office, and there were no maps or literature on the round-leaf birch available. I was ready to leave when one of the women clerks asked, "Did you see the big round-leaf birch right in front of our building? It was planted about twenty years ago."

"You mean there's a tree out there that I can photograph that isn't fenced in, that I can just walk right up to?"

"Of course." I was out of there in five seconds, and for the next twenty minutes I was taking pictures of the tall tree from all angles, and getting close-ups of the round leaves, the bark, and this year's and last year's catkins. What a stroke of luck! And to think I almost drove right past that place! This was a great ending to my 1999 Appalachian trip.

The search for rare and endangered plants in Ohio also continues. In May 1999, I was extremely fortunate to find a guide who could lead me to the best site in Ohio for the **running buffalo clover** (*Trifolium stoloniferum*–E), a federally endangered plant with a strange history.

In the early years of this century, running buffalo clover—one of only four native clovers east of the Mississippi, as listed by *Gray's Manual*, although at least thirteen species had been introduced from Europe—was reported from eight states, mostly those watered by the Ohio and Missouri Rivers; *Gray* (1950) lists its original range from "West Virginia to South Dakota, south to Kentucky, Missouri, and eastern Kansas." Throughout the clover's whole range, populations declined precipitously for unknown reasons, probably related to loss of habitat and competition with European clovers, until by 1940 it was found only in southern West Virginia. (It hadn't been seen in Ohio since 1907.)

After the species had been lost nationally for forty-four years, two tiny populations were rediscovered in West Virginia in 1984; at one site there was only one plant, and at another, eleven. However, since the Endangered Species Act was now in effect, protective measures could begin, and the clover was declared federally endangered in 1987.

Ep-16 The viewing platform next to an enclosure inside a wire fence, all built to protect a few **round-leaf birches** from vandalism or herbivores. They were also protected from photographers.

Ep-17 The ranger station closest to Cressy Creek. Tall tree in front is a fine specimen of **Betula uber**.

Ep-18 Closer view of the tree, which was planted in the '70s.

As has happened many times in the past quarter century, federal involvement has unleashed a great wave of rediscovery and intensive study of endangered plants and animals. Thus, in 1987 it was no accident that a small population of *T. stoloniferum* was discovered in Indiana and a very large one in Kentucky.

With this impetus, a search team of five botanists from ODNR, aided by federal funds, planned to track down the elusive clover in southwestern Ohio, where it had been known almost a century before, at the height of its blooming season, mid-May to mid-June of 1988. First, they would view the Kentucky sites to find out what sort of habitat to concentrate on, and how to distinguish the running buffalo clover from its European look-alikes—especially the **white clover** (*T. repens*), probably found on every lawn and roadside in eastern North America.

After noticing that *T. stoloniferum* seemed to thrive in disturbed open areas like paths and roadsides as well as in moderate shade, as under large trees, the search team from ODNR returned to Ohio ready to look for disturbed grassy habitats, such as dry meadows, prairies, open woodlands, and parks. Within five weeks they had found eight new populations scattered over three counties in southwestern Ohio, amounting to 250-270 individual plants, enough to make Ohio's population the second largest in the country. Another piece had been returned to the ecological jigsaw puzzle, and another X-rated plant was now E.

In spring of 1999, by calling people in southwest Ohio, I was able to contact Dan, an amateur botanist who worked as a landscaper and by himself in his spare time had discovered new colonies of *T. stoloniferum*. Everyone I talked to said he was the most knowledgeable person on the subject of the clover. On May 26, Carol and I made the long drive down from Cleveland and met Dan at a preserve that I will call "Miami Bend," known for its large, prosperous colonies of running buffalo clover.

Within a few hours we found extensive stands of T. stoloniferum along paths and roadsides and in a large meadow dominated by **Kentucky blue grass** (*Poa pratensis*). The clover seemed to prefer the shade of the scattered trees—including **Kentucky coffee tree** (*Gymnocladus dioica*) and **pawpaw** (*Asimina triloba*). Dan taught us how to distinguish the rare clover from the European white clover: both have **stolons**, which send up leaf stalks and flower stalks, but the flower stalks of *stoloniferum* each bear two leaves beneath the flower head, whereas T. repens bears none. (Perhaps for this reason—more leaves to each individual plant—a recent government bulletin, summarizing some of the benefits

Ep-19 Close-up of the round or slightly heart-shaped leaves of **Betula uber**.

Ep-20 Close-up of one of this year's **catkins** containing unripe seeds. Last year's catkins were brownish and broken, strewing the ground with seeds.

of the Endangered Species Act after twenty-five years, states: "One species, the running buffalo clover, an endangered species once believed to be extinct, is now being screened as a possible forage crop because of its higher protein content and perennial nature.")

As if all this weren't enough, Dan took us to a rocky wooded slope in another part of Miami Bend, where he pointed out about ten specimens of **Guyandotte beauty** (*Synandra hispidula*) in bloom. This is a large-flowered mint with white petals speckled with green dots, that later turn purple, and one that I had been looking for, on and off, in southern and central Ohio for the last ten years. Apparently it has a short blooming season. Though it was once listed as T in Ohio, in the course of years, enough populations to take it off the list completely have been found.

Ep-21 The only other round-leaved birches in North America grow mainly in the Arctic as dwarf species. In Ohio, one exception is the **swamp birch** (*B. pumila*–T), a creeping shrub with matted leaves. Shown here in Cedar Bog in central Ohio.

Ep-22 **Finding the Long-Lost Running Buffalo Clover**: a good view of the Miami River from Miami Bend in southwestern Ohio.

Ep-23 **Running buffalo clover** (*Trifolium stoloniferum*–E) in a grassy roadside meadow at Miami Bend. Note its close resemblance to the European **white clover** (*T. repens*).

Ep-24 Close-up of the flower head of **running buffalo clover**. Note a pair of leaves, with three leaflets, attached to the flower stalk directly under the flower, a feature lacking in the European white clover.

Ep-25 For comparison, a close-up of the **buffalo clover** (*T. reflexum*–E), currently lost in Ohio. The three leaflets are pointed, not rounded. (Photo taken at a botanical garden.)

When we were saying good-bye, Dan mentioned that he is actively looking for a second rare clover, the **buffalo clover** (*T. reflexum*–E), originally found in Vinton County in 1955, then lost until rediscovered in Pike County in 1990 on a sandstone slope, and at present lost again. If anyone finds it in Ohio in the near future, my best bet is that it will be Dan.

*　　　*　　　*　　　*　　　*　　　*　　　*

As I look back on the last twenty-five years of searching for rare and endangered species, reporting to ODNR on my sightings each year (and there are always a few good ones), and visiting Herrick Fen and reporting to The Nature Conservancy on its condition, I feel that I'm doing some good in the ever-changing field of plant conservation.

Ever since I joined TNC, Carol and I have attended many of this fine organization's annual meetings, usually held in the fall in a different part of the country every year. They always include many field trips to the unspoiled TNC-owned nature preserves and provide a real education in the plant and animal life of an unfamiliar region.

In Florida we visited so many subtropical rain forests that it whetted our interest in seeing the real thing in Latin America. Fortunately many travel companies now provide a new form of tour, called the ecology tour, or **eco-tour**, for short, which stresses plants, animals, native peoples, unique habitats, and ancient ruins and eliminates cruise ships and shop-till-you-drop forays in every port. So far, Carol and I have visited seven tropical American countries plus Hawaii to see the endangered rain forests via eco-tour, and many of the touring companies have a tie-in with TNC and are advertised in the bimonthly Nature Conservancy.

We have also visited the Arctic several times via eco-tours, either planned out by ourselves, as in our visit to Churchill, Manitoba; or by way of Canadian companies, as in the tour of Newfoundland and Labrador; or through the Cleveland Museum of Natural History, when we went to Alaska.

With my cameras and record books at my side, I am constantly gathering information on rare and endangered species, whether I'm on a three-hour walk in Ohio or a two-week tour in another continent or climate. As a popularizer in the field of conservation, I find the possibilities of new articles are so many that it's sometimes hard to choose. Will my next one be on the Florida Panhandle or the Labrador coast? Or how about the Siskiyous of the Pacific

Ep-26 Flowers of a showy mint found in a rocky, shaded ravine at Miami Bend, **Guyandotte beauty** (*Synandra hispidula*) or just synandra, once considered very rare in Ohio but later taken off the Heritage List.

Ep-27 **Natural Bridge State Park, Kentucky, Autumn, 2003: Gray's Arch**, seen from beneath, is typical of the huge eroded rock formations in the east-central part of the state. Despite the rocky soil and the lack of sufficient light and moisture, a large variety of plants thrive in this region, including the endemic white-haired goldenrod.

Ep-28 The rare **white-haired goldenrod** (*Solidago albopilosa*), seen at a distance in a half-reclining position and with many broad leaves to take advantage of the little sunlight that reaches it. First described and named by Ohio botanist Lucy Braun.

Ep-29 In close-up, the **white-haired goldenrod** has such few flowers per stem (and with petals of a greater size than in most species in its genus) that it hardly resembles a goldenrod at all. Note white hairs on stems.

Northwest, where new species of plants have been discovered even in the '90s? The granite barrens of Georgia in the spring? Or the dunes at Mentor Headlands on Lake Erie, thirty miles away?

As an amateur botanist, I try to popularize the work of the laypeople and scientists who are involved in restoring the missing pieces to Ohio's and America's jigsaw puzzle. Like them, I sometimes feel frustrated with so much to do and so little time. But then I write something about the real world that touches some of my readers, and when they write back, I feel a great deal of satisfaction.

One thing I can be sure of, whether I'm on a three-hour walk, planning a new trip, looking over a newly developed roll of film, or finishing another article—I'm never bored.

Ep-30 **The author**, as usual loaded down with camera bag and binoculars, kneeling down inside a **rockhouse**, an eroded formation resembling a cave entrance, to point out a specimen of **white-haired goldenrod**. (Photo taken by David Dvorak.)

Appendix

NO-1 **The Grand River of Northeast Ohio, a Clean River System and Its Inhabitants:** Spanning the river at Harpersfield, Ashtabula County, is an old covered bridge, supplemented by a modern steel structure—a symbol of the dilemma involving habitat conservation: preserving the original state despite the pressures of the modern world.

NO-2 Thanks to the clean water of the Grand River, amphibians like the **mud puppy** (*Necturus maculosus*) can thrive. Here we see Tim Matson of the Cleveland Museum of Natural History, demonstrating how to catch this 20-inch salamander in order to band it.

NO-3 The head of the **mud puppy** crad in Tim's hand. Note the smooth skin lacking scales, characteristic of salamanders and fro

Appendix A:
Plants not discussed in the text that are found in Northern Ohio with NO- numbers in the captions

NO-7 **Wetlands of Northeast Ohio:** at Fern Lake, a tree, unmistakably felled by **beavers**, provides the clue for the resurgence of wetlands in northeast Ohio. Like many rare animals and plants, the beaver is enjoying a comeback.

NO-8 Among the wetlands of northeast Ohio, Morgan Swamp of Ashtabula County, which started out as a **beaver pond**, is perhaps the most extensive. The emergent water plants in the photo are probably **spatter-dock** (*Nuphar advena*), a yellow-flowered water-lily.

NO-9 **Bogs and fens**, characterized by mats of sphagnum moss or sedge meadows respectively, flourish especially in Portage, Summit, Ashtabula, and Wayne Counties. The **Canada burnet** of the rose family (*Sanguisorba canadensis*) was once considere rare, but because its fen habitats are increas it has been taken off the Heritage List.

NO-4 Because the Grand River has been so undisturbed through the years, rare plants such as the **few-flowered St. John's-wort** (*Hypericum ellipticum—E*) still live on its banks.

NO-5 The pristine headwaters of the Grand River in Ashtabula County have been acquired by the Cleveland Museum of Natural History in the last two decades and named **Grand River Terraces**. In the undisturbed beech-maple forest on the Terraces, many rare northern plants make their home, such as this **Robin-run-away** (*Dalibarda repens—T*), a member of the rose family, closely related to the wild blackberries (*Rubus spp.*).

NO-6 Puzzle picture: Find the nesting **woodcock** (*Scolopax minor*), a nocturnal, seldom-seen, forest-dwelling member of the shore-bird family, as it blends in with the leaf cover at Grand River Terraces. (Hint: look at the center of the scene. Its long bill faces left.)

NO-10 **Wild calla** (*Calla palustris—T*), a relative of the Jack-in-the-pulpit, is found mainly in small ponds and forest streams. In Canada, with its bright white shield, or **spathe**, protecting the flower head, or **spadix**, wild calla is often seen covering acres of wetland along railroad tracks.

NO-11 Aquatics that spend their whole life cycle in ponds and still waters are often the most difficult plants to spot and identify. In Ohio they account for a large percentage of Heritage plants. A very striking aquatic is the **water stargrass** (*Heteranthera dubia*, of the pickerelweed family), whose six narrow petals against a background of dark green, stringy leaves makes an almost unreal pattern.

NO-12 At Fried Swamp in Geauga County, I spotted a strange duckweed floating in the water on a Northeast Ohio Naturalists outing, in 1980. It had four tiny flattened stems, instead of the usual single stem for most of the **duckweeds** (*Lemna*). When I pointed out the odd specimen to Jim Bissell, who was wading in the knee-deep water next to me, he gasped, "Oh, my God, that's **star wolfiella**! It's rated X on the Heritage List!" And thus another aquatic species considered extirpated (*Wolfiella gladiata—T*) was brought back to the living world.

NO-13 On the other hand, **American lotus** (*Nelumbo lutea*) of the water-lily family has always been the most visible of aquatics. Found mainly in calm bays along the Lake Erie shoreline, its creamy-yellow petals contrast with the golden seed-head in the center, shaped like a shower-head when it dries later in the season. Archaeologists believe that the extensive shoreline distribution of this species may be due to its edible seeds being relished by Native American tribes, who planted them in convenient places along their foraging routes.

NO-14 **Northern Conifer Forests:** mature forests of **white pine** (*Pinus strobus*) are rare in northern Ohio as well as in Michigan, where Hartwick Pines State Park is a well-known tourist attraction. Pictured here is the white pine forest at Snow Lake, in Geauga County, which is surrounded by a sphagnum mat that is the next step to a bog.

NO-15 One of the outstanding associates of white pine is a common plant of the northern conifer forest but a rarity in northern Ohio—**bunchberry** (*Cornus canadensis*–T) of the dogwood family. As in the arboreal flowering dogwood (*C. florida*), the four white "petals" are really modified leaves called **bracts** that attract pollinators to the tiny flowers gathered in the center.

NO-16 **Beech-Maple Forests:** Cathedral Woods in Ashtabula County is one of the most mature beech-maple forests in Ohio. It is unusual that the large **hemlocks** (*Tsuga canadensis*) in these woods grow right beside the beeches and sugar maples rather than on rocky slopes nearby.

NO-17 The flowers of **striped maple** (*Acer pensylvanicum*–E) are greenish rather than white, but under the dark canopy there are so many in each bunch that they look white. Stripes of green alternate with whitish on the bark of this rare northern tree.

NO-18 Some of the rarer wildflowers associated with mature beech-maple forests often bear white petals, conspicuous in the deep shade of the leaf canopy, for example, **starflower** (*Trientalis borealis*) of the primrose family.

NO-19 Similarly, **goldthread** (*Coptis trifolia*) of the buttercup family, a low plant on the forest floor with leaves of three leaflets resembling those of strawberries, adds a touch of white to the deep shadows from the forest canopy.

NO-20 A bush with white puffs of flowers— **hobblebush** (*Viburnum alnifolium–P*)—also follows the same pattern. One of a large genus of woody plants in the honeysuckle family, hobblebush ranges from the Northeast through the Appalachians, barely reaching northern Ohio.

NO-21 **Plants of Open Areas, Wet or Dry:** With its long thin leaf, the **lance-leaved violet** (*Viola lanceolata–P*) differs radically from ordinary violets with their heart-shaped leaves. Loves wet, sandy habitats, usually near ponds or creeks.

NO-22 One of the largest and most colorful mints in Ohio, the deep-red **Oswego-tea** (*Monarda didyma*), familiar as a garden plant, prefers wet, open woodlands. Common in northeastern Ohio, it blooms in mid-summer. I have seldom seen it in bloom. Photo taken in Geauga County in July.

NO-23 **Lilies:** the **wood lily** (*Lilium philadelphicum–T*), found in northeastern Ohio, is the only large lily with upright flowers.

NO-24 Only when one is looking directly down at a group of **wood lilies** are the dark freckles apparent against the reddish petals. These black spots are probably **honey guides**, zeroing in pollinators, such as bees, to nectar glands in the center of the flower.

NO-25 The flowers of the **Canada lily** (*L. canadense*) in Ohio are usually reddish, as opposed to yellow in other areas. The usual growth habit of their flowers is to hang directly down.

NO-26 The **Turk's-cap lily** (*L. superbum—P*) has nodding flowers with the petals reflexed, or bent back. The tallest of the true lilies in Ohio (almost 8 feet), it is most easily found in the northeastern counties near water.

NO-27 The colorful but scarce **painted trillium** (*T. undulatum—E*) is confined to extreme northeast Ohio, to which it has extended from its Appalachian homeland. This specimen was found in a forest dominated by hemlocks.

NO-28 Another rare Appalachian species, the **bluebead lily** (*Clintonia borealis—E*) has yellow flowers. It is found in Ohio only in the extreme northeast, where it favors sandy soil in an open forest next to a large sand barrens.

NO-29 **Miscellaneous Plants of Northern Ohio, Mostly from the Prairie Openings of the Northwestern Counties:** TNC's Kitty Todd Nature Preserve, shown here, is a treasure house of rare species adapted to open, sandy-soil habitats.

NO-30 A bicolored legume, the **wild lupine** (*Lupinus perennis*–P), is well known in dry habitats around the Upper Great Lakes but scarce in Ohio. The larva of a rare butterfly, the **Karner blue** (*Lycaeides melissa ssp. samuelis*–E) feeds only on the leaves of this species.

NO-31 **Plains frostweed** (*Helianthemum bicknellii*–T), belonging to the rock-rose family, a poorly represented group in North America, also favors Kitty Todd Preserve. It is distantly related to the violets.

NO-32 Another bicolored legume, **goat's-rue** (*Tephrosia virginiana*), is much more commonly seen in Indiana and Illinois than in Ohio. A genus of mainly Southern Hemisphere plants.

NO-35 Only when it shows its bright red berries does it become unmistakable. Much rarer than its cousin, the **white baneberry**, or **doll's-eyes** (*A. pachypoda*), it really belongs to the buttercup family. As in the case of many members of this family, its fruit is poisonous.

NO-33 **Fireweed** of the evening-primrose family (*Epilobium angustifolium*–E) is famous for having colonized burnt-over areas of London after the World War II blitz. Most common in weedy, disturbed areas, such as beside railroad tracks, where I first saw it in Ohio.

NO-34 **Red baneberry** (*Actaea rubra*–T), when in flower, looks as if it might be from one of a half-dozen families, such as the umbels, composites, roses and others.

NO-36 Seen in Irwin Prairie on the outskirts of Toledo, the **Skinner's foxglove** (*Agalinis skinneriana var. parviflora*–E) is one of many pink, snapdragon-like plants, once called **gerardias**. This specimen was found in a wet, sandy location.

NO-37 Specimen of **Kalm's St. John's-wort** (*Hypericum Kalmianum*) a Great Lakes region **endemic** (found only in one area). It is a much smaller shrub than the common **shrubby St. John's wort** (*H. prolificum*).

NO-38 **An Odd Goldenrod:** having so far refrained from including any of the 23 native Ohio goldenrods among my photos, because outwardly they all look alike, I feel I must mention one of the rarest—**stout goldenrod** (*Solidago squarrosa*–T) because it blooms in one of the Cleveland Metropolitan parks, a half hour from my home; it has one of the skimpiest flower-spikes of any of the goldenrods; and its habitat is dark, mature forests, on rocky slopes, not in open grasslands. I wouldn't have found it if a friend hadn't given me explicit directions.

NO-39 Is It or Isn't It in Ohio? The first and only time I saw the **white wood-sorrel** (*Oxalis montana*–X) in Ohio was at Holden Arboretum in August 1978. Later ODNR called this colony of the wood-sorrel "escapees from cultivation." A station in Ashtabula County, known in the 1980s, can no longer be found. Perhaps some day in a dark, wet, mature woods, with plenty of hemlocks, and probably on private property, another site for this elusive forest-dweller will be revealed. (Photo taken by author in western New York, 1983.)

P.S. 2006: this species was rediscovered in Eastern Ohio, in Belmont County, a few years ago. The heritage rating is now E.

SO-3 The red spots on the petals of **mountain laurel** flowers are actually depressions that hold back the pollen-bearing anthers under tension. When a pollinating insect lands on the flower, the anthers are suddenly released and shower the insect with pollen.

SO-1 **Woody Heaths:** among the woody members of the heath family, the **great rhododendron** (R. maximum–T) is perhaps the largest and best known. A preserve in the Hocking Hills has both this species and the equally glamorous **flame azalea** (R. calendulaceum–E). (See Epilogue.)

SO-2 Like the great rhododendron, **mountain laurel** (Kalmia latifolia) is commonly cultivated as a garden plant.

> **Appendix A, continued:**
> Plants not discussed in the text that are found in Southern Ohio with SO- numbers in the captions

SO-4 **Other Woody Plants:** I have seen the next three woody plants in the South but not in Ohio. **Cross-vine** (Bignonia capreolata) with its large, bicolored flowers, a member of the catalpa family, is at the northern edge of its range in six Ohio River counties. It was on the Heritage List until recently.

SO-5 **Sweet-shrub** or **Carolina-allspice** (Calycanthus florida var. glaucus–X), also named C. fertilis, is in a family all its own, between the magnolias and the papaws. Other members of the same genus live in eastern Asia—a pre-glacial distribution pattern suggestive of great geological age.

SO-6 **Fringe-tree** (Chionanthus virginicus–T) of the olive family, has a multitude of white stringy-petaled flowers, all blooming at the same time.

SO-7 **A Miscellany of Southern Ohio Wildflowers:** The white form of **shooting-star** (*Dodecatheon meadia*) of the primrose family is a handsome member of the prairie flora in southwest Ohio. Its completely reflexed petals are the clue that its nearest relatives are the **cyclamens** of the Mediterranean.

SO-8 The genus *Silene* of the pink family has produced a large number of showy prairie species in Ohio, such as **royal catchfly** (*S. regia*–P). (See Chapter 3.) Pictured here is a smaller but equally colorful relative, **fire-pink** (*S. virginica*).

SO-9 This close-up of **fire pink** shows the typical notched petals. **Pinking**, as in the phrase **pinking shears**, is an old word that means to make a notched or saw-toothed edge in a material such as cloth.

SO-10 Although the **smooth ruellia** (*Ruellia strepens*), a low-lying prairie plant, resembles the **garden petunia** of the **nightshade family**, it actually comes from the tropical **acanthus family**, not well represented in the northern United States.

SO-11 A relative of the **poinsettias**, the **glade spurge** (*Euphorbia purpurea*–E) is one of the strangest-looking member of a strange family, ranging worldwide from cactus-like trees in East Africa to ground-hugging weeds in every suburban garden. Long considered extirpated in Ohio, it was rediscovered in a prairie in one southern-Ohio county in 1990.

SO-12 The **beard-tongues** (*Penstemon*) are handsome relatives of the garden snapdragons and flower in tall spikes like foxgloves. There are scores of very showy, colorful beard-tongues out west, but in Ohio most are gray-white. **Smooth beard-tongue** (*P. laevigata*–E), which I first saw in Adams County in 2002, is the exception, being a pale pink.

SO-13 **Two Milkweeds:** in West Virginia, when I first saw the **white milkweed** (*Asclepias variegata*–P), I had no idea that this roadside plant was also a southern-Ohio rarity. The flowerhead is almost globular, like a popcorn ball.

SO-14 Green and purple are an odd combination of colors, more typical of some orchid flowers than in the milkweed family, except for the **spider milkweed** (*A. viridis*–P), which has green flowers with tiny purple centers. It favors dry, open habitats, including roadsides, where I found this specimen in Adams County.

SO-15 **Two Lilies:** Jack and Florence Selby helped me out one March in locating the tiny flowers of the elusive **snow trillium** (*T. nivale*) in a park north of Columbus. Later we saw it in two parks near a river in the heart of the city, growing on limestone ledges.

SO-16 The green leaves of the **snow trillium** have a grayish cast that blends in well with the limestone rocks it grows among. Perhaps this is one way to avoid being eaten by deer, which are notorious for feeding on the **great white trillium** in northern Ohio. This distance shot also shows how tiny the flowers of snow trillium are.

SO-17 The tightly-flowered stalks of the **fairy-wand** or **Devil's-bit** (*Chamaelirium luteum*) from a distance resemble certain species of coral fungi, an illusion enhanced by the inconspicuous leaves and the dark forest habitat.

SO-18 **Two Members of the Rose Family:** a tall, many-flowered plant similar to **feather-bells** of the lily family (*Stenanthium gramineum—T*) (See Chapter15), **goat's-beard** (*Aruncus dioica*) has mainly an Appalachian distribution from the Catskills to Alabama.

SO-19 I have often seen **bowman's-root** (*Porteranthus trifoliatus*–P) as well as its look-alike, the **American-ipecac** (*P. stipulatus*), on trips to the South, but I never noticed either in Ohio until the Botsocs Field Meeting in 2002 (See Chapter 15.) when bowman's-root was seen growing along the roads in Shawnee State Forest. The unsymmetrical flowers, typical of this species, are not a sign of wilting. Also classified as *Gillenia trifoliata*.

SO-20 **Two Composites:** a common member of the aster family in the Deep South, **golden-knees** (*Chrysogonum virginianum*–T) reaches Ohio only in five southeastern counties. I have seen it only once: in a roadside colony in a nature preserve near Marietta.

SO-21 A prairie species common in Indiana and Kentucky, the **compass-plant** (*Silphium laciniatum*–E) in Ohio is strangely restricted to only one hillside in one county and nowhere else in the state. Needless to say, the hillside field has been designated as a state nature preserve. Since there was no sign visible from the road, in August of 1986, when I visited the area, I had to knock on the door of a nearby farmhouse to make sure I had found the right field. Incidentally, the English name is derived from the fact that the edges of the large, lobed leaves line themselves up in a north-south plane to get maximum sunlight.

SO-22 **Southern Ohio Rarities Found in Kentucky, in October 2003: Small-flowered alum-root** (*Heuchera parviflorum*–T, of the saxifrage family) flowers July through October on rocky ledges in only three Ohio River counties. Note the tiny white flowers and the lobed leaves that are wider than long.

SO-23 Known for its narrow leaves and shapeless heads of pink flowers, **Curtiss' milkwort** (*Polygala curtissii*–E) is found in Ohio in only one Ohio River county, but has a large range in the Southeastern and Appalachian states. Likes open woods and rocky to sandy soil.

SO-24 **Silk-grass** (*Crysopsis graminifolia*–E) has an identity crisis: plant systematists can't agree on whether it should be placed in the present genus or in *Heterotheca* or *Pityopsis*. In Ohio, it is found in only one county on a sandy ledge overlooking the Ohio River. Its huge range extends into the Deep South, Florida, Texas, and Mexico. Its grass-like leaves are virtually unique in the aster family.

SO-25 **Round-leaved catchfly** (*Silene rotundifolia*–P) differs from the equally bright-red **fire pink** (*S. virginica*) in that it has large, wide, rounded leaves, mostly arising from the roots, as compared with the long, narrow leaves of the latter. It also takes root on rocky ledges and edges of cliffs.

GL-1 **Northern Evergreen Forest:** Ile Royale in the middle of Lake Superior is America's least visited national park and still clings to its wild heritage to a great degree. Tobin Harbor, shown here, is dominated by trees of the northern conifer forest, probably **red spruce** (*Picea rubens*), judging by their silhouette in this photo.

GL-2 **Plants of the Forest Floor:** most of the northern evergreen forests have disappeared from Ohio and with them many small plant associates. **Twinflower** (*Linnaea borealis*–X), a delicate member of the honeysuckle family, has nodding flowers in pairs. It is named after the founder of systematic botany, Linnaeus.

Appendix A, continued:
Plants not discussed in the text that are found in the Upper Great Lakes region with GL- numbers in the captions

---

GL-3 **Three-leaved false Solomon's-seal** (*Smilacina trifolia*–X), like many plants of the dark northern forest, has tiny white flowers, perhaps useful in attracting night-time pollinators, such as moths.

Note: Many of these photos were taken in Michigan (Ile Royale, Wilderness State Park) and in Ontario (Manitoulin Island, Bruce Peninsula). In the past many of these species reached Ohio but are now classified as E, T, or X.

GL-4 One of the homelier orchids (See Chapter 10.), **Hooker's orchid** (*Platanthera hookeri*–X) is dirty white but has a distinctive petal formation that resembles claws when viewed from the side.

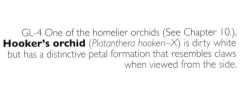

GL-5 Another forest dweller, the **Alaska orchid** (*Piperia unalascensis*) is a curious **disjunct**: Alaska to Wyoming, Utah, and California; then skipping 1,000 miles of prairies, it is found on the Canadian shores of Lakes Superior and Huron. Its small flowers are almost invisble.

GL-6 Another one of the "homely orchids," the tall **northern green orchid** (*Platanthera hyperborea–X*) perhaps has the northernmost distribution of any in the mainly tropical orchid family. It is found commonly from Alaska to Greenland south to the Great Lakes.

GL-7 Related to the heaths, almost all the pyrolas have attractive white flowers. The **pink pyrola** (*P. asarifolia*) with its numerous pink flowers and wrinkled, circular leaves is an exception.

GL-8 **Nodding trillium** (*T. cernuum–X*) doesn't merely nod; it hangs vertically upside-down. Dwells in wet, peaty woods.

GL-9 Close-up of the flower of **nodding trillium**, with oddly folded petals.

GL-10 More orchid-like in appearance than most orchids, **gaywings** (*Polygala paucifolia–E*) is almost a "dead ringer" for the grass-pinks (*Calopogon orchids*) with its bright coloration and one petal modified as a brush to pick up pollen. The **milkwort family**, to which gaywings belongs, was once considered to be closely related to the legumes.

GL-11 **Two Ferns of the Northern Evergreen Forest:** one of the oddest-looking ferns, having an **entire** (undivided) frond with a leathery texture, the **hart's-tongue fern** (*Phyllites scolopendrium var. americanum*) occurs discontinuously around the Great Lakes—in limestone areas of the Upper Peninsula of Michigan and in four counties in Ontario, including the Bruce Peninsula, where it is most common.

GL-13 **A Northern Rattlesnake:** the **eastern massasauga** (*Sistrurus catenatus–E*) is a shy, non-aggressive rattlesnake associated with forests in Ontario and the Great Lakes states. Photo taken on the Bruce Peninsula on a forest path near Lake Huron. After I heard the loud rattle, I realized the snake itself was only six feet in front of me and desperately trying to crawl away.

GL-12 The northern fern that fern hunters get most excited about is the **moonwort** (*Botrychium lunaria*). It has one set of spore-bearing fronds which, when ripe, look very much like flowers gone to seed; and another set of fronds resembling a set of Japanese fans or half-moons. An ancient species, found on all the Northern Hemisphere continents and on both Atlantic and Pacific coasts. (Photo courtesy of Tom Sampliner)

248

GL-14 **Wetlands of the Bruce Peninsula:** the Large Flowerpot, a rock formation that often serves as a symbol of the Bruce Peninsula, although it actually occurs on a small island near the tip of the peninsula.

GL-15 Oliphant Fen on the lower Bruce Peninsula. Note sedges rather than sphagnum moss characteristic of bogs, and a large stream. Conifers in the distance are probably **black spruce** (*Picea mariana*) in the background and **northern white-cedar,** or **arbor vitae** (*Thuja occidentalis*–P), towards the front. Other great wetlands are Dorcas Bay and Petrel Point.

GL-16 **Three Colorful Woody Heaths:** Heaths, of the family *Ericaceae*, are often associated with wetlands around the Great Lakes. Shown here is **bog-rosemary** (*Andromeda glaucophylla–X*).

GL-17 **Bog-laurel** (*Kalmia polifolia*) is much smaller than its bushy Ohio relative, **mountain laurel** (*K. latifolia*).

GL-18 **Labrador tea** (*Ledum groenlandicum–E*) with its clusters of white flowers. When the leaves, coated with white, woolly hair underneath, are bruised, a fragrant odor is detected, which probably gave the common name to the plant.

GL-19 **Carnivorous Plants:** the **butterworts** (*Pinguicula vulgaris*) of a family allied to the **scrophs** (or **snapdragon family**) have basal leaves of the same yellowish color and stickiness as in old-fashioned fly-paper and perform the same function. The leaves secrete gastric juices to digest any insects unlucky enough to be caught.

GL-20 A half-opened flower of the **butterwort**. When fully opened, it has lavender petals and a white throat and superficially resembles an ordinary violet in size and growth habit.

GL-21 The characteristic **sundew** of the Upper Great Lakes is the **long-leaved sundew** (*Drosera anglica*). The Latin specific name, meaning "English," reflects the European and Asiatic distribution of this species before the North American range was known. Perhaps one of the few plants in the world native to both Alaska and Hawaii.

GL-22 **A Common Iris:** the **northern blue flag** (*Iris versicolor*). Although this species is listed by Lucy Braun as common in 16 northern counties of Ohio, I can recall seeing it in bloom in Ohio only once. Photo taken at Dorcas Bay on the Bruce Peninsula.

GL-23 **A Bruce Peninsula Orchid: Bog-candles**, or **tall white bog-orchid** (*Platanthera dilatata*) is never found away from wetlands and perhaps qualifies as one of the handsomest plants on the Bruce Peninsula.

Appendix B:

Federally Listed Plant Species of Ohio and the Upper Great Lakes States (as of 1999)

E= Federally Endangered   T= Federally Threatened

Common Name	Scientific Name	U.S. Status
Ohio		
Northern Monkshood	*Aconitum noveboracense*	T
Lakeside Daisy	*Hymenoxys herbacea*	T
Small Whorled Pogonia	*Isotria medeoloides*	T
Eastern Prairie Fringed Orchid	*Platanthera leucophaea*	T
Virginia Spiraea	*Spiraea virginiana*	T
Running Buffalo Clover	*Trifolium stoloniferum*	E
Illinois		
Mead's Milkweed	*Asclepias meadii*	T
Leafy Prairie Clover	*Dalea foliosa*	E
Lakeside Daisy	*Hymenoxys herbacea*	T
Small Whorled Pogonia	*Isotria medeoloides*	T
Eastern Prairie Fringed Orchid	*Platanthera leucophaea*	T
Decurrent False Aster	*Boltonia decurrens*	T
Pitcher's Thistle	*Cirsium pitcheri*	T
Indiana		
Mead's Milkweed	*Asclepias meadii*	T
Pitcher's Thistle	*Cirsium pitcheri*	T
Eastern Prairie Fringed Orchid	*Platanthera leucophaea*	T
Running Buffalo Clover	*Trifolium stoloniferum*	E

Common Name	Scientific Name	U.S. Status
Michigan		
Michigan Monkey-flower	*Mimulus glabratus var. michiganensis*	E
Pitcher's Thistle	*Cirsium pitcheri*	T
Houghton's Goldenrod	*Solidago houghtonii*	T
Dwarf Lake Iris	*Iris lacustris*	T
Eastern Prairie Fringed Orchid	*Platanthera leucophaea*	T
American Hart's-tongue Fern	*Asplenium (Phyllitis) scolopendrium var. americanum*	T
Lakeside Daisy	*Hymenoxys herbacea*	T
Small Whorled Pogonia	*Isotria medeoloides*	T
Minnesota		
Minnesota Dwarf Trout Lily	*Erythronium propullans*	E
Western Prairie Fringed Orchid	*Platanthera praeclara*	T
Leedy's Roseroot	*Sedum integrifolium ssp. leedyi*	T
Wisconsin		
Prairie Bush-clover	*Lespedeza leptostachya*	E
Fassett's Locoweed	*Oxytropis campestris*	T
Eastern Prairie Fringed Orchid	*Platanthera leucophaea*	T
Northern Monkshood	*Aconitum noveboracense*	T
Pitcher's Thistle	*Cirsium pitcheri*	T
Dwarf Lake Iris	*Iris lacustris*	T

Selected Bibliography, Annotated

Part I: General References

Braun, E. L. 1967. The Monocotyledoneae [of Ohio], cat-tails to orchids. Ohio State
Univ. Press, Columbus. This reference, plus Fisher 1988 and Cooperrider 1995,
are part of a series The Vascular Flora of Ohio, which still lacks one volume
at this date (2003)—The Dicotyledoneae of Ohio, Part 1. Excellent illustra
tions in all three.

Cooperrider, T.S. 1995. The Dicotyledoneae of Ohio. Part 2. Linaceae through
Campanulaceae. Ohio State Univ. Press, Columbus. See note after Braun, E. L.
1967.

_____, A. W. Cusick, and J. T. Kartesz. 2001. Seventh catalog of the vascular plants
of Ohio. Ohio State Univ. press, Columbus. The most useful and up-to-date
source for common and scientific names of Ohio seed plants, ferns, and fern
allies. Also includes sections co-authored by J. Furlow, B. K. Andreas, and J. V.
Freudenstein.

Fernald, M. L. 1950. Gray's manual of botany, 8th ed. American Book Co., New York. My
main reference for northeast US and eastern Canada, superseded by
Gleason, 1991. Highly technical keys and descriptions. Line drawings in the
case of difficult genera.

Fisher, T. R. 1988. The Dicotyledoneae of Ohio. Part 3. Asteraceae. Ohio State Univ.
Press, Columbus. See note after Braun, E. L. 1967.

Gleason, H. A., and A. Cronquist. 1991. Manual of vascular plants of northeast US and
adjacent Canada, 2nd ed. New York Botanical Garden, Bronx, N. Y. Replaces
Fernald 1950. Pen-and-ink illustrations in a separate volume. Excellent for
up-to-date common and scientific names, which incorporate forty years of
scientific study since Fernald's time.

Lafferty, M. B. 1979. Ohio's natural heritage. Ohio Academy of Science, Columbus.
With a state with so many different habitats, this sort of book becomes a

necessary reference, with each habitat deserving of a separate chapter. Each chapter written by a different specialist in the field. Well illustrated.

McCance, R. M., Jr., and J. F. Burns. 1984. Ohio endangered and threatened plants, abstracts of state-listed taxa. ODNR, Columbus. Deals only with Heritage plants, currently listed E or T, as of 1984, but includes much valuable information on reasons for rarity, type of habitat required, time of blooming, and distribution throughout Ohio, with maps. Covers 367 species. Regrettably, the many X (extirpated) species are not included.

Milne, L. and M., 1967. Living plants of the world. Random House, New York. This beautifully printed, large-sized, hardcover volume with outstanding color photographs is the ideal popular-style plant survey with chapters arranged by families in evolutionary order. Stresses plants of economic, horticultural, and agricultural value, as well as those that are remote, curious, and downright bizarre.

Mohlenbrock, R. H. 1983. Where have all the wildflowers gone? A region-by-region guide to threatened or endangered US wildflowers. Macmillan Publishing Co., Inc., New York. Covers the whole country but mainly non-woody plants. No ferns, grasses, sedges, or obscure families. Illustrated with pen-and-ink drawings as well as color photos. Good historical background on the discovery and distribution of each plant listed. The closest thing to a Peterson guide to rare species. Thirteen species of plants in Mohlenbrock are also mentioned in the present volume.

ODNR staff (editors not listed by name), "Rare Native Plants 2002-03 Status List." ODNR, Columbus. A biennial, 25-page handout listing up-to-date common and scientific names of all plants on the Ohio Heritage List, including lichens and mosses. A one-page bibliography is included to explain deletions from and additions to the 2001-02 List.

Voss, E. G. 1972, 1985, and 1996. Michigan flora, vols. I, II, and III. Cranbrook Inst. of Science, Bloomfield Hills, Mich. and Univ. of Mich., Ann Arbor. Especially good for many northern Ohio rare and extirpated plant species, which are still fairly common in Michigan.

Part II: References Useful for Specific Chapters

Introduction: "The Three-Hour Walk"

Kinkead, E. 1976. The search for *Betula uber*. The New Yorker, Jan. 12, 1976: 58-69. The original of the article that began my interest in endangered and lost plants, in this case, the rediscovery of the round-leaved birch of Virginia, considered extirpated from 1914 to 1975.

_____. 1976. The search for *Betula uber*. The Explorer (magazine of the Cleveland Museum of Natural History), 18: 12-22. A reprint of the text of *The New Yorker* article above, but supplemented with 13 photographs, presumably supplied by the author.

Chapter 1: "A Walk Through Lucy Braun's Prairie"

Stuckey, R. L., 2001. E. Lucy Braun (1889-1971): Ohio's foremost woman botanist, her studies of prairies and their phytogeographical relationships. RLS Creations, Box 3010, Columbus, Ohio. A privately printed book of reprints of Braun's articles of prairies, but also includes short biographies, such as Stuckey's own 1973 article from *The Michigan Botanist*, 12: 83-106. Author also provides a bibliography of Braun's works and photographs of Braun and her family.

Chapter 2: "Four Species in Search of a Habitat"

Case, F. W., Jr. 1964. Orchids of the western Great Lakes region. Cranbrook Inst. Of Science, Bloomfield Hills, Michigan. The standard reference for northern Ohio orchids.

Luer, C., 1975. The native orchids of the United States and Canada, excluding Florida. New York Botanical Garden, Bronx, N.Y. The standard reference for the orchid family in temperate North America.

Prance, G. T. and T. S. Edison, 1977. Extinction is forever, New York Botanical Garden, Milbrook, N.Y. Proceedings of a symposium held at the New York Botanical Garden. Covers rare plants of the world, in the early days of the Endangered Species Act of 1973, when the problem was not clearly understood.

Chapter 5: "...Halophytes..."

Cusick, A. W. 1970. An assemblage of halophytes in northern Ohio. Rhodora 72: 285. One of the first articles to warn of a new flora invading Ohio in the wake of over-salted interstate highways.

Reznicek, A. A. 1980. Halophytes along a Michigan roadside, Mich. Bot. 19: 23-30. The Michigan equivalent of Cusick's Ohio article.

Stone, D. M. 1983. The Lives of Plants, New York: Scribner's. Section on halophytes mentions the amino acid proline that some possess and the physiology of plants living in salt water.

Chapter 6: "Mallows"

Spooner, D. M., A. W. Cusick, et al. 1985. Observations on the distribution and ecology of *Sida hermaphrodita (L.)* Rusby (Malvaceae). Sida 11: 215-225. An important article on the Virginia mallow.

Wieboldt, J. F. and A. Wieboldt. 1998. Special collections. Castanea: 23: 88. Reports the recent discovery of *Napaea dioica*, the glade mallow, in Virginia. Allison Cusick of ODNR is credited with determining the identity of the species and that it is a native of the New River valley area in Virginia.

Chapter 7: "Faribault Diary"

Pleasants, J. M. and J. F. Wendel. 1989. Genetic diversity in a clonal narrow endemic, *Erythronium propullans*, and its widespread progenitor, *E. albidum*. American Journal of Botany 76: 1136-1151. Shows the relationship between the endemic dwarf trout lily and the white trout lily.

Chapter 8: "The Knotted Dodder..."

Dawson, J. H. 1967. Soil-applied herbicides for dodder control. Washington Agricultural Experimental Station Bulletin 691: 1-7. Tells how "dodder mills" work.

Kuijt, J. 1969. The biology of parasitic flowering plants. Univ. of California Press, Berkeley and Los Angeles. Excellent, readable guide to the parasitic plant families of the world.

McCormac, James S. and Windus, Jennifer L. 1993. *Fire and Cuscuta Glomerata (Choisy) in Ohio: a Connection?* Rhodora 95, No. 882: 158-165. Update to authors' article in Mich Bot.

Peskin, P. K. 1990. Knotted dodder (*Cuscuta glomerata,* Convolvulaceae) in Ohio. Michigan Bot. 29: 125-127. The author's article based on the specimen he collected in Liberty Fen. Concentrates on the past distribution of the knotted dodder in the Midwest.

US Dept. of Agriculture, Agricultural Research Service and Extension Service, 1984.
Dodder and its control. Farmer's bulletin 2276. *Cuscuta campestris,* the field
dodder, as a farm pest in California, and methods to control it.

Chapter 11: "Pennsylvanian Nature Trail"

Chitaley, S. and K. B. Pigg. 1996. *Clevelandodendron ohioensis,* gen. et sp. nov., A slender
upright lycopsid from the late Devonian Cleveland Shale of Ohio. American
Journal of Botany 83 (6): 781-789. The first description of a tree-sized
ancestor of the modern club-mosses called quillworts from a period earlier
than the Pennsylvanian.

Taylor, T. N. 1981. Paleobotany. McGraw Hill, New York. One of the most reliable single
texts in the field of paleobotany. Good section on the origin and structure of
coal balls and the process of making peels.

_____ and A. C. Scott. 1983. Interactions of plants and animals during the
Carboniferous. Bioscience, 33: 418-493. Good source for paleoecology.
Mentions horse-shoe crabs using *Cordaites* roots as a refuge from their
salt-water enemies. Also describes evidence of insect herbivores from
plant fossils.

Chapter 13: "...Grasses"

Pohl, R. W. 1954. How to Know the Grasses (in the Pictured Key Nature Series).
Wm. C. Brown Co., Dubuque, Iowa. Excellent for any amateur botanist trying
to make sense of the huge grass family.

Index

If items in the index are in regular type, these items will appear in the text. If items are in boldface type, these items will appear in the captions.

A

AAF Bees, 9
acanthus family, **SO:10**
achene, **14:6**, 189
Adams County, **3:27**, 47
    prairies in, 48
Adam's needle, **3:8**
aerial roots, **11:12**, **11:15**, 160
agave family, **3:9**
Age of Fishes, 167
alkaloids, **9:17**
allspice, Carolina, **SO:5**
aloe, false, **IN:5**, 20
alpine tundra, 209
alum-root, small-flowered, **SO:22**
alvar area of Misery Bay, **4:26**
    habitat, 10
alvars, the, **4:20**, 56, 217
American Association of Field Botanists. (See AAF Bees.)
anemone,
    Canada, **4:5**, **4:6**, 39
    false, **7:7**, 103
    red, **4:2**
    western, 62
anglepod, 20
annuals, 120
anthers, **4:6**, **7:2**, 101
Appalachia, Edge of, 24
arbor vitae, **GL:15**, 122
Archeopteris (fossil plant), **11:17**
arethusa orchids, 5, 13, 32, 33, **IN:14**
aroids, **IN: 9**
arrowhead, 60
aster, 118,
    annual salt-marsh, **5:8**
    family, 137 (See also composites.)
    salt water, 73
    weak, 32
    western annual, **5:9**, 77
author, **7:15**, **EP: 30**

avens, 64
awns, **13:1**
azalea, Cumberland, 22, 220, **EP:13**,
    early, 32
    flame, **EP:14**, **SO:1**, 22, 220
    roseshell, **2:14**, **15:24**, 205

B

badger, 51
bamboo, **13:12**, 183
baneberry, **NO: 35**
    red, **NO: 34**
barley, 183
    squirrel-tail, **13:3**, **13:4**, 184
bartonia, yellow, **12:5**, 174
bayberry, **EP:5**, 218
beach grass, American, **13:2**
beaks (on sedges) 188
bean, bog, 176
    wild, **9:30**
bearberry, **EP:3**, 216
beard-tongue, smooth, **SO:12**
beaver, **NO:7**
beaver pond, **NO: 8**, 218
beech, American, **8:10**, 121
beech drops, **8:10**, 121
beech-maple forest, **NO:16**, 174, 218
bees, as pollinators, **2:18**, **10:18**, **NO: 24**
biennial, 177
big bluestem, **IN:15**, **2:7**, **13:6**, **13:7**, 185 *See also* little bluestem
Bigelow Cemetery, **3:23**, **3:24**, 45
bindweed family, 115
biodiversity, def. of, 10
birch, river, 198
    round-leaf, **EP:15-19**, 8, 222
    swamp, **EP:21**
birds at White City Beach , **9:1**
birds, salt-water, found at Mentor Marsh, 76
Bissell, Jim, **EP:11**, **NO:12**
bittersweet family, 19, 208

Black Brook, 76
black haw, southern, 197
bladders, structure of, 125
bladderworts, 125
    horned, **8:23**, 126
blazing star, dense, 42
    large, **3:7**
    scaly, 44, 198
    slender, **3:28**
block mountains, 209
blowout at Grand Sable Dunes, **4:10**
bluebells, Virginia, 28
blue-eyed Mary, **2:5**, 29
bluehearts, **8:25**
bog clubmoss, 5
bog cotton, **14:5**
bog habitats, **IN:6**
bog-rosemary, **GL:16**
bogs and fens (See succession stages)
bogs, quaking, 32-33
boneset, 22
borrow pits, 170
BotSocs Annual Field Meeting, southern Ohio, May 2002, **15:2**
bottomlands, 170
bowman's root, **SO:19**
boxwood, Oregon, 209
brachiopads, 160
bracts, **NO:15**, 184
Braun, Lucy, **IN:15**, **IN:16**, **IN:17**, **IN:18**, **EP:13**, **EP:28**, **14:7**, **15:28**,
    10, 22-23, 47, 178-181, 195, 206, 209-10, 220
brine fly, 76
broom-rapes, 120-121
Bruce Peninsula, **4:13**, **10:3**, 57, 62, 65
buckbean, **12:11**, 176
buckthorn, alder-leaved, 33
    Carolina, 20
    European, 218
buffalo-berry, Canada, 45
bulrush, **14:2**, 187
bumblebee, pollinator of orchids, 33
bunchberry, **NO:15**
bunchflower, **EP:7**, **EP:8**, **EP:9**, 218-19
bur, buffalo, **9:17**, 138
burnet, Canada, **NO:9**, 32
buttercup, **2:4**, 28, 59, 68
butterfly, brown-eyed, 33

Harris's checkerspot, 33
Karner's blue, **NO:30**
Butterfly-weed, **3:12**, 44-45
butterwort, **GL:20**
Buzzard Roost Rock, Adams County, Ohio, **3:27**, **3:28**, 47-49

C
cabbage family, **9:27**
cacti, **3:8**
    prickly pear, **3:10**, **3:11**, 45, 58, 88
Caesar weed, 82
Calamites (fossil plant), **11:1**, **11:2**, **11:3**, **11:14**, 16
calciphile, 104
calla, wild, **IN:9**, **NO:10**
calypso, 67, 146, 206, **10:19**, **4:29**
camass, death, **EP:10**
    white, 218
camellia, mountain, 220
Canalway Metropolitan Park, Cleveland, Ohio, 59
cancer-root, 121,
    one-flowered, **8:11**
cane, giant, **13:12**
    sugar, 197
canebrakes, **13:12**
Cannon Falls Prairie, Minnesota, **7:8**
caper family, **9:24**, **9:25**
Carboniferous Period, 161
cardinal flower, **15:1**, 196
carices (plural of Carex), 188
carnivorous plants, 115, 165, **IN:13**
    butterworts, **GL:19**
    pitcher plant, purple, **8:21**
catchfly,
    round-leaved, **SO:25**
    royal, **SO:8**, **3:22**, 45
catkins, **EP:20**
cattail,
    common and narrow-leaved, **5:6**, 72, 218
cecropia, 87
cedar,
    eastern red, **1:1**, **1:2**, 48, 191
    northern white, **GL:15**, 62-64, 122
cemeteries, **3:22**
cereals, 183
chaff, 184
Chagrin River, **IN:17**

chamomile, **4:30**
Chaparral Prairie, Adams County, Ohio, **15:2**
chenopod, **9:10**, 73.See orach
cherry, Great Lakes sand, **4:2**, 60
chickweed, 91
chlorophyll, 114
Chincoteague Island, Virginia, **6:3**, **6:7**, 82
Chiwaukee Prairie, Illinois, 65
chives, wild, 68
cinquefoil,
    bushy, **EP:2**
    shrubby, **2:10**, **2:11**, 32-33, 141
circumboreals, 63
clammy-weed, **9:25**
Claridon Prairie, near Marion, Ohio, **IN:3**
clay banks, **3:13**
Clevelandodendron (fossil plant), **11:19**, 167
cliff-brake,
    slender, **4:14**, 63
    smooth, **IN:12**, 20
cliff green, **15:36**, 208
clifftop species, **15:35**
climax vegetation, 174
clover, buffalo, **EP:25**, 227
    prairie bush-, 110
    running buffalo, **EP:23**, **EP:24**, **EP:25**, 223, 227
    white, **EP:23**, 224
club-moss, **IN:15**, **11:13**, **11:18-19**, 166-7
    northern bog, **IN:12**
Coal Age, 161
coal ball, 164
    peel, **11:10**
cocklebur, **9:11**, 137
coelocanths, 160
coffee tree, Kentucky, 225
colic-root, 202
colombo, American, **12:3**, **12:4**, 174
column, 81, 84
comfort root, 82
compass plant, **SO:21**
composite family, **3:24**, **4:31**, **9:10**, **9:31**, 18, 141
compressions (type of fossil), 164
coneflower,
    gray-headed, 41, 104
    prairie, **3:4**
    purple, **3:24**, 41, 45

cones, spore, 160
conifer, 160
Conrail system, **3:19**
coralroot,
    early, **10:27**, 127
    crested, **8:19**, 124
    spotted, 124, **8:18**
    striped, **4:12**, 62
Cordaites (fossil plant), 160
coriander, 138
corm, **11:20**, 183
coreopsis, golden, 57
corydalis, 68
    pale, **2:19**
cottongrass, green, **2:6**
cottonwoods, **IN:1**
cow wheat, **8:24**
crab, horseshoe, 160
cranberry,
    large, **IN:10**, 33
    small, 5
Cretaceous Period, 166
cross-pollination, 81
crowfoot family, **2:4**, 28, 30
crowns, 57
crucifers, **9:27**
Cruickshank Glen, **2:15**, 34-36
culm, 184, 188
Cup-and-Saucer Trail, Manitoulin Is., **4:13**
Cusick, Allison, 193
Cuyahoga
    River near downtown Cleveland, **IN:4**
    Valley National Park, **2:19**, **3:14**
cyclamens, **SO:7**

D
daisy, Lakeside, **4:22**, **4:23**, 57
daisy family, **3:24**, **9:10**, **9:31**, 118, 141
    (See also composites and aster family.)
Deciduous Forests of Eastern North America, The, **IN:14**, 22
Denny, Guy, **8:2**, 117-8
devil's-bit, **SO:17**
devil's club, **4:30**, 60
Devonian Period, 167
Devonian plants, **11:17**
dicots, **4:7**, 60, 101

disjuncts, 18-20
dissected foliage (definition of), 68
disturbed-area habitat, **IN:3**, **IN:4**, 12
dodder,115-116, 119, 129
    buttonbush, 118
    common, 116-119, **8:5**
    definition of, 12
    field,127, 129
    hazel, 118
    knotted, **8:3**, **8:4**, 114, 118, 127, 129
    smartweed, 118
dogwood, flowering, **IN:11**
doll's eyes, **NO:35**
dolomite, **IN:12**, 209
    ledges, 15:2
dragon's mouth, **IN:14**, **10:16**, 33
Driftless Area, Minnesota, 12, 34, 86, 96-97
dropseed, sand, 44
ducks at White City, Cleveland, 135
duckweeds, **NO:12**
dunes,
    inland sand, Ohio, **IN:2**, **3:8**
    of Assateague Island National Seashore, Maryland, **5:1**
    of Carter Bay, **4:9**
    of Mentor, Headlands, **IN:1**
Dutchman's breeches, **7:6**, 102-103

E

ecological succession, 74
ecology, 27
    definition of, 12
eco-tour, 228
Edge of Appalachia, southern Ohio, 209
egret, snowy, 76
elm,
    American, 28
    cork, **7:8**,104
    rock, **7:8**, 104-106
"endangered" (a Heritage listing), 30, 215, 252-53
Endangered Species Act, 6-7, 10, 13, 27, 82, 112
endemic (plant found in limited area), **15:33**
equatorial rain forest, 15
escapees from the garden, 9:13
Eurasian plants adapted to wastelands, **9:10**
Explorer, 9
"extirpated" (Heritage List term), 7, 215

F

fairy slipper, 67
    albino form, **10:20**
Faribault, Minnesota, 98-101
featherbells, **15:14**-17, **50:18**, 198, front cover
Federal Heritage List (See also Heritage List.)
fen Indian plantain, **8:9**
fens, **IN:6**, 218
    or alkaline bogs, 32
    Canadian, 116
    Midwestern, 116
    prairie, **8:1**, 116,
fern,
    American climbing, **15:10**
    bulblet, 20
    hart's tongue, **GL:11**
    limestone adder's tongue, **15:4**, 197
    Mackay's brittle, 107
    moonwort, 149
    seed, 160
    tree, **11:15-16**, 159
    walking, **7:11**, 63, 107
Fern Wall, a rocky ledge in northern Adams County, **15:7**, **15:10-11**
fescues, 183
fig family, 87
"Fire and *Cuscuta glomerata* in Ohio: a Connection?", 129
fire-pink, **SO:8-9**
fire, use of , 37, 41
    at Mill Prairie, 44
fireweed, **NO:33**
flag, northern blue, **GL:22**
flax, 138
floating-heart, **12:11-12**
flood plain, 82, 84
forb (definition of), 43
forest,
    mixed hardwood, 207
form genus (fossil plants), 165
Fort Hill, Ohio, nature preserve, **15:29**
fossil plants (See Chapter 11.)
Foxey Prairie, Manitoulin Is., 63-64
foxgloves, false, 87
    mullein, **6:13**, 84
    Skinner's, **NO:36**
    yellow false, 129
fringe tree, **SO:6**

fronds, sterile, **4:14**
frostweed, plains, **NO:31**
fumitory family, **2:19**
fungus associates (See under *mycorrhizae*), 123

G

gaywings, **GL:10**
gentian,
    blind, **12:9**, 176
    bottle, **12:8**
    fringed, **12:2**, 170
    pine barren, **12:18**
    pink, **12:6**, **12:13**
    pleated, **12:17**
    Plymouth, **12:15**, **12:16**
    small fringed, **IN:17**, 170
    stiff, **12:7**, 176
    yellow, **12:10**
gentian family, 170
gentians from outside Ohio, **12:12**
geranium, Bicknell's, 68
gerardias, **NO:36**
ginger, long-tipped wild, 104
gingko, **11:10**, 166
Girdham Road dunes at Oak Openings Park, **IN:2**
glacial erratic, **4:5**
glaciers, 18
glades (definition of), 85
gland (definition of), **12:4**
glassworts, 73
glaucous bloom, **8:8**
globeflower, spreading, **2:1**, **2:2**, 28, 36, 220
    growth conditions, 37
    nectaries, function of, **2:2**
    petals, function of, **2:2**
    sepals, function of, **2:2**, 30
goat's beard, **SO:18**
goat's rue, **NO:32**
golden knees, **SO:20**
goldenrod, 22, 71, 118
    Great Lakes, 124
    Riddell's 42
    seaside, **5:1**, **5:2**, 70, 72, 76
    stout, **NO:38**
    white-haired, **EP:28**, **EP:29**, **EP:30**, 222
goldenthread, **NO:19**

goldflower, stemless, 57-58
goosefoot, **9:10**, 73
Gore Bay settlement, 62
Grand River of Northeast Ohio, **NO:1**
grass,
    alkali, 73
    American beach, **IN:1**, **4:10**, **9:7**, **13:2**, **EP:1**, 61, 136, 184
    beach, **13:2**, 136, 184
    beard, 183
    bent, 183
    big bluestem, **IN:15**, **2:7**, **13:6-7**, 41, 185
    bottlebrush, 23, 178, 183
    canary, 183
    cord, 183
    cotton, 188
    ditch, 72
    foxtail, 183
    giant cane, **13:12**
    giant plume, 197
    green cotton, **IN:11**, **14:5**, 5
    Indian, **13:5**, 41, 184
    Johnson, 84
    Kentucky blue, 225
    little bluestem, **13:8**, 41
    Marram, 61
    northern wood-reed, **2:16**, 34
    orchard, 183
    panic, 183
    prairie cord, **13:10**
    purple love, 184
    reed (also called phragmites), **5:4-5**, 72-3, 218
    reed canary, 185
    saw, 42, 188
    side-oats grama, 49
    silk, **SO:24**
    silver plume, **15:3**, 197
    switch, 44, , 137, 184
    turkey-foot, **2:7**, 41
    twisted yellow-eyed, **15:20**, 203, 206
    velvet, 183
    Virginia cut, 185
    Walter's barnyard, 185
    white, 185
grasses, reproductive structures of, **183-4** (Fig. 1)
ground-cherry, large white flowered, 58
ground squirrel, thirteen-lined, 108-9

growth rings of trees, 160
gulls at White City, Cleveland, 135
Guyandotte beauty, EP:26, 226

H

halophytes, 5:7, 13:10, 61, 70- 74, 77
    definition of, 12
    future in Ohio, 77
    Michigan, 76
haustoria, 119
hawkweed,
    Canada, 9:31
    Savoy, 9:31
heath family, **IN:10**, **IN:15**, 122, 216
heaths, woody, **SO:1**
hemlocks, **NO:16**
hen and chickens, 108
henbit, 138
herbarium (plural herbaria), def. of, 6
    sheet, 146
    slip, 6
herbicides, **3:19**
herbivores, 165
Heritage List, **IN:13**, **EP:11** (See also Federal Heritage List.)
herons attracted by salt marshes
    Louisiana, 76
    tricolored, 76
Herrick Fen in Portage County, Ohio, **IN:4**, **EP:4**, **EP:7**, 218-19
hibiscus, 83
    pineland, 82
    rose of Sharon, 80
    shrubby, **6:1**, **6:2**, 80
    sleeping, 82
    Waimea Canyon (of Hawaii), **6:11**
hickory, butternut, 107
hobblebush, **NO:20**
hollyhock,
    garden, 80-1, 93
    mountain, 88
honey-creeper (family of birds), 83
honey guides, 6:9, **NO:24**
honeysuckle family, 197
horehound, water, 118
horsetail, 11:4
    giant (fossil plant), **11:1-3**, 160, 166
    woodland, **11:14**

I

Ice Age, 161
Ile Royale, Michigan, 60, **14:15**
index species, 6
Indian paintbrush, scarlet, **4:4**, 19, 45, 60
    yellow color phase of, **4:4**
Indian pipe, **8:17**, 123
Indiana Dunes National Lakeshore, 61
indigo, prairie false, **3:20**
inflorescences, types of, 179, 184
insect mimics: the crane-fly orchid, **10:29**
insects, fossil, 165-6
inter-dune pond, **EP:1**, 216
ipecac, American, **SO:19**
iris,
    common, **GL:22**
    dwarf, **15:25**, 205
    dwarf crested, **15:26**, 206
    dwarf lake, **15:27**, 61
Irwin Prairie Preserve, Ohio, **3:1**, 42, 49

J

Jack-in-the-pulpit family, **IN:9**
jasmine, western rock, 104
jimsonweed, **9:12**, 138
Johnny-jump-ups, 79-80, 204
juniper,
    common, 45
    ground, **3:15**

K

Kelley's Island, Ohio, 67
kettle-hole, def. of, 5
    bog, **IN:15**
    lake, **IN:16**
Keweenaw Peninsula, Michigan, 60
Kitty Todd Nature Preserve, Ohio, **NO:29**
koki'o ke'oke'o, (Hawaiian mallow), 83

L

labium (part of orchid), **10:10**
lady's slipper, **10:1**, **10:2**, 146. See also orchid
    Andrews', **10:10**
    Kentucky, **15:6**, 197
    large yellow, **10:9**, **15:6**, 63, 197, 216
    pink, **10:7**, 80, 204

albino, **10:8**
ram's head, **10:5**, 67-68,155
albino, **10:6**, 155
showy, **10:3**
albino, **10:4**, 31
small white, **2:7**, **10:10**, 28, 32, 39, 43
small yellow, **10:10**, 63
Lake Erie
dunes, 44
plants, **9:7-32**, 130-43
Lakeside Daisy Preserve, Ohio, 67
Lake Warren, (prehistoric lake), **IN:2**
lamb's quarters, 138
land stewards, 218
larch, American, **IN:4, 5**
larkspur, dwarf, **15:29**, 34, 209
latex, 9:9
laurel,
bog, **GL:17**
mountain, GL:17, SO:2, SO:3
leafcup, 92
leaf-scars, 11:11
leather-flower, **IN:8**
leather-leaf, **IN:15-16**
leatherwood, 106
leaves,
basal, **IN:6**
palmately compound, **15:23**
succulent, 73
ledges, wet sandstone, **2:15**
Lepidodendron (See scale tree), 11:1, **11:2**, **11:6**, **11:13**
lily,
adder's tongue, 206
white, 207
yellow, 7:1, 109, 206
bluebead, **NO:28**
Canada, **NO:25**
dwarf trout, **7:3**, **7:4**, **7:17**, 12, 94, 97, 207
fawn (same as trout lily), **IN:13**, 7:1,**15:8**
glacier, 96
golden star, **IN:13**, **15:28**, 206
Michigan, **3:2**, 42
trout, **7:1**, 94, 103
white, 101, 109
Turk's cap **3:2** , **3:12**, **15:15**, **NO:26**, 42
wand, 218

white, **EP:10**
wood, **NO:2**, **NO:23**
limestone cliff species, **4:13**
limestone quarry at Marblehead, **4:21**
lip petal (orchid structure), **10:18**, 13, 202, 124
lobelias, tree, 82
lotus, American, **NO:13**
lumpers, 153
lupine, wild, **NO:30**
Lynx Prairie, southern Ohio, **1:1**, **3:29**, 17-19, 24, 47

M
Magnolia,
bigleaf, **15:8**, **15:9**
umbrella, **15:7**
mallow, 80
common, 81
desert globe, **6:8**, 83
glade, 85, 88
globe, 82- 8
Kankakee, 83, **6:18**, **6:20**, **6:21**, **6:22**
marsh, 82, 93
Mohave, 6:9
musk, **6:6**, 81
Peters Mountain, 83
Rio Grande, 82
rose, 82
seashore, **6:7**, 82
swamp rose, **6:3**
Virginia, **6:14**, 82-83, 86-88
Waimea Canyon, **6:11**, 85
mandarin, nodding, **15:13**
mangrove, 160
mangrove swamp, 158
Manitoulin gold, **4:20**, **4:21**, 56, 64-65
Manitoulin Island, **4:4**, **4:17**, **4:33**, Chapter 4
maple,
mountain, 34
striped, **NO:17**
Marblehead Peninsula , Ohio, 57
marigolds
bur, 138, 141
nodding, **9:21**
fetid, 77, 143
marsh, **2:4**, 29, 62
marl, 201

marsh-pink, slender, **12:13**, **12:14**
Mary, blue-eyed, 29
Matson, Tim, **NO:2-3**
maypop, **IN:10**
McCormac, Jim, **6:18**, **6:20**, **15:3**, 20-22, 83
meadow-beauty, Virginia, **3:6**
Medullosa (fossil fern), **11:9**, **11:10**, 160
melastome family, **3:6**
Mentor Marsh, Ohio, **5:4**, 72, 75
Milford Center Prairie, Ohio, **3:25**
Milk-vetch, Cooper's, **3:17**
milkweed,
    cross-leaved, **15:19**, 202
    spider, **SO:14**
    Sullivant's, **E:21**
    white, **SO:13**
    whorled, 19
milkweed family, 141
milkwort family, **GL:10**
milkwort, Curtiss', **SO:23**
    purple, 202
millet, broomcorn, 138
Mill Prairie, **2:7**, 31-32, 42, 44
Misery Bay, Manitoulin Island, **4:20**, **4:26**, 64
Mississippi Highlands (of southern Minnesota), **7:10**
mistletoe, 121
    American, 122
    dwarf, **8:14**, 122
miterwort, naked, 62
moccasins, 79-80
monkshood, northern, **2:17**, **2:18**, 28, 34, 36, 86, 97
    nectaries, 34
    sepal, 34
    temperature and light requirements, 37
monocots, **4:7**, 60, 101, 178
moonwort fern, **GL:12**
Moorhead Forest, 2:2, 29-30
moose, **14:16**
morning glories, **9:22**, 115
mosquito, salt-water, 75
moss,
    haircap, 176
    sphagnum, **IN:7**, **IN:13**
mountain-lover, **15:36**, 206, 208
mud puppy (salamander), **NO:2**, **NO:3**
mycorrhizae (of fungi), 123

N
National Audubon Society, 219
Natural Bridge State Park, Kentucky, **EP:27**
Natural Heritage Program in Ohio, 27
Nature Conservancy, The, 217-18
NEON (See Northeastern Ohio Naturalists.)
Nerstrand-Big Woods State Park Minnesota, **7:6**
nettles, tall, 86
Neuropteris (fossil fern), **11:9**
Niagara Escarpment, Manitoulin Is., **4:13**
nightshade family, **SO:10**, 138
Northeast Ohio Naturalists, 197
northern conifer forests, **NO:14**, **GL:1**

O
oak,
    bur, 118
    mossy cup, 118
    valley, 112
Oak Openings Park, Ohio, **3:8**, **3:10**, 44, 51
oats (a grass), 183
ODNR. (See Ohio Department of Natural Resources.)
Ohio,
    Biological Survey of 1978, 41
    Department of Natural Resources, 53, 216
    Division of Natural Areas and Preserves, ODNR, 6
    Historical Society, 219
    Natural Heritage Program, 42
    Nature Conservancy, 48
Ohio River counties, 196
    disjuncts, **15:12**
Ojibways, **13:11**, 185
Oliphant Fen, Bruce Peninsula, Ontario, **GL:15**
old field habitat, 84
orach, 73, 77
orchids, **IN:15**, 12, 149 (See also lady's slipper.)
    Alaska, **GL:5**
    arethusa or dragon-mouth, **IN:14**, **2:13**, **11:15**, 4, 10, 28, 32-33, 39
    bog candles, **GL:23**
    calypso, or fairy slipper, **4:29**, **10:19**, 56, 206
    coralroot, spotted, **8:18**
    crane-fly, **10:29**
    fringed, 146, 201
    prairie, **10:13**, 20
    western, 110

ragged, **10:23**
small purple, **10:12**, 220
yellow, **10:11**, **15:18**
fringeless, **15:21**
    purple, *15:21*
grass-pink, **IN:14**, **10:16-18**, 202
ladies'-tresses, hooded, **10:24**, 220
Hooker's, **GL:4**
long-bracted, **10:28**
northern bog, **10:15**
northern green, **GL:6**
pogonia, rose, **10:16**, 13
    whorled, **10:22**
        small, **10:22**
rattlesnake plantain, downy, **10:25**, 149
three birds, **8:20**, 123
turbercled rein-, 124-125
orchis, showy, **10:21**
Ortt, Marilyn, **15:14**, 198
Oswego-tea, **NO:22**
osmosis, 73

P
pahute weed, 72
paleobotany, 161
paleoecology, 165
palynology, 165
Pangaea, 161
panicle, **15:15**, 198
papyrus, 187
parasites, **8:10**, 114
    host-specific, 116
parasitic plants (See Chapter 8.)
parsley family (formerly called umbels), **3:29**
pasque-flower, 105
passion-flower,
    yellow, **1:9**, 20
    purple, **1:10**
pawpaw, 225
pea,
    inland beach, **9:26**
    wild, **3:26**, 47
peat mining, 32
peels (of fossil plants), 164
Pennsylvanian Period, 161

perigynia (singular is perigynium, reproductive structure of
    sedges), 188-189, Fig. 2
permafrost, 97
Permian Period, 161
petrifactions, 164
phlox,
    downy, **3:14**, 45
    moss, **15:31**, **15:32**, 210
    spotted, 198, 203
photosynthesis, 73, 114
pickerelweed family, **NO:11**
pine,
    red, 64
    scrub, 48
    white, **NO:14**
pinxter-flower, **15:24**, 205
pistils (female reproductive structures), 84, 184
pitcher plant, California, 111
    purple, **8:21-2**
plantain,
    common, 29, 197
    heart-leaf, **2:3**, 29
plasmolysis, 73
poinsettias, **SO:11**
Point Pelee, 58
poison ivy, **2:12**
    northern, **9:32**
poison sumac, **2:12**, 33
pokeweed, 138
ponds, fresh water, **IN:8**
pondweed, Hill's, **EP:11**, 219
poppy, wood, **15:30**, 209
portulaca, garden, **9:23**, 13
power-line corridors, **3:22**
prairie, 10
    chicken, 51
    dock, **1:3**, **1:4**, **2:7**, 18
    smoke, **4:17-18**, 63-4, 104
prairie fires, 93
Prairie Peninsula, 126
prairies, 4:17, 37. 8
    Ohio, 42, 3:18
    ecology of and types of (See Chapter 3.)
    hanging (See Chapter 3), **3:28**, 47, 209
    power-line corridors, **3:22**
    railroad (See Introduction and Chap. 3), **IN:3**

sand, **15:18**
    wet, **3:1**
preservation, 42
primrose
    birds'-eye, **4:26**, 68
    family, **NO:18**
prince's feather, **9:14**, 138
proline 74
progymnosperm, 166
Psaronius (fossil fern), **11:1-2**, **11:10-11**, 159
purslane family, **9:23**
pyrola,
    family, 122
    pink, **GL:7**

Q

Queen Anne's lace, **3:29**
queen-of-the-prairie, **8:6**, 117
quillwort, **11:18**, **11:21**, 161
    Appalachian, **11:20**, 167

R

racemes (type of inflorescence), **13:7**
radioisotopes, 76
Ramsey, Dr. Gwynn, **6:19**
rape, oil-seed, 127
rattlesnake, eastern massasauga, **GL:13**
rattlesnake master, **3:29**
recovery plan, 12, 92, 110, 112
redbud, 49
red-cedar openings, southern Ohio, 45, 191
reed, giant (same as phragmites), 218
rhizomes (type of underground stem), 124
rice, wild, **13:11**, 183-185
river banks, 82
River Bend Nature Center, Faribault, Minnesota, **7:17**
roadsides, as a habitat, 82
Robin-run-away, **NO:5**
rock cress, lyre-leaved, **9:27**
rock harlequin, **2:19**, 68
rocket, inland sea, 136
rockhouse, **EP:30**, 222
Romine, Trella, **3:18**
root hairs, 73
rootlets, 118
roots, stilt, 160

roseroot, common, **7:14**
    Leedy's, **7:13**, 105
rubberweed, 57
ruellia, smooth, **SO:10**
runners (type of stem), 160
rush,
    beak, 188
        white, **14:4**
    chairmaker's, **14:2**
    nut, 188
    spike, **14:3**, 188
    four-angled, **14:3**
    three-square, **14:2**, **14:6**
    twig, 188
rye, 183-185
    Canada wild, 185
    downy wild, 185

S

St. John's-wort, few-flowered, **NO:4**
    Kalm's **EP:12**, **NO:37**, 37
    shrubby, **NO:37**
salt pollution, 76
sand-barrens area, 124
sand spurrey, salt, **5:7**, 73
sandstone, **IN:17**
sandwort, rock, **15:37**, 212
saphrophytes, **8:10**, 115
saprophytic orchids, **4:12**, 62
savanna, **15:2**
saxifrage, swamp, 29
scouring-rush, **11:4**, 166
scrophs (abbrev. of snapdraggon family), **GL:19**
sea-blite, western, 72-75
sea-rocket, inland, **9:8**
sedge, **IN:11**, **IN:15**, 12, 187
    aquatic, **14:3**
    bladder, **14:11**
    broom, common, **13:9**, 185
    low umbrella , **14:1**
    Gray's, **14:10**, **14:11**
    green cottongrass, **2:6**
    juniper, **14:13**, 191, 193
    long-fruited, **14:12**
    meadow, 32
    Michaux's, **14:15**, **14:16**

plantain, **14:9**, 23
purple wood, **14:14**
spike-rush, 188
    four-angled, **14:3**
tassled, **14:8**
three-square, **14:2**, **14:6**
umbrella, 187
white beak-rush, **14:4**
sedge, reproductive structures of (See Fig. 2, p. 189)
seed dispersal, 120
self-pollination, 92
Serpent Mound, Ohio, 17
settling ponds, 71
Seventh Catalog of the Vascular Plants of Ohio, 193
shale bank, **IN:17**, 170
shale barrens, 91
shinleaf, 122
Shipman Pond at Mentor Headlands, Ohio, **5:7**
Shorebirds at White City, Cleveland, 135
shrub, sweet, **SO:5**
silverweed, 141, **9:29**, **GL:13**
silverwood, **9:29**
slippage slopes, def. of, **3:13**
slumps, def. of., **3:13**
    clay, 45
smartweed, water, 118
snapdragon family, **GL:19**, 29, 87
soil horizon, 32
Solomon's seal, starry, 31
Solomon's seal, false, 31
sorghum, 138
sorrel, white wood, **NO:39**
southern Ohio,
    habitats, 196
    prairies, 3:27
spadix, **NO:10**
spathe, **NO:10**
spatter-dock, **NO:8**
spearwort, **4:7**, 59-60
spider-flower, **9:24**, 137
spike-moss, limestone, **15:5**
    midwest, **15:5**
spleenwort, **4:15**, 63
splitters (as opposed to lumpers), 153
spore cases, 197
    cones, **11:6**

sprangletop, 77
spring beauty, **9:23**
spruce,
    black, **GL:15**
    red, **GL:1**
spurge,
    glade, **SO:11**
    seaside, **9:9**, 136
squaw root, **8:12**, 121
stamen, def. of, **3:11**, 84, 184
starflower, **NO:18**
stargrass, water, **NO:11**
stigma, 101
stipes, 188
stolons, 225
stonecrop ditch, 118
stoneroot, early, **15:12**
Straight River bottomlands, southern Minnesota, **7:2**
succession, plant, stages in, 32, 58
sullivantia, **15:33**
sundews: **IN:15**, **GL:21**
    round-leaved, 33, 202
    spatulate-leaved, 20
sunflower, 118
    ashy, **3:5**
    common, **1:3**, **9:16**
    Kansas, 127
    saw-toothed, 41
swamp forest, 218
    at Carter Bay, Manitoulin Island, **4:12**
symbionts, **8:10**
synandra, **EP:26**

T
tagging, 76
tailings, 72
tamarack, **IN:4**, **IN:7**, **IN:16**, 5
tansy, Huron, **4:31**, **4:32**, 61
tassels in corn, 184
tea, Labrador, **GL:18**
Teays, River, 85, 86
thistle family, **9:11**
    Pitcher's, **4:11**, 56, 61
thistle, Russian, **9:10**, 137
timothy, 183
Titus bog, Pennsylvania, **IN:7**, **IN:8**, 4

Titus Canyon at Death Valley National Park, California, **6:8**
TNC (See Nature Conservatory, The.)
toadshade, 29
Tobermory harbor, 61
tree, scale (fossil plant), **11:6**
   seal (fossil plant), **11:5**
tree ferns, **11:1-2**
Triangle Lake, northern Ohio, **IN:16**
trillium, great white, **SO:16**
   nodding, **GL:8**, **GL:9**
   painted, **NO:27**
   sessile, 29
   snow, **SO:15**, **SO:16**
tundra, 97
Turk's cap, **6:10**, 82
turtle, Blanding's, **4:8**, 59
twayblades, 149
   common, **10:30**
twig rush, **3:1**, 42
twinflower, **GL:2**

U

V

valerian, large-flowered, **15:34**, 209
Vascular flora of Ohio, Volume I: Cat-tails to
   Orchids, The, 5, 23-24
vascular system (of plants), 73
veins, netted, of leaves, **11:9**
vetchling, yellow, **3:16**
Vickers, Lindley, **2:6**
vine,
   cross, **SO:4**
   sand, **9:18**, **9:19**, 141
violet,
   bird's foot, **15:23**, 80, 205
   lance-leaved, **NO:21**
virgin's bower, purple, **4:24**, 68

W

water flea, 125
waterfowl (at White City, Cleveland), 135
water-lily, white, **IN:8**
West Bay, Manitoulin Is., **4:5**
wetlands, **IN:6**, **2:12**, **15:2**
   of the Bruce Peninsula, Ontario, **GL:14**

of northeast Ohio, **NO:7**
wheat, 183,
   cow, **8:24**
wheat rust, 119
white-cedar, northern, **4:33**
White City Beach, Cleveland, Ohio, 132-157
whitlow-grass, wedge-leaf, 212
whitlow-grasses, 104
whorl, 160
Wilderness Preserve, Adams County, Ohio, 47
Wildflower magazine, 9, 24
Will County, Illinois, 65
willow,
   autumn, 33
   blue-leaved, **8:8**, 117
   bog, **2:9**, **2:13**, 13, 31-33, 37, 39
   heart-leaved, **4:3**, 60
   hoary, **2:9**, 33
   sandbar, **IN:1**
Windus, Jennifer, **15:9**
wintergreen, 122
Wisconsinan Glacier, 60
witches' broom, 122
wolfiella, star, **NO:12**
woodcock, **NO:6**
Woody Plants of Ohio, The, 23
woolly bean, annual, **9:30**
Wormwood, annual, 91

X

Y

yellow star-grass, 31
yew, Canada, **4:24**, 34, 64
yucca species, **3:8**, 45

Z